BACHELOR GIRL

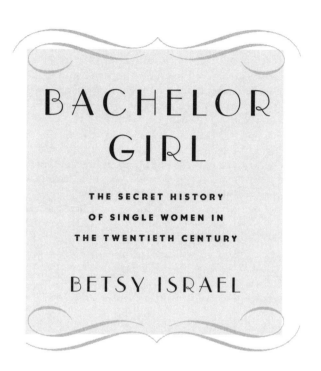

BACHELOR GIRL

THE SECRET HISTORY
OF SINGLE WOMEN IN
THE TWENTIETH CENTURY

BETSY ISRAEL

WILLIAM MORROW
An Imprint of HarperCollinsPublishers

Grateful acknowledgment is made to the following agencies for sup-plying the illustrations for this book:

Page 13, © Ecoscene/CORBIS; page 55, © Lewis W. Hine/Hulton/Archive/PictureQuest; pages 113 and 207, © Bettmann/CORBIS; page 149, © Hulton/Archive/PictureQuest; page 243, PEOPLE Weekly © 1986 Time Inc., all rights reserved; and page 265, unit production photograph from *Bridget Jones's Diary* by Alex Bailey, provided cour-tesy of Miramax Films.

HarperCollins books may be purchased for educational, business, or sales pro-motional use. For information please write: Special Markets Department, HarperCollins Publishers Inc., 10 East 53rd Street, New York, NY 10022.

FIRST EDITION

Designed by Gretchen Achilles

Printed on acid-free paper

Library of Congress Cataloging-in-Publication Data

Israel, Elizabeth, 1958–
    Bachelor girl : the secret history of single women in the twentieth century / Elizabeth Israel.—1st ed.
        p. cm.
    Includes bibliographical references and index.
    ISBN 0-380-97649-8
    1. Single women. 2. Single women—United States. I. Title: Secret history of single women in the twentieth century. II. Title.
HQ800.2 .I85 2002
305.48'9652—dc21   2002066011

02 03 04 05 06 JTC/RRD 10 9 8 7 6 5 4 3 2 1

CONTENTS

ACKNOWLEDGMENTS

This book would not exist without the foresight, goodwill, and patience of two extraordinary people. My agent, Susan Ramer, has been with me through three proposals, five drafts, and an epic spell of writer's fog. She has devoted so much time to this project, worked through so many of its problems, and been such a terrific friend that I cannot thank her enough. Jennifer Hershey is the most thoughtful, good-natured, and enthusiastic editor I've ever worked with. She helped me to find a way through what was, in essence, a great dark mass of material, and never did she seem to doubt it would take shape. Despite an enormous workload, she personally edited this book down to the tiniest detail. I am indebted to my research assistant, Jeryl Brunner, the woman who can find anything, anywhere. Thanks, too, to Jeanine Barry, Carleen Woolley, and Ariana Calderon for their assistance and fact-finding. Donna Brodie at the Writer's Room gave me much-needed early encouragement, and Amy Gross offered me the chance to write about single women, in *Mirabella*. Thanks, too, to all the friends, colleagues, and relatives who have listened and commented throughout. In particular I am grateful to my husband, Ezra Doner, and to Nan Friedman, Betsy Zeidman, Priscilla Mulvihill, Lorraine Rapp, Fleur and Sheldon Israel, the late Alex Greenfield, Sally Hines, and Dalma Heyn; to Teriananda, who took care of my household; and to Susannah Israel Marchese, who had an easy answer to my hardest question. My beloved Hayley and Timothy have been more tolerant and patient than any children should ever have to be. Finally, inestimable thanks to the many women who described their lives and gave me my story.

I THINK WE'RE ALONE NOW

> *Commands sent through highways and byways . . . drawing rooms, workshops, by hints and suggestions . . . lectures . . . the imploring letter . . . essays . . . sermons . . . as if a voice . . . din[s] in the ears of young women: Marry! Marry! For the unmarried woman fails at the end for which she was created.*
>
> —"THE WAY OF ALL WOMEN," HARPER'S, 1907

We all grow up with images of single life. For me, these were brightly colored fantasies that drew on TV heroines—*That Girl* Marlo Thomas, Avenger Emma Peel, Catwoman, the Mary-and-Rhoda duet—and a vision of how I'd look in the tight little blue suits of UN tour guides and stewardesses. A young woman plotting out a single life circa 2002 has a broader, more eccentric range of iconic singles to play with, each wearing her own unique single suit: Ally McBeal, cute, hallucinating miniskirted lawyer; Bridget Jones, "singleton," who sees clearly the masochism inherent in both her single life and her own ill-fitting tiny skirts; and the *Sex and the City* foursome, who, like doctors or madams, discuss clinical aspects of sex, while dressed for sex, in restaurants.

More so than any other living arrangement, the single life is deeply influenced—*haunted* may be a better word—by cultural imagery. And the single woman herself has had a starring role in the mass imagination for many years. Admit it or not, most of us have our fixed ideas of single womanhood and at some point we all indulge in the familiar ritual of speculation: How did she end up that way? How can she stand it? And how might she correct what must be a dull, lonely, and potentially heartbreaking, meaning possibly childless, situation?

One hundred and fifty years ago, Sarah Grimké, tough "singleside" and "womanist," wrote that marriage had ceased to be the "sine qua non of female existence." In every decade since, many, many women have come to agree with her. And they have inspired more than the familiar ritual of pitying speculation and disdain. Single women seem forever to unnerve, anger, and unwittingly scare large swaths of the population, both female and male.

Writing from an academic viewpoint, historian Nina Auerbach notes, "Though the nature of the [single] threat shifts . . . the idea remains of contagion by values that are contrary to the best and proudest instincts of humanity."

A woman writing in the *New York Times* some years back put it plainly: "There's something about a woman standing by herself. People wonder what she wants."

The media, in all its antique and more recognizable forms, has long served as the conduit for this stereotypical single imagery. Reporters, novelists, and filmmakers again and again have introduced the single icons of the moment by organizing them into special interest groups with neon nicknames: Spinsters! Working Girls! Flappers! Beatniks! Career Women! That's the job, of course, to discover and explore newly evolving social phenomena. In the process, however, they've repeatedly turned the new single into a nasty cartoon or a caricature.

Most of the standard single icons have been portrayed as so depressing, so needy and unattractive, that for years women who even slightly matched the descriptions had a hard time in life. But gradually all variety of single types began to flourish within their own tiny worlds and eventually found that they might stake a claim in the larger one. And contrary to the melancholy depictions, the weepy confessionals, many audacious and self-supporting single women had a lot of fun along the way. They continue to. And so the press continues to cover them as well as what is still perceived as their "condition."

My own young single life, and how it abruptly ended, makes a strong case study in the power of single imagery and the way our mass media distorts it. That particular ending also marks the beginning of this book.

SNAPSHOTS FROM A SINGLE LIFE

In 1986, I was twenty-seven, living alone, and working in publishing—a youthful life phase that I'd spent years trying to organize and had enjoyed, until the day I got up and heard the news. According to bulletins on the Today show, National Public Radio, and every local newscast, I had officially become a Single Woman. To summarize briefly what newscasters milked for half an hour: A study now infamous for its flaws had revealed an alarming decrease in marriage "prospects" among women anywhere in age between twenty-five and forty. If, like me, you'd "postponed matrimony" due to your career or your generational tendency to cohabit, you'd now confront the tragic reality of your birth cohort: There weren't enough men and potential husbands for you and all of your friends.

It seemed ridiculous—a prespinster at twenty-seven? No hope of marrying at forty? Yet two researchers from Harvard and Yale were assuring me that my life and the lives of just about everyone I knew were now ruptured.

Before all this—as in the day before—I had been merely me: an attractive, short, nervous person who did well in jobs requiring "girls" with excitable temperaments. At the time I was a writer for several similar lifestyle magazines. On any given day I'd find myself celebrating the "flippy sandal," then skipping my way through a list of topics that might include thighs, parental death, the penis, betrayal, the truth of bagels, and a story inevitably called "Abortion Rights Are Still with Us."

I was smart, or as some ex-boyfriends liked to say, I really was in my own way very clever. For example, I had struggled against the single fates ("live at home" or "have five roommates") and had won. I had a place. No matter that at first—and second—glance it seemed situated inside a tenement. It was "rent-stabilized," a phrase that, for young New York women of the time, was a lot more exciting, filled with more possibility and the hint of adulthood, than "marry me." The details—cabbagey, narrow hallways; spindly, crooked Dr. Seuss–like stairs—didn't bother me. The point was to learn certain survival skills. How did you negotiate with landlords who conversed with your breasts? How to deal with the roaches my neighbor referred to as "BMW's," for "big mothers with wings"? And how to get past the grannies, the babushka ladies who hissed as a group when they saw me? Every day I ran an obstacle course—bugs, ladies, landlord—not stopping until I shoved open door #5 with my hip and stepped inside.

My decorating efforts had been devoted to painting over wallpaper (maypole theme) the landlord had refused to remove, and that had left little time and money for things like furniture. The primary piece, and the center of all activity, was the "divan," a bed/couch/office made up of three futons stacked and transformed by a shiny black red-fringed cloth of my grandmother's. Layered with pillows, newspapers, typewriter, phone, it formed a bountiful square in the midst of my large, naked space. (It was important at the time to describe any area as a "space," a potential venue of art, even if referring to a closet. Not that I had a closet.)

I shared this bounty with the expected singular companion, a black Siamese cat I called "Py-Not," a negation of Pywacket, the magical witch cat in Bell, Book, and Candle, and the only single cat name less clichéd than Cat, of Breakfast at Tiffany's. Rarely were my Py and I home alone. I had boyfriends, "fellas" as my mother called them, plus my girlfriends and just-friends, the many acquaintances who lacked their own spaces and stopped in at mine, then stayed for hours.

Never did I believe that this was it—My Space! My Cat! My Three Plates!—but it had seemed part of a definite forward progression. When I was fifteen, no one had gone on dates. This was during the 1970s and "dating" consisted of standing in parental basements alongside boys and getting high. Hardly anyone spoke. It was bad form to cough, indicating that you, as a girl, could not hold your smoke.

In college, it was bad form to smile. As a "womyn," a last-dregs junior feminist, one found all men suspect. If they smiled or, rather, "usurped" you with their "gaze," you demythologized them with your death stare. We'd learned well from our unmarried female professors: No sister, meaning us, was to mate before making of herself a coherent, unified being, a new woman, as there'd forever been new women who—

"Shut the fuck up!" some guy would shout. "Who the fuck's gonna marry *you?*"

Still, despite such hostile repartee, the many stilted conversations, and analogous sexual encounters, I assumed, as I had always vaguely assumed, that I'd get married. Somehow. To someone. In my apartment life, age almost 28, I was technically no closer. But I had met certain males whom, in my journal, I referred to as interesting men, not inscrutable or angry *myn.*

I WANNA BE SEDATED

I had arrived in my late twenties at one of those moments—one of those recurring spells of media frenzy in which single women appear as marginal creatures most frequently described as "pathetic." But, hey, I *worked* in the media, as I told every concerned, lip-biting woman I met, and these overblown, underverified stories were deliberately slanted to terrify the reader. I had personally manufactured, or manipulated, such terror stories on a variety of subjects, minimum, five times a year. And because I'd once been a womyn, I knew that this kind of media harassment had a history that stretched back for decades.

Despite my special knowledge, however, I was annoyed. People kept asking me questions, and essentially the same questions: Did I still live alone? And if so, why? What kind of life was that, and where was I going in that "bigger picture"? And what about (the Laundromat lady really said this) my "need for the babies"? After a while I stopped answering the questions "Seeing anyone?" "How old are you?" and "Big date?" I refused to speak to people who used the phrase "biological clock." As I saw it, the only relevant clock was the immense cultural one that seemed to be running backward into the 1950s, where a wan Frank Sinatra song was playing and in a few more bars it would be autumn.

In 1956 one women's magazine polled 2,220 high school girls on the unfortunate social plight of the single woman. As the authors paraphrased, 99 percent of participants rigorously agreed that "single career women [had] . . . so thoroughly misunderstood their central role and identity that they had failed to achieve even the most basic task of establishing a household." One teen elaborated on this spiritually homeless female: "They're misfits. Out there alone. It's crazy. And hard to understand. . . . They are not in the normal range."

Apparently, without our even suspecting, that view had held and here we all were in the wrong range. For some time I'd been receiving unsolicited mail from matchmaking and other single services. These packages ("Jewish?" "Jewish, culturally?" "Jewish, downtown?" "Like Jewish men?") included booklets on writing personals that sold "the you *you* alone can see," as well as pamphlets entitled "Accepting, Grieving, Dating" and, in true 1950s form, "How to Make a Normal Life You Can Live With." My favorite piece of advice came from a brochure entitled *Out There Alone— Guerilla Tactics:* "At the movies, or theatre, should you feel self-conscious by yourself, attempt to convey, using hand gestures, that you are with the couple, or individuals, seated next to you."

That's when I began to collect evidence of single pathos. On a large bulletin board in my kitchen, I pinned up anything that commented subtly, or not so very subtly, on single women. For example, I compiled an unrelated series of ads featuring female executives, each in standard eighties-era floppy-bow suits, each placed in a large, impersonal office, and each holding a hand to her abdomen, back, or head in pain. But the products advertised had nothing to do with physical ailments. Two were for Caribbean/Bermuda airline getaways; one was for an adjustable bed; and one showed a new lightweight leather briefcase. The subtext was louder than the copy: These attractive, successful women suffered the disease of the mistaken path, a condition familiar from popular T-shirts. (NUCLEAR

WAR? WHAT ABOUT MY CAREER? and OH, MY GOD, I CAN'T BELIEVE I FORGOT TO HAVE CHILDREN!)

My best find, however, was a cartoon pulled from a local newspaper I found in an airport. In it, seated on a double bed, surrounded by teddy bears and Chinese-food containers (incriminating signs of singleness), was a thirty-fivish woman in bra and underpants. This would seem commentary enough but for the fat bubbling out from her abdomen to form six fleshy rings. It looked as if the classical spinster had lost her neat bun and excellent posture and given up tea for Snickers bars smeared with peanut butter.

Then several developments interrupted my work.

I got married. Immediately we moved across country and back, only to move within New York City twice in two years. After a while we had kids, moved again, and began to lose track of certain friends, in particular, I found, my single friends. They resented my distraction while on the phone. ("Being always out of breath is *not* a status symbol!") In person, they did not like the way I spoke to them while looking and making faces at my baby. They didn't like the way that, exhausted, I often fell asleep mid–hilarious anecdote. Someone said I snored. It hadn't been that long since I'd been single. But so much had happened in so short a time that my apartment life with Py-not seemed kind of foreign, exotic, like a year spent abroad sometime in college. I had pictures from the trip but the actual details were starting to blur.

Then one night I began to recall that time, the entire trip, more coherently. I was seated, at the moment, with my children in the emergency room. We'd been playing a game; I was "asleep" and to wake me one child had shoved a tiny stiletto Barbie shoe up my ear. Now it was stuck. Oh, they were sorry, twisting themselves around my legs and crying, but I had trouble reassuring them and seeming "fine." I was aware only of stupid pain, ambulance sounds, and, from the smell of things, other patients hiding day-old French fries in their coat pockets.

I closed my eyes. As if it were a taxi, a Red Cross flying carpet, the lost divan pulled up in my brain. Easing back the silky black covers, I climbed in.

A DIVE INTO THE SINGLE FILES

There is an incredible amount of written material on single women out there. Amazon.com lists 787 current titles, most fitting into one of several single niches. The most obvious is the advice from "the woman who knows" (usually a doctor who goes by a first name such as Dr. Paula or Dr. Joan) to the woman who clearly doesn't. Nonexpert advice and guidebooks for single women could fill a New Age college catalogue—finding soul mates; learning to love yourself first; identifying obstacles and creatively crashing through them; and how to drag him back using every imaginable part of your body as an arsenal.

There are hundreds of relevant novels, ranging from *The House of Mirth, Sister Carrie,* and *After Leaving Mr. Mackenzie* to *Fear of Flying, Looking for Mr. Goodbar,* and *Bridget Jones's Diary.* There are some fascinating academic studies. And there are many interesting if sometimes repetitive journalistic offerings, usually magazine articles (a day/night/week in the life of a single) that grow into books and/or oral histories.

Some of the best oral histories become meditations, as in *The Improvised Woman,* a wonderful book by journalist Marcelle Clements, in which she alternates subjects' remarks with her own thoughts—all to explain how thousands of women, thirty-five to fifty-five, found themselves permanently single and raising children alone. This she viewed as nothing less than a radical rewriting of the social contract. Because of this proposition, the book was trashed by critics as "too seventies," meaning that it seemed too celebratory, too self-consciously groundbreaking—*too feminist.*

I may as well warn you that there is no way to discuss single life at this point without getting "feminist." Nearly all American women will for some part of their adult lives exist singly—that is a statistical fact. Some of us will enjoy it, some will feel relieved or depressed or will have no particular views on the subject. And yet we all know that "single" as a social entity has its unique complications. Namely, other people's sexist attitudes.

A Columbia University senior sighs and says, "You know that, as a woman, single is childlike, younger, and that a mature individual forms combinations. . . . If, as a woman, you do not, you will come to understand that 'single,' as a word, begins with the same letter as 'stigma.' . . . 'Cancer,' I am sorry to say, has the same number of letters."

A thirty-six-year-old graphic designer is less glib: "I see my married friends and female relatives mostly when the 'other half' is away. They come down to my loft and it's, like, they're so amazed to find that it's really specifically decorated. . . . And this is even if they've *been there before*. It's so insulting. I had one friend, a school chum, who seemed paralyzed by my having Le Creuset cookware. It was, like, do you have to have a wedding license to apply for heavy French pots?"

No one has the ability to make the many presumptuous views of single women disappear. But the impact might be diminished by some clear sense of where these sad-girl stereotypes originated, and how, as in a mass game of telephone, they became sadder and more grotesque over time. To track evolving views of single women, I read selectively through one hundred years of newspapers, magazines, and novels. I studied advertisements, caricatures, photographic style, fashion, theater, movies (silent, serial, sound), radio, and TV. I collected high school artifacts (filmstrips, home-ec primers, yearbooks). And I've encapsulated relevant academic opinion and research as it filtered down into the mainstream culture.

Most interesting to me and in many ways most useful, I read diaries of women who'd lived singly in 1866–69, 1884–88, 1900, 1942, 1951, 1961–62, 1973–76, and 1999.

A FEW NOTES ON APPROACH

The roots of single phobia curl back into antiquity. But I've started my investigation with the industrial revolution, and the emergence of displaced single women, specifically the middle-class spinster and the immigrant working girl. I've organized the chapters according to the single icons that came after—factory girls, "shoppies," steno girls, new women, bohemians, Gibson Girls, and the numerous other types that followed them across the twentieth century and into the present. But *Bachelor Girl* is not a simple pictorial timeline, a semiotic tour that charges through decades, admires the era's single pinup, then rushes on. Nor is it encyclopedic history. I have combined my historical single archetypes with their rough counterparts now—mostly women in their midthirties and early forties, the point that marks what one magazine editor, forty-four, calls "The Pass-Over Ceremony." As she explains: "In your twenties, you're a free bird. You are an unmarried person who has options she hasn't yet exercised. After the pass over . . . it's metamorphosis. . . . You are viewed, and you know it, as a different woman. An unmarried, as opposed to a merely single, person."

Along with this primary peer group, I interviewed all over the age map: women in their late teens and twenties, a big eager group now in their fifties and sixties, a few in their seventies, one voluble eighty-five-year-old, plus the occasional ten- or twelve-year-old with strong views about independence as it might affect future careers in veterinary science. Except for the under-twelves, all but one wanted their name and any identifying detail changed. I agreed, of course, but asked that my subjects choose their own pseudonyms. This request seemed appropriate, since many of the earliest single working girls invented fantasy names for themselves. Whether stuck in a factory, behind a store counter, or cleaning someone's house, the Marys, Hannahs, and Bridgets of the world became for ten to fifteen hours a day Absintheia, Serenissima, Cassamandrina, or my favorite, Briar Desdemona Woods, née Mary O., a seamstress circa 1870 noted for her speed and small stitches.

Because I've drawn from the popular media, in its infant and more mature forms, I have narrowed my dig to the feminine icons most consistently held out to represent American womanhood. My primary iconography, therefore, is white, if not always predictably middle-class. Of course women of (all) color have lived out, and continue to live, the single drama, and their personal narratives intersect at many points with those I've emphasized. But they make few primary appearances in the public record until occasional stories on the "sad," "dreary," or "dead-end" world of the "Negro single," circa 1966. (It would be impossible, anyway, to do justice to the complexities of the black single experience in this volume. It requires and deserves its own study, and I sincerely hope someone takes on the challenge.) Likewise, I have not included much material on self-defined lesbian women. But I do work through the various ways that "spinster" and "lesbian" have overlapped at times to describe an afeminine woman who, according to prevailing dicta, ranked as a human mutation.

Finally, I have pretty much settled the single woman in New York City, specifically Manhattan, where right now an estimated 1.95 million single women live among some 1.4 million single men. Of course the historical trail of the single leads through Europe and New England, San Francisco, Los Angeles, Chicago, and just about every abandoned suburb and small town in America. (As early as 1868, *The Nation* noted ". . . the city is the habitat of the single. The country town or small city is an uncongenial clime for the species.") But New York City exaggerates the trends and figures—as well as the nasty remarks—that are prevalent everywhere.

As of this writing, 42 percent of the American female population over age eighteen is technically single. Most have never married, although I must note that it's difficult to say precisely how many in this grouping are gay. (Census takers cannot by law ask, most gay-rights organizations are too financially strapped to conduct precise nationwide counts on their own, and of course many respondents would not answer truthfully. Thus, figures vary dramatically.) The never-weds are followed in number by widows and then the divorced, a number that fluctuates constantly.

Some census officials, and the professors and authors I'll call census spectators, predict a drop in the age of first marriage (now 26.1 for men; 25.2 for women) and an "increased post-collegiate married cohort." Others predict just the opposite, describing a country inhabited by urban "tribes," groups of thirtyish women and men who have extended the college-era concept of the group house into adult life. (The TV phenomenon *Friends* picked up on this years ago.)

Whatever the prevailing trends, most every woman will one day find herself in the single subcategory, marked as I was as a single type, an inexplicably stubborn and undesirable female alien. And there will be no escaping it. As a prescient single woman wrote, in 1955, for *Mademoiselle:* "We are never allowed to forget what the billboards, television, movies, and the press would have us remember."

That is the story *Bachelor Girl* has to tell.

CHAPTER ONE

THE CLASSICAL SPINSTER: REDUNDANTS, THE SINGLY BLESSED, AND THE EARLY NEW WOMEN

*My dear, to a brighter future—when there will not be so many forced
marriages, and women will be taught not to feel theirs a destiny manqué,
nor the threat of poor spinsterhood, should they remain single.*
   —BRITISH WOMAN, NINETEEN, WRITING TO A "MOST-BELOVED"
      (PRESUMABLY UNHAPPY) MARRIED SCHOOL FRIEND, 1859

He: Who's the fat lady with the heavy brows and all the hair?
She: A spinster aunt.
He: Where are you, taking the picture?
*She: I'm the fat lady with the heavy brows and all the hair. I'm poor
Aunt Charlotte. And I'm still not well.*
   —BETTE DAVIS, HAVING LOST WEIGHT, NOW, VOYAGER, 1942

*The woman of a certain age is a very charming concept in French. In just
about every other language it is a euphemism for having lost, through age,
whatever charmant thing it was that made you charming. And for a
woman who never married, there are no euphemisms. The "losing" in*

her case is a condition, a pathology. It is about as far removed from a
charming concept as a brain tumor.

—DORIAN, THIRTY-EIGHT, NATIONAL
PUBLIC RADIO PRODUCER, 2001

IN THE SPINSTER MUSEUM

It seems safe to say that in 2002 nobody is a spinster and that a certain
percentage of the population is not entirely aware of what a spinster is. For
those in the latter category, I offer a brief tour of the Classical Spinster
Museum.

WHAT THE OLD GIRL LOOKED LIKE:

". . . grey-haired . . . desiccated . . . with a funny little tic that
twitched her left eye-brow, and a mole on her upper lip. . . ."

—A DESCRIPTION OF MISS SKIDMORE FROM *EDNA, HIS WIFE,*
MARGARET AYERS BARNES, 1935

WHAT SHE DID EACH DAY:

"I went upstairs to my flat to eat a melancholy lunch. A dried-up
scrap of cheese, a few lettuce leaves for which I could not be bothered to make any dressing, a tomato and a piece of bread and butter followed by a cup of coffee . . . a woman's meal, I thought, with
no suggestion of brandy afterwards."

—MILDRED LATHBURY, HEROINE,
EXCELLENT WOMEN, BARBARA PYM, 1951

WHAT OTHERS THOUGHT (IN ADDITION TO "IT'S SO SAD"):

"A woman alone is an atrocity! An act against nature. Unmarried
women pose a grave danger . . . our great civilization could decline . . . the larger health of the nation is at stake."

—A BRITISH MP, FROM A SPEECH GIVEN IN 1922

THUS HER POTENTIAL TO BECOME A MONSTER:
"It was the third house on the right side of our street . . . gray ranch, white curtains, and this lady who lived there . . . she lived all alone and she never came out . . . It was the 'cootie's house' because all you saw was one eyeball peeking out the corner bay window. In my child sense, she was only an eye and not a body. You had to run past."

—EDITH, FORTY-FOUR, DANCE COMPANY ADMINISTRATOR, 2001

It's an odd and dusty exhibition, and yet pieces of the collection are still scattered about the culture. A forty-two-year-old pianist who called herself "Mildred—definitely Mildred" says that her relatives give her money as she leaves any family event, in case, as an unmarried, childlike person, she doesn't have her own. Another woman, thirty-eight, describes phone calls from relatives and friends who are "really calling to make sure I have not died and, as no one noticed, I've gone ahead and decomposed." A single stockbroker, thirty-six, says, "My sister asks me to do errands that often require me to stand on long lines and this is 'reasonable' to her because she has children and I do not. What *is* this presumption?"

I'd call it an essential part of the spinster legacy.

IN WHICH THE SPINSTER ARRIVES

The first spinsters appeared in thirteenth-century France and a bit later in Germany and England as spinners of cotton and wool. They were not yet spinsters but *femmes seules*—unwed young girls, orphaned relatives, and widows of the Crusades who performed their tasks within the self-sustained family home. Most stayed there. Yet there were some who lived independently, dealing for themselves with weavers and textile merchants and often earning their praise. As late as 1783, in a *Description of Manchester*, we learn that "weavers were . . . obliged to pay more for the spinning than the price allowed by the merchants 'but darst not complain . . . lest lose the spinner.' "

Long before the industrial revolution—and before the implementation of a restrictive British common law—single women worked on their own in other ways. Town and city records, portions of which have been published in academic papers, indicate that unwed women in medieval France, England, and Germany traded in raw wool, silk, and rare spices. Some engaged in foreign trading and owned their own ships, and a few are said to have managed large estates and breweries.

On into the seventeenth century, *spinster* was used to identify a respectable employment category. When later that century the French began using *spinster* to indicate an unwed woman, the term was understood to be descriptive: a woman on her own, for any number of reasons, and in need of an income.

In England, however, another spinsterly model was in the making: the Old Maid, who first took form as a loud, bosomy theater grotesque known as "the Dame." Here was a new female creature so vain, so rabidly flirtatious she seemed unaware that the men she desired found her repulsive. For best effect, the dame was played by a man. Even in France, where the view of the serious, dedicated spinner prevailed, the playwright Molière created a protospinster, his own prehistoric Old Maid, in the form of Bélise, a conceited and oblivious character in *Les Femmes savantes* (1672). Bélise has never wed, and without companionship, talking to or arguing with herself or whomever happens to be standing there, she has come to believe that she's a genius. Just as the British recognized the dame as a harridan with access to rouge pots, so French spectators recognized this blathering female as a deluded *idiote*.

By the late eighteenth century, these apparitions—the spooky lone woman who was neither brilliant nor beautiful—had coalesced. The resulting character, often set down at the edges of good society, appears first in *The Expedition of Humphry Clinker* by Tobias Smollett (1771), a novel reexamined in a 1990 doctoral thesis, "Singleness of Heart," by scholar Susan Leslie Katz. The spinster part is small but highly detailed, as if the curtain had risen on a sitting-room drama and there, standing rigidly far stage left, was an odd-looking woman in conversation with herself. As the creature inches her way center stage, a male voice relates the woeful tale of one Tabitha Bramble. (The name Tabitha is classical spinster—similar to Tituba, the Caribbean servant at Salem, Massachusetts, who allegedly taught the spells and charms that led Sarah Good and nineteen others to be burned or hanged for witchcraft. And "Tabitha" would be long associated with single women—tabbies, tabby cats, would become common nineteenth-century single nicknames—and with witches. The baby witch on the beloved 1960s TV series *Bewitched* was named Tabitha. The grandmother witch, Endora, was exceptionally catty, a real Tabby. And, to switch popular forms, Dorothy L. Sayers's Lord Peter Wimsey called his troops of excellent war-widow detectives "the Cattery.") But back to the tragically appointed Miss Bramble:

> In her person, she is tall, raw-boned, aukward, flat-chested, and stooping; her complexion is sallow and freckled; her eyes are not grey, but greenish, like those of a cat, and generally inflamed. . . . her forehead low; her nose long, sharp, . . . her lips skinny, her mouth extensive, her teeth straggling and loose, of various colours and conformation; and her long neck shrivelled into a thousand wrinkles—In her temper, she is proud, stiff, vain, imperious, prying, malicious, greedy, and uncharitable.

And I leave out her dog, a cursed animal. Tabitha kicked it.

Before the debuts of the Dickensian sideshow freaks—the world-renowned bride, Miss Havisham, Miss Wade of *Little Dorrit*, and Rosa Dartle of *David Copperfield*—and even before Hawthorne's Hepzibah, the "mildewed piece of aristocracy" wandering her way through *The House of the Seven Gables*, many voices articulated the case against the old maid. In 1748 the *Oxford English Dictionary* defined her as "any spiteful or ill-natured female gossip or tattler." Alexander Pope made it personal: "My soul abhors the tasteless dry embrace/of a stale virgin with a winter face." Wordsworth commented with cool remove—describing a maiden withering on a stalk—while Henry Fielding expressed pure and immediate disgust: "She did not resemble a cow so much in her breath, as in the two brown globes which she carried before her." A few years later he added this advice: "Young ladies" dared not venture too close to one of these "types for the girl was sure to be bitten by one, as by a mad dog." That is, if the maid in question still had teeth. A widespread public discussion had established that the old maid's teeth were rotting at a faster-than-average rate. Without explaining exactly why, one medical treatise, circa 1766, featured a spirited debate about whether or not the maid should have them all pulled to avoid embarrassment "to one's relations" caused by rotting incisors.

In her early incarnations, the old maid was not associated with the industrious and respected spinner. Rather, she was a toothless parody of the uneducated minor noblewoman who had been trained for nothing more than marriage and then had failed to capture a husband. Just think of Cinderella's stepsisters. (It's not surprising that this groping sadistic duo emerged in their distinctive modern form in the Perrault version of the fairy tale published in seventeenth-century France.)

But the industrial revolution and its aftermath would permanently blur the distinctions between the goodly spinner and the crazy old maid.

Once the self-sustaining mercantile household—the entire working system of artisan, apprentice, and journeyman—collapsed, those who'd worked there, the spinners included, were left to negotiate a place within the new economy. Many spinsters sought work inside the textile mills, although the mills favored the very young girl and then usually fired her when she turned twenty, or at whatever point she began to seem "older," meaning tired and likely to complain. More mature spinsters took custom sewing or quilting assignments known as "out work." When they could. The competition was intense, there was never enough work to begin with, and many were forced to quit. A few daring misses took more public positions in small token or "cent" shops, but the large majority moved in with former employers or distant relatives, who supplied room and board in exchange for household work and child care. Those without any connections advertised. Governess, companion, nurse, fine seamstress—these positions would be pinned onto the spinster's image like a wilted, brown-edged corsage.

Among the castaways were hundreds of unlucky upper-class girls. In some cases they'd been orphaned and their family homes lost to male relatives through the machinations of British inheritance laws. And some stood to lose prospective mates. With the industrial revolution, it had become common practice among the upper classes to postpone marriage until the groom had established himself financially. But in both Europe and the United States, many men had quickly learned to live well as bachelors, renting private rooms, joining private clubs, taking mistresses. Now, when the intended had suffered so drastic a setback, there was even less urgency to wed. As one MP put it, "Before us lies the disaster we have . . . watched coming. A girl who has trained for the arts of wifehood . . . schooled in the gracious arts, who fails so much as to wed? We witness the unfolding of a tragical redundant class."

These perceived changes were amply documented in the 1851 British census. It seemed that there were in England 405,000 more women than men, creating a surplus in all segments of the female population.* Known as redundant or superfluous women, they officially became a social problem, and one with no easy remedy. Those who worked would compete for a limited number of jobs. And there were those who could not quite bring themselves to work. The pamphlet *Dedicated to the Refined Young Lady*, reprinted consistently from 1860 to 1905, dictated that one might make her way, without loss of station, in lace making, fancy needlework, or as a "paid reading partner." She might also, under an assumed name, sell canned jams and jellies, write love stories for magazines, or give "dramatic readings." The pursuit of an actual job, however, was impossible, for to work in an office, "to stamp envelopes . . . would greatly decrease the likelihood of marriage." The better girl might work "for cake" but not "for bread." (It should also be said that this girl might not be cut out to do real work of any kind. The résumé of Mattie Silver, the central female character in Edith Wharton's *Ethan Frome*, typifies the situation: "Her equipment, though varied, was inadequate. She could trim a hat, make molasses

---

*Some early feminists pointed out that the numbers needed interpretation. Women lived longer because, never soldiers or bar brawlers, they often kept their bodies intact past age thirty. They didn't leave home as often as men, meaning that when census inspectors called, they were in. There also now simply *seemed* to be more women, because so many formerly hidden middle-class women were out on the streets.

candy, recite 'The Curfew Shall Not Ring Tonight,' and play 'The Lost Chord,' and a pot-pourri from 'Carmen.' ")

Yet many, of course, were left with few choices. The Brontë sisters, Charlotte, Emily, and Anne, were among those who routinely made visits to local "intelligence," or employment, offices to apply for the scant number of jobs hundreds had applied for already. In Charlotte's case, the jobs she eventually secured provided background and details for three of the most complex single heroines in all literature: the stoical Jane Eyre, Caroline Helstone of *Shirley* (1849), and, my favorite, Lucy Snowe of *Villette* (1853), a boarding-school teacher so fiercely self-contained—she has suffered a severe trauma she cannot speak of—that Jane Eyre, in comparison, seems like a gay lady at Mr. Rochester's house party. When left alone at the school during a holiday, Lucy suffers one of the most realistic nervous breakdowns in all literature. If not strictly autobiographical, this episode suggests that the author at a young age knew the misery of enforced, impenetrable solitude.

William Makepeace Thackeray wrote, intending to praise Charlotte Brontë, that she was "that fiery little eager brave . . . tremulous creature!" As he explained, "[I] see that rather than any other earthly good . . . she wants some Tomkins to love her and to be in love with her. But you see this is a little bit of a creature, without a penny of good looks, thirty years old, I should think, buried in the country." She was a spinster. But at least a spinster with talent.

With so many others lacking literary or any other talents, what was Great Britain to do? The most famed proposal, entirely serious, came from one W. R. Gregg, a conservative commentator, in 1862. In his view it was essential that the British "restore by emigration of women that proportion between the sexes in the old country and in the newer ones." The difficulty, he imagined, would be "chiefly mechanical. It is not easy to convey a multitude of women across the Atlantic or the Antipodes by an ordinary means. . . . To transport the half million from where they are redundant to where they are wanted at an average of 30 passengers a ship would require 10,000 vessels, or at least 10,000 voyages." (To clarify, the only transport of women out of Great Britain for reasons of marital status had occurred years earlier, when "purchase brides" had been shipped to the Virginia Colony for the "price of transport.")

Gregg was ready for his critics. Should his scheme fall through, he had another, more practical solution for surplus waste. Under this plan, redundant women would be trained to behave like courtesans, thus attracting more men. Those too stubborn or proud to do so would, as promised, live out their miserly unadorned and childless lives as social lepers.

It should be noted that "stubborn and proud" in this situation referred at least in part to those women—educated, politically astute, or rebellious—who believed that a surplus of women existed only because nobody before had bothered to count them. Victorian men, as many saw it, lived to count, to document, to arrange and to name every detail of the physical world. This generation had drawn a map of the universe allowing for every phylum and genus; unmarried women fit no known categories.

In many ways, England offers up a textbook case history in spinsterism: A creature found in folklore and literature—the old maid—is dredged up, her traits grafted onto a segment of the female population that has become threatening—in this case, all those seemingly unwilling to wed. These women are assigned a subsecondary status and become, as a group, a cautionary icon for younger females: This Could Be You.

AMERICAN GOTHIC

Early America, early New England specifically, still holds the record for extreme intolerance toward single women. For years after the Salem hysteria, Americans regarded the unwed female, whether she was outspoken or mysteriously shy, with grave suspicion. The Puritans herded women into marriage, viewing it as a holding pen within which to grow the population and keep a firm lock on those deemed potentially threatening to it. Puritan doctrine preached that a woman possessed her own soul, as opposed to a soul meshed with her husband's. She would be judged alone for her acts in this life, and it was her husband's responsibility to be sure she remained true to God and that she behaved chastely for the greater good of the community. It was a job that required close scrutiny.

Throughout the late seventeenth and eighteenth centuries, an unwed

Boston woman of twenty-three was labeled a "spinster"; at twenty-six she plunged into the leprous zone of the "thornback," a name derived from an ugly spiny-backed fish. If a thornback belonged to no family—and life spans were so short, many girls at twenty-six were on their own—then she needed to seek out a well-respected, churchgoing male whose wife was schooled in female piety. She would live with them, doing chores and, like a moral orphan, studying Bible and proper conduct. She would never leave the property unless escorted by an adult family member or a male of good repute.

To quote a Boston bookseller, circa 1788, who'd seen his share of thornbacks: "Nothing can exceed it and [it is] look'd on as a dismal spectacle."

Outside New England there seem to have been few such complications. One British traveler, Nicholas Crestell, called late-eighteenth-century America "a paradise on earth for women." Excluding Massachusetts, a place with three times the usual number of spinsters, the colonial life was "luck incarnated." Crestell wrote home: "That great curiousity the Old Maid, the most calamitous creature in nature, is seldom seen in this country." So rare was this creature that she was called, so Crestell wrote, an "ancient maid."

The phenomenon of the ancient maid was due largely to the "westward trek," the monumental task of fulfilling America's manifest destiny. Now here was a mighty concept that appealed to many men and drew thousands away from New England. As one historian would later put it: "Wives were as scarce in Idaho as husbands were in New England."

Put another way, very few unwed New England women were inclined to trek after men into the wilderness. The self-educated spinster, in particular, understood just what was in store for her "out there." At least one in twenty-five pioneer wives died in childbirth, and they were quickly replaced—the farms had to run; more children were needed to work the farms—and these next women, if they died, were quickly replaced and often replaced again.*

Back in the East, spinsters were evolving an early singular culture,

---

*Some single women headed west—by themselves. The Oregon Land Donation Act of 1850 was originally intended to entice spinsters and younger women to come west and marry homesteaders. Changes to the law during the next decade allowed several hundred women to stake land claims of their own.

based in friendships, books, teaching jobs, and tea parties that begin to suggest parlor scenes out of Henry James's *The Bostonians*. Officials were quick to reassure the city's men (of course some had stayed behind) and safely married women that these "other" women represented an aberration. To quote from an issue of the Farmer's Almanac, 1869, "They've been left behind, as they are always left behind, and as they have diminished resources . . . they become diminished goods." One very literal example: reputable Boston doctors began to report that spinsters were likely to develop shriveled ovaries, a natural occurrence, it seemed, if one did not make good use of them early on. (Sperm, God-blessed, was safe.) The 1855 census confirmed that the aberration was far more widespread than suspected: There was a surplus of forty-five thousand females in the New England states. Rather than ship them off to Canada—the Massachusetts governor's initial declaration—politicians, essayists, and concerned married women decided it was time to clarify just what it was a spinster might do, and what natural restrictions could be applied to her actions.

This first public etiquette for American spinsters called for a muted surrender, as if a spiritual hysterectomy had been performed, leaving behind as scars an insecurity and chronic melancholia.* Typically spinsters helped with the chores at home and moved between the homes of married siblings who needed help. And as in England, they hired themselves out as paid companions, tutors, schoolteachers or assistants, and seamstresses. Within the household, even if this was her original family household, she was made to seem unimportant and childlike—for a woman's adult life began at marriage—and she was expected to keep herself well occupied

---

*There were a few categories of spinster exemption. For example, if a woman had lived a privileged life on the stage or been a famous painter's model or dancer, she would be presumed to possess a stage trunk full of romantic stories forever putting her out of the banal spinster category. The other "out" was the widow-manqué, the spinster who had been engaged to a brave soldier, dead in battle, his picture forever on her bureau. An excellent widow-manqué can be found in Jane, one of the two spinstered Sawyer sisters in *Rebecca of Sunnybrook Farm*, who lost her great love to the Civil War. Although Jane had "never left Riverboro in all the years that lay between and [had] grown into . . . [a] spare New England spinster . . . underneath was still the faint echo of that wild heartbeat of girlhood." Her sister, in comparison, was hard, unyielding, and nasty. And occasionally a spinster character might redeem herself by marrying late, miraculously shedding her dusty paper chains. A great twentieth-century example is Miss Parthenia Ann Hawks of the musical *Show Boat* (1926), who'd lived "a barren spinster's life" before her marriage to Cap'n Andy.

and out of the way. One force-fed book, *The Afternoon of Unmarried Life* (1858), suggested that the maiden female not engage in any taxing physical activity, including walks, unless they were limited to the periphery of one's property. The poor thing might wander off and happen upon a preacher, some itinerant revivalist who might excite her, and as this and other manuals explained, these women, naïfs, were prone to outbursts of ecstatic piety. "She must never risk to be made enthusiastic by religious fervour . . . or agitated," warned the author, hinting obliquely at sexual arousal. But an "industrious, independent, cheerful" spinster (the words of a bishop) need not be treated like a neutered pet (my own). She made an excellent companion for aging parents; in short, she was like a walking retirement benefit.

Of course "spinsters," having perfected this meager act, still hoped for future union—whether with like friends or, still, yes, perhaps a man. Consider this excerpt from an 1867 "storiette" (a very short story, usually romantic, published in early magazines and compilations). In this one, a thirty-eight-year-old woman awaits the arrival of a man she was once engaged to, a man who went off to find fortune and has now returned. Here she is before her looking glass:

> "A lavendar gown," said Miss Cambron, with a stiff and critical survey of herself in the glass . . . quite suited to thirty eight; some lines about the mouth and eyes; a mere ghost of color . . . a look not specifically young. He won't come again! He'll want some little blue eyes—with pink cheeks and a coral necklace! It's not his fault [still] she stood at her mirror contrasting the image it gave her with another from the deepening glass of her memory—that of a young girl.

She goes on at some length about her lack of "bloom," the rosy-colored cheeks that define a woman as happy and young. (The concept of "bloom" figures heavily into many nineteenth-century spinster novels; in Jane Austen's *Persuasion* it is mentioned twenty-one times.) Once it goes, the skin is pallid, symbolizing inevitable and rapid decay.

But it is important now to pause and state that not all women shared this belief in slow evisceration or found it at all relevant to their futures.

TRUE WOMEN AND THE SINGLY BLESSED

They are not a widely known group of women. They led no particular movement, formed no political cells, did not even qualify as a peer cohort—still, they made some small history by saying no. No to marriage proposals, in which the concept of "forever," as Florence Nightingale famously said, slid into "never." As in never being wholly oneself; never being permitted to make up one's own mind; never to be able to move about freely. In some sense, buried alive. Especially if one was marrying just to marry. As one Eliza Southgate wrote to a friend in 1841, "Which is more despicable? She who married a man she scarcely thinks well of—to avoid the reputation of 'old maid'—or she who . . . preferred to live her single life?"

She who "preferred to live her single life" lived it most often in New England, from the 1830s through the mid-1870s. This was the era of "single blessedness," an almost devotional phrase used by a fairly elite and intellectual band of single women to describe a state of unmarried bliss. To sketch a quick composite of this early rebel, we can say that she grew up amid intellectuals, preachers or writers, with left-leaning principles and a love of oration. Household conversation ranged from abolitionism, transcendentalism, or trade unionism to any other radical topic then debated at public meetings and in Unitarian church sermons. She may not have received an education like her brother's, but on her own she had trained her mind the way others had worked to play delightfully upon the pianoforte, or to sing lieder (not that she lacked these more delicate talents). Living across an expanse of cities, towns, and states, these single women did not create a declaration of their beliefs. But if they had, it might have been this: a desire to elevate singlehood from its status as horrifying fate to "an expression of self-reverence."

Dr. Lee Virginia Chambers-Schiller, author of *Liberty: A Better Husband*, a dazzling book on these women, derived the term "singly blessed" from a letter, written in 1820 by a frustrated young woman, Eliza Chaplin, to her friend Laura Lovell. As Chaplin wrote of marriage and singlehood: "[rather than] endure the unhappiness that exists where minds are 'fettered to a different mold,' and rather [than] be subject to the 'eternal strife' which . . . prevails [I prefer] ever to remain in 'single blessedness' and deem it felicity thus to live."

The list of women who described themselves this way was long: the abolitionist Grimké sisters, Florence Nightingale, the poet and onetime mill girl Lucy Larcom, Louisa May Alcott, Susan B. Anthony, Dr. Elizabeth and nurse Emily Blackwell, Vida Scudder, and M. Carey Thomas, second president of Bryn Mawr and one of the first women to attend Cornell. There were even a few men who agreed; commentator Aretemus B. Muzzy wrote during the 1840s: "A single life is not without its advantages; while a married one that fails . . . is the acme of earthly wretchedness."

Single blessedness had its roots in the eccentric nineteenth-century New England household but, more important, in new attitudes toward female education. Starting at midcentury, many middle-class families began to send pubescent girls to boarding schools, and later a smaller number would send their most insistent marriage-aged daughters to "girls' college." (Among the elite schools, Vassar opened in 1861, Wellesley in 1870; Smith in 1871, and Bryn Mawr in 1885.) A few of the most determined enrolled in the small number of all-male schools admitting women, while the majority of the education-minded daughters attended the teaching academies known as "normal schools."

No matter how unusual and enlightened her upbringing, no adolescent girl started out in life aspiring to a state of single blessedness. She entered boarding school understanding what any average woman knew: Marriage served as a woman's only practical life solution. Moreover, it served as her moral and spiritual duty. If any aspect of this observation had been left unclear, every political, religious, educational, and literary force in the culture, every leader, of anything, wrote out or recited for girls the female life agenda: to make and maintain the family home, populating it with no fewer than five children (allowing for inevitable miscarriages), and to create within it a calm, well-decorated realm for her hardworking, exhausted husband.

Author Catherine M. Sedgwick, writing circa 1835, summarized the primitive female media blitz in this way: "By all the talk that we hear from old and young, married and single . . . marriage is not only the felicity of woman, but [the source of] her dignity, her attractiveness, her usefulness . . . her very life depends on it!"

By the second or third year of school, the more intuitive, rebellious girl had come to grasp the underpinnings of the institution. Perhaps she'd learned that *nuptial* came from *nupta,* the Latin word for veil, or covering. In French the word was *couverte,* which gave rise to the full-surrender marital state known as couverture. As adapted in the United States from British common law, married women had no legal rights and were in essence the property of men, who owned and got to keep it all, including any children, in the case of divorce. As that translated on a day-to-day basis: He ventured forth into the world; she stayed inside. As it was said of these appointed spheres: "He for the world and commerce; she for the domestic, the nursery." Or, as Milton had earlier expressed it: "He for God only; she for God in him."

By graduation, such a girl would have understood the mechanics of Victorian marriage, and what historian Barbara Welter dubbed "the Cult of True Womanhood." True womanhood was the brainchild of the "domestic feminists" (oxymoron notwithstanding), a group of reform-minded women who sought a conservative way to mediate their problem. Their problem, roughly summarized: What exactly should intelligent married women do, given that they didn't belong in the world but had opinions and ideas too big for the house?

The best-known domestic feminist was Catherine Beecher, sister of Harriet Beecher Stowe (she watched the kids while Harriet wrote *Uncle Tom's Cabin)* and Henry Ward Beecher, the preacher now best remembered for his role in a sex scandal. As she and others viewed it, the Wife, exercising subtle manipulations—an exquisitely hypnotic feminine style— might exert some quiet influence over her husband, encouraging him to take certain desired actions out there in the world. At the same time, she'd project a radiant moral force over her children. Think of her as a human aerosol can, her sweet lingering residue infusing the house with calm, a sense of order for her brood, and, when needed, an undetectable means for mesmerizing her husband to get her way.

Not all marriages followed the stage directions—one partner set to play the whispering, encouraging angel and one to play the boss. But there was an inherent deceit in many male-female transactions. Consider that most men and women, husbands and wives, did not always know each other at the start of marriage. They knew only what to expect. No matter how pleasant on the surface, marriage could be what one young college girl called "a trial of inequality." And not always in the ways expected. Activist Mary Dodge, who preferred instead of "singly blessed" the term "nobly discontent," had put it this way: "True, he may be as good as she, but he might not be good enough for her."

The best relationship a woman had was often with her girlfriends.

Sketches from the mid- and late nineteenth century show two women huddled together at the center of a dark velvet davenport, holding hands. During the Civil War era, they were dressed in crinolines so wide that the women look like matching parachutes—ready to jump, together. Later, in photographs, they're shown strolling, bustles out and arms linked. A magazine illustration common throughout the Victorian age shows one writing a letter to the other, who is pictured inside a daydream cartoon balloon, the edges frilly, like a valentine, the beloved's imagined face angelic.

Special friends usually met at boarding school, and typically their parents encouraged the duet. In the ideal parental scenario, two young girls would be "smashed"—think of best friends going steady—and once smashed, they'd learn trust, loyalty, tolerance, patience. Once they'd mastered these skills they would be able, theoretically at least, to transfer them onto a marital relationship. Even if those who wed never felt quite the same about their husbands.

At the time there were far fewer taboos on touching between same-sex friends and it was common for affectionate girls to kiss each other, to sleep in the same bed, and to engage in what we'd consider foreplay—and possibly more. The term "lesbian"—the very idea—did not in its current sense yet exist. Until it was redefined, circa 1919, to discredit "new spinsters," that is, independent, professional singles, the word conjured a series of images from antiquity, usually transvestites, for example, a medieval French-woman clad in armor and perched on a horse. Many girls' school profes-sors, prime examples of the singly blessed, lived with special friends—smashes that had turned into lifelong partnerships. To their stu-dents, what could have seemed more natural than women in pairs?

The intense devotion of many a smash is revealed in girls' most secre-tive correspondence. One girl wrote of "the thrill of our pet dovey times" and a "burning sensation, both when I am with you—as you will know—and when I am alone and imagining back." Studies made in 1900 of twenty thousand "Boston marriages"—two women who lived as sisters or lovers—and of numerous smashes revealed episodes of mutual masturbation. Other couples give no hint of overt sexual activity—or what we'd consider overt sexual activity—but were, rather, said to be playful and affectionate.

Whatever the precise nature of the bond, smashed girls likely re-mained friends for life, whether or not one of them married. "My every nerve springs forward at attention when I hear the post arrive!!" wrote a married friend to another who was far off and unwed. In long letters illus-trated with ink drawings—self-portraits, fancy matching gowns, two women out strolling—they reaffirmed their feelings for each other and helped each other negotiate the requirements of married life. One engaged New Englander revealed to her dearest friend in 1782 a shocking decision: she would never change her name. "I think it a good [name] and am de-termined not to change it without a prospect of some great advantage. I am sure to confront a tribunal."

Threatened by these connections, some men called them immature, proof that women underneath were really children who could not put away girlish toys and dolls and sit properly alongside their mates. As far back as 1847, a visitor to the United States, one Domingo Sarmiento, concurred: "Americans have developed customs which have no parallel on this earth—the unmarried woman flies about with her friends as if it were a butterfly."

The more unusual man found beauty in these friendships, sometimes collecting and reading aloud women's letters to one another. For this odd connoisseur, female love letters were refined works of sentimental expression, the prose equivalent of a hand-carved miniature or cameo. Scholar Carroll Smith-Rosenberg writes that Goethe published the love letters sent between his fiancée, Bettina, and a countess she was deeply attached to; Margaret Fuller, respected New England intellectual, found a U.S. publisher for the volume. To underscore how important these bonds were in the young (and older) female life, consider the life span of one early study on the subject, *The Friendships of Women*, by William R. Alger. It was published in Boston in 1869 and by 1890 had reached its twelfth printing.

It was obvious still that to marry was to win at the era's female lottery—if not necessarily hit the jackpot—but the point is that a few women actively, and without trace of pathos, had begun to question the contest. In articles entitled "A Loyal Woman's No," and "The Difficulties That Accrue to Our Sex from the Marriage Bond," they argued for allowing some female lives to evolve on their own terms, possibly with their own chosen friends or family. As one midcentury woman, a self-styled biological researcher, wrote to her "dearest dear": "I cannot wait these days to turn 30! Then I may put away all pretense of being marriageable and concentrate on my interests."

SEND ME NO FLOWERS

Starting in the 1870s, the marriage rate among educated women plummeted to 60 percent, compared with 90 percent of all women in the general population, and the figure would remain low until 1913 or '14. Remember that these women lived in an era that celebrated feats of daring and genius in the visual and dramatic arts, social and physical sciences, transportation, politics, and archeology. Explorers, doctors, even realist novelists were heroes, secular gods lauded for their intellectual gifts and their bravery. A talented woman would have been acutely aware of her potential.

And she also would have been acutely aware that marriage carried with it specific dangers. One in every thirty women died in childbirth. And there was plenty of opportunity to witness a live unanesthetized birth before marriage, an experience that Susan B. Anthony herself called "a very nasty business." (The entire nature of the business would become far nastier in 1880, when the U.S. government declared abortion and the few extant forms of contraception illegal—a ban on all abortions that would remain in place until the 1973 *Roe* v. *Wade* decision.)

Then one had to contemplate husbands.

Even the loyal and genuinely loving ones couldn't help but domineer, and many of them, even the very best, were likely to drink. In fact, it was widely accepted that all men drank, just as all men used spittoons and knew their way around a rifle. (Some even claimed drinking was healthy. Mid-century it was often argued that whiskey was cleaner and safer to drink than New York City public water.) Earlier in the nineteenth century the little-known but remarkable Women's Moral Reform Society had railed against alcohol as the primary cause of spousal battering, rape, and the use of prostitutes. There were always pious groups who specialized in social cleanup, "municiple housekeeping," as it was called. But none had made the explicit link between male drinking and male abuse of women. In its women-run newspaper, *The Advocate*, Moral Reform editors listed the names of men seen leaving brothels. As they saw it, this was "The Everyman" and they also called him "The Destroyer." One *Advocate* writer stated, "I'd as soon bed down with a nice clean dog as with a man . . . holding a bottle."

That's not to say that the singly blessed used terms such as "The Destroyer" or that they refused to hear marriage proposals. Many young women had simply learned to reject them—no matter how often they were repeated.

In one famed case, a Boston woman refused the same man sixteen times; another allegedly turned down twenty-six different men. Poet Lucy Larcom, who worked for years as a mill girl in Lowell, Massachusetts, reported that her first proposal left her with hives for a week. Florence Nightingale seems to have turned them down weekly, pausing to consider just one man so exceptional, famed, and intelligent that only the most beautiful and brainy of the famed Nightingale girls would do. She spent six months writing furiously in her journals to explain her refusal, a grueling narrative alternating between rage and self-loathing, a suspicion of mental illness, and a tenuous pride in following the secret pledge she had made to her herself about her duties. My favorite terrorized-fiancé story belongs to Jane Austen, a young woman said by one of her closest friends to "shift," to be charming and decorous and yet to possess "eyes the color of a viper's." Once, while visiting friends, she listened warily as a young suitor made so passionate a case, she stunned herself by accepting, then left for home. But not long into the ride she began to feel queasy. One hour later, she had her driver turn back, despite bad weather, to rescind her agreement. After seven hours of additional traveling she arrived home physically ill but relieved.

As more unattached women seemed to be working, giving speeches, or just out walking around at odd hours, the Massachusetts governor once again proposed direct action. This time he hoped to ship the state's twenty-one thousand redundant women to Oregon or California, where wives, as always, were in short supply. (As historians would later point out, so were prostitutes, although this particular need the governor did not publicly address.)

The proposal died, but not the paranoid views of single women. What seemed to be changing was the way some single women, the "blessed" in particular, responded. In public situations, even the youngest had been trained to ignore nasty epithets and walk proudly. College women took an eager part in debates, for example, at Oberlin, "Is Married Life More Conducive to a Woman's Happiness than Single?" or "Is the Marriage Relation Essential to the Happiness of Mankind?" True, for girls at coed schools it was hard, in almost any situation, not to run off crying. But there are records of girls who braved the taunting ("The Co-ed leads a wretched life/She eats potatoes from a knife!"). In an 1863 diary one college girl remarks that she is developing "a natural armor, which seems attached and fastened tight on to my body and brain. I hope someday I may step out of it."

Professional women out on the road needed an even stronger suit of armor and perhaps a sword. The original abolitionists were typically booed off stages. Men called them hags who'd never had men and wanted to free the black "species" only so they could snag themselves a black male. Social workers and nurses typically slept in the worst parts of a city, sometimes among people who had contagious diseases. Others, traveling for pleasure, to see friends who'd married or gone to teach at far-off schools, suffered nasty comments along the way. Still, a trip for the single woman was a test, an adventure that would have been unimaginable to her as a girl; some stayed on the road for up to six months. (Elizabeth Cady Stanton, founding feminist and the mother of seven, once wrote jokingly to her single and suddenly absent colleague, Susan B. Anthony: "Where are you? Dead or married?")

Back at home, Theodore Roosevelt, an up-and-coming public figure, accused them of committing "race suicide," meaning that they were failing to produce healthy white babies amid the many (I paraphrase) filthy, copulating immigrants. But as single women saw it, that was the vision of a paranoid man who happened, by chance, to be a politician. Ignoring him, they continued their school studies, their work, and their travel. Clara Barton's sister, Mary, had an idea for them all. Like everyone else, she had "viewed from a safe distance the exquisite happiness of marriage." In response, she declared, "Let us form an Old Maid's Hall!"

THE MAKING OF A FEMALE COMMUNE

There was no precedent for group life among American single women who were not nuns. Most unmarried women ended up back where they'd started—at home, tending to the usual family crises: illnesses, pregnancies, and the usual miserable complaints. Poet Lucy Larcom put it this way: "I cannot think my own thoughts in the thick of other people's lives."

Louisa May Alcott echoed the sentiment in 1868: "I want to realize my dream of supporting the family *and* being perfectly independent. Heavenly hope!" This she is said to have written in her journal, so we may assume she wrote it in secret, separate from the diary her relatives would

have seen. In many households anything a family member wrote, any letter received, was considered open for reading or recitation. This passed the
time and served also as a means—especially in houses occupied by teachers or writers—for exercising one's critical faculties. Or just for criticizing.
(Louisa May Alcott's father, the famed preacher and educator Bronson Alcott, noted that, of his daughters' journals, "Anna's was about other people.
Louisa's is about herself.")

One contemporary, Ellen "Nelly" Wheeton, was caught with the contraband: a journal hidden beneath some papers in a drawer. In it, she had
apparently expressed disdain for the married state. As she managed later to
write: "[Mother] found it necessary to prohibit the use of pen and ink, or
slate and pencil, except while receiving instruction from her or the writing
master. My brother was made to spy upon my actions . . . he often threatened to tell mother when he had seen me writing upon the wall with a pin,
which I sometimes did when I had no other resources."

But could such a young woman have simply moved in with like-
minded female friends? Consider it: a house, a self-sustained universe,
where women could live happily among themselves, refusing marriage and,
more important, childbearing. The idea was blasphemous. It was as if *Her-
land*, the utopian 1915 novel by Charlotte Perkins Gilman, had sprung to
life. (In this work, serialized in the author's own magazine, a British expedition sets out to find a hidden country populated solely by genius women
warriors; as they discover, men of all classes have been extinguished.) In
short, the idea of an all-female house incited alarm.

Yet there was a long tradition of communal living among single
women. In Great Britain it dated to A.D. 385 and the founding of the Ur-
suline and Pauline orders, religious communes that were actually more like
early social-work agencies. Lone girls from all over England arrived daily so
desperate and grateful that, from the descriptions, it's not hard to imagine
them standing on the steps and shouting "Sanctuary!" These groups—and
there were constantly new ones—quickly earned the title "bastard flocks,"
for their loose approach to devotional life. Without quite meaning to, they
had devised the only viable escape for unwed women stuck at home: an
unquestionably proper religious setting in which girls could learn some-

thing useful. In fact, to claim a religious calling—whether fantasized or cleverly invented—would become the means for many determined single women to break free. Florence Nightingale, for example, claimed that she'd had an epiphany as opposed to a rebellious fit and this calling, this quasi-religious mission, allowed her slowly to extricate herself from her controlling family.

But the conventual life was a hard one. The novitiates, or the new girls, spent a year working through strictly regimented days on the grounds. After that they were trained to perform charitable works for the poor. These works—nursing, child care, housecleaning, cooking—were physically draining and carried out in places so run-down, in weather so bad, few girls told their parents just what they did. (One communard, a nurse trainee, returned home, told her family what she did, and found that no one would come near for fear of disease.) But the rewards! A justifiable life outside the house! A job, a place, procured on her own! Most thrilling was the chance to be judged for one's skills and bravery and not one's ability to please a man.

Some communards were tremendously influential. Annie Macpherson, a young Scottish woman, established a fund to take in Arab street kids who'd been abandoned all over London. Working with a small team, she arranged for their safe transport and adoption by families in Canada. That's how I describe her achievement. One of her male contemporaries saw it differently. Here was yet another woman blindly ignoring her responsibilities. Instead of marriage she was determined to "explain the world to swarthy students."

She had her American counterparts. Single abolitionist Fanny Wright, along with her spinster sister, established an all-women commune on some uncleared land in Tennessee and called it Nashoba. Their goal was to educate freed slaves, but the effort was cut down by charges of free love and unfair labor practices; poor finances ultimately forced the school to close. As if in penance, Wright at thirty-six entered a loveless marriage.

But another sort of British commune, this one originally male, would have a serious and lasting impact on American spinsters. That was the settlement house, a social-work institute set down in the worst parts of major cities and, in America, run by corps of women, often college friends who then lived there together for the rest of their lives. Jane Addams, founder of Hull House in Chicago, and Lillian Wald of New York's Henry Street Settlement are the most famous, and their "houses," of course, are still in business. But there were many others that did the same—offered to poor women, and especially immigrant women, necessary services, whether medical referrals, English-language classes, or specific items such as blankets, food, and clothing.

And their sights were set higher. Senior staff trained young women "of promise" (meaning girls with a clean appearance, a serious demeanor, and a college diploma) and sought out others with political backgrounds. House leaders formed alliances with one another to construct what scholar Carroll Smith-Rosenberg calls "a delicate web of interlocking social justice organizations." Over time, settlement leaders and their allies campaigned for child-labor legislation, women's unionization, and the founding of the NAACP (despite all the justified charges of early white feminist, specifically suffragist, racism). And many settlement causes, suffrage for one, eventually became U.S. law. Some of their residents would later move into positions of power, especially during the 1930s, when Eleanor Roosevelt tapped them to run New Deal agencies that dealt with women.

As professionals, these women had a uniform, similar to that of academics: shirtwaists, high-collared white blouses that buttoned down the back and stood up stiffly, worn with long skirts, hair pulled back from the face in a bun. Spectacles, keys, crucifixes hung like necklaces. It was a presentation of self that read: I am serious, not girlish and frilly but so somber, so plain I can mean nothing to you sexually; I have a cause. This warrior wear may be viewed as the sartorial ancestor of the early dress-for-success professional gray-out.

Using their somber appearance, their impressive credentials, and their emphasis on feminine good works, the settlement women gained national respect. The causes they worked for did not have anything to do with the rights of women to live alone or in groups. But their group-house experiment, so exotic and yet so sensible, influenced thousands of girls to sign on. Thousands of parents and would-be fiancés dissolved in panic.

THE GIRL GROUP AS TERRORIST CELL

Suspicion of women living in groups shows up in the earliest of Western mythologies. In the Greek myths, we find the Graeae, three eerie spectral sisters, who lived in some indefinite realm beyond the space and time of the human world. The Graeae shared among them one eye, which they passed to one another at regular intervals. It was this eye that Perseus stole to use in his search for the Gorgons, a sister band of outcasts. The eye revealed the group and his special prey: Medusa, whose phallic snakey head he then chopped off and paraded as proof that the world was safe once more for men. (Medusa, of course, could turn any man to stone just by looking at him.)

Not so easily defeated were the Amazons, a ferocious band of warrior women who lived on a mysterious island, hidden from the world, where they practiced their "arts. . . . To draw the bow, to hurl the javelin." According to Herodotus, each Amazon cut off a breast to make it easier for her to handle the weaponry. Eventually, Theseus, king of Athens, waged a severe, relentless battle and won their queen as his wife. Another select group of single women, the Muses, daughters of Zeus, watched over male lives. Each had the power to give to men specific artistic or intellectual gifts; they also possessed control over men's imaginations, their ability to love and remember, although they could not directly affect a man's destiny. That was left to the most feared female gang of all—the three Fates, those morbid shrouded beings who rolled out the string of life, stretched it, and raised the knife.

A mistrust of female communality turns some unexpected corners. Bronson Alcott summed up the patriarchal view when he said of Louisa, "She has involved herself with a group of women who are ridiculed and condescended to. . . . she [will be] tolerated as an eccentric . . . a faded woman . . . fit only for the fringes of family and social life." But some early feminists objected, too. Mary Wollstonecraft, author of what would become the feminist constitution *On the Vindication of the Rights of Woman* (1792), worried that women together were forming "unnatural organizations," behaving without regard to the outside world, and thus developing a "grossness," too great a degree of "intimacy," among one another that would make it impossible for them to function as adult women the world would take seriously. Writer Eliza Lynn Linton, circa 1875, referred to shared group houses, or any too-close female organization, as "the shrieking sisterhoods."

The sound of women talking together—gossiping, chattering, even whispering—seems always to have evoked negative images, shrieking or otherwise. Nathaniel Hawthorne complained famously of the many hack women writers, "damned scribblers," as he called them, whose dreadful blathering books outsold his own. He often added to his usual tirade the secret belief that they worked somehow together, having masterminded a female word machine. "They speak endlessly to one another in private letters and they keep diaries which they are only too pleased to have others read out loud." *The Strand* magazine, in 1894, only hinting at satire, called for the reinstatement of the brank, or gossip's bridle, a sixteenth-century device that was, until 1824, used to "silence the talkative shrew." The brank or branks consisted of an iron framework that locked like a helmet onto a woman's head. Attached to the front was a small metal flap, or "gag," that was inserted into the woman's mouth so that she could not move her tongue. The bridle had extra features. The sharp gag was positioned so that if our shrew spoke at all, her tongue would be slashed.

The paranoid belief that women, when gathered in groups, will plot gossip, using words as Amazons used their weapons, is a recurring theme throughout history.

A fascinating document of this dread is a little-known 1916 anti-abortion film called *Where Are My Children?* In this story, a small-town district attorney prosecuting a doctor for performing a deadly abortion learns that the doctor has performed abortions on many single women the lawyer knows—in fact, he's assisted married women and, as it turns out, most of the women in the town. It soon becomes clear that the local women have for years secretly helped one another to terminate pregnancies, passing the doctor's information around like contraband. One member of this under-ground network is the lawyer's wife, who may have had an abortion and, like all others in her spy circle, *without telling her husband*. The thought of abortions was awful enough.* But worse almost was the thought of women plotting together to control their fertility. The lawyer, played by Tyrone Power, Sr., seems about to break down. To comfort himself, he declares that if women pose such "a danger to mankind," they will be monitored. Male spies will be turned on the crazy female spies, and they will stop them! And their antisocial insanity.

Single women in particular were often written off as crazy. "Their talk-ativeness, violation of conventions of feminine speech, and insistence on self-expression. . . . [that] was the kind of behaviour . . . that led to their being labeled 'mad,' " writes scholar Elaine Showalter. Although it was im-possible to prove, it was often said that single women in the late nineteenth century made up more than half the population of mental institutions.

By the 1960s, when critic Elizabeth Janeway revisited female collec-tivity, incessant chattering and potential madness no longer seemed to be the issue. The problem, as she saw it, lay in the social distancing of "un-wanted unloved tribe(s)," whether single women, homosexuals, or any ex-cluded group. Stuck together in a quarantined state, group members began to "externalize" or project their self-hatred onto outsiders. And the same dynamic would often work inside the group itself. In this self-loathing and paranoia she foresaw the spread of internal anarchy and betrayal.

The Women, George Cukor's 1939 film version of the Clare Boothe Luce play, more enjoyably makes the same point. True, the characters technically are married, but we never see the husbands; the women act as though the men don't exist and spend their days wandering from home to store to spa in a state of heavily subsidized singledom. With little to do, without connection to the larger world, they live to gossip and to plot against one another. *The Women*, both as play and film, turns verbal spar-

*The corollary of the single woman who refused to bear healthy white children was her married contemporary who sought ways to abort unwanted children. During the mid-nineteenth century, in the decades just before the abortion outlaw, a common image in the American press was "the Aborting Matron," a piggy, self-satisfied wife downing poison or else portrayed as demonically pos-sessed.

ring into a spectator sport, a fur-draped "pardon *me*" teacup kind of wrestling match with destructive results. The idea of manless women turning on one another, proving that these women are vile and imbecilic, has endless appeal. Both Wendy Wasserstein and Julia Roberts have attempted to revive the play, and a campy new version debuted on Broadway in the fall of 2001.

LIVES OF THE LONE RANGERS

Let's briefly examine the lives of three nineteenth-century single women—Louisa May Alcott, Clara Barton, and, with special emphasis, Florence Nightingale. They are all members of that traditional grade-school book-report list of famous women, the one that includes Eleanor Roosevelt, Madame Marie Curie, and Helen Keller, who was for years presented as the consummate female role model (deaf, dumb, and blind but through intensely hard work making the most of it). Each of these women had to wait miserably at home before starting her career at about age thirty. And all struggled for years with intense frustration, guilt, and heavy bouts of depression.

Florence Nightingale will live always on record as history's greatest and bravest nurse, as well as one of history's most effective medical reformers. But the brave "Lady of the Lamp," unlikely heroine of the Crimean War and England's most celebrated medical statistician, spent much of her life until age thirty-three battling her mother. Frances Nightingale was a rich, socially prominent woman who expected her daughters, Parthenope and the younger, more beautiful Florence (named for the city where she was born), to participate fully in the season's activities—balls, concerts, visiting rounds—then to move on to the family's winter estate and start up again. Florence loathed social life, the hours spent dressing and chatting and smiling, all of it engineered to culminate in her early marriage. Her only solace was in the lessons she had with her father, a Cambridge graduate who'd insisted on teaching both girls mathematics, Latin, Greek, and literature. At sixteen, Florence wrote in one of her many journals that she could happily spend the next year seated with her father in the library. That, however, was impossible; her mother, Florence wrote, was intent on "raising female slaves" she could marry off for good profit.

As she continued: "I don't agree at all that a 'woman has no reason—and not caring for anyone else—for not marrying a good man who asks her,' and I don't think Providence does either. . . . Some have every reason for not marrying, and . . . for these, it is much better to educate the children who are already in the world and can't be got out of it, rather than to bring more into it."

When she was seventeen and out for a walk in the garden, Florence received what she referred to as her "calling." The voice of God told her plainly that she was to do good works, although he did not specify exactly which ones. She had always been interested in "social conditions," and much to her mother's horror, Florence began visiting poor, sick neighbors near the family's summer estate in Derbyshire and near the winter manor at Hampshire. Through a friend of her father's, she arranged to tour local hospitals, and as a teenager she first posed the question she'd spend the rest of her life attempting to answer: How can any person get well in such depressing and horrible places? She started reading, often secretly by candlelight, about nursing technique and hospital administration. Soon she was the only London belle to have extensive knowledge of bedsores, sutures, and the average number of patients stored like animals in underlit institutional rooms.

This "dank obsession" (her mother's words) mortified her family. Nursing at that point ranked close to servant's work—dirty, unsuitable, and just possibly, not that one would say it, involving what we would call bedpans. The fights between Florence and her mother gradually escalated. Florence assured her she did indeed find herself pretty and that, yes, she did like attention but that she wanted to do something useful. She wanted—and she was sorry to hurt them—but she wanted to train to be a nurse. At that point several of her relatives, including possibly her sister, began to moan, literally throwing themselves on the ground at the thought of Florence near sick people. After long years of subterfuge, argument, and many crying fits, the Nightingales sent Florence on a chaperoned tour of the world.

In letters home, the chaperones described Florence as moody and adamant in visiting not museums but hospitals. At important social situations, she fell into odd muttering trances; at other times she remained silent for so long she seemed catatonic. Silence had become her refuge, a trick she had taught herself to persevere. Many Victorian women, trapped between the desire for work and family duty, famously became ill. But Florence Nightingale brought the conflict, and its torments, to new highs. She was silent, indisposed, bizarre in public, but always, even in the midst of fits, scheming a new life for herself. Unlike most of her neurasthenic peers, she had decided to "serve," and as a first step she had decided to "avoid at all costs marriage." As she told her journal: "Marriage . . . is often an initiation into the meaning of that inexorable word *never*; which does not deprive us, it is true, of what at their festivals the idle and inconsiderate call 'life,' but which brings in reality the end of our lives, and the chill of death with it."

On their way back to England, her traveling party passed through Germany and stopped at a school renowned for its teaching hospital. Florence felt she'd at last found a place. Ignoring extreme disapproval, she announced her intent to take a three-month nursing course at the German facility and promptly left, convinced her entire life was about to change. When she triumphantly finished, she returned home to find that it hadn't. There were invitations and calling cards, outings and theater—an engagement calendar that seemed to be full for several years.

As she later wrote, "I . . . dragged out my twenties. Somehow, I don't know how." Locked in her room, she tore at the world in her journals: "Why," she asked at age thirty-two, "are women given passion, intellect, moral activity . . . and a place in society where no one of the three may be exercised?"

During this time she channeled her rage into an unusual novel called *Cassandra,* a series of monologues delivered by numerous characters who, like the prophetess, could see the future, discourse with great fury for hours (and pages), then suffer outrage when no one believes a word. It was published in 1860, once Florence was famous, but for her parents it was, even in an unfinished state, a baffling and embarrassing enterprise.

In 1853 she got her first real job, as superintendent of the London Establishment for Gentlewomen During Illness. More significant, that same year, at the age of thirty-three, she took a London flat of her own, a move so shocking her mother is said to have fainted. Florence was never able to confront her mother directly, but in a journal she addressed her and the situation this way: "Well, my dear, you don't imagine that with all my talents . . . that I'm to stay dangling about [your] drawing room all my life! . . . You must look at me as your vagabond son . . . you were willing enough to part with me to be married . . . and I should have cost you a great deal more."

In 1854 her "calling" at last seemed to materialize. The Minister of War, a social acquaintance greatly impressed with her work, called on her to recruit nurses and to help organize the field hospitals in the Crimea, where Britain, France, and Turkey were fighting Russia. The tricky part was that no women had ever before served as battle nurses. Florence gathered thirty-eight nurses and went off, with a secret allowance from her father, into the war at Scutari.

The female nurses at first were scorned, dismissed from operating rooms, jeered at, served dinner hours after the male staff. But the work so absorbed Florence—she was the lone woman to assist at amputations—that people came to respect her for her stoicism, her amazing speed, and her genuine empathy. As "the lady in chief," she acted as the soldiers' friend. She learned their names, sat with each one, read to them or wrote letters for them and made sure they were mailed. She also took care of their finances, sending home checks and corresponding with wives who needed money. And she taught the squeamish by example. Florence was known around camp for her friendship with a man who had half a face.

At the war's end Florence returned home famous, a woman adventurer and living saint. Some also saw her as a genius. In the Crimean War she used statistical calculations to determine how many men could be kept alive if rooms were sanitized according to her specifications. She was credited with inventing the pie graph to demonstrate her estimates—how many would live, how many die according to conditions—and she was usually right. The British government created a fund so that Florence could organize civil hospitals along the same lines as she had in the Crimea. At thirty-five, the raging girl locked in her room now had a rare and meaningful life before her.

Louisa May Alcott, author most famously of *Little Women*, likewise spent much of her young life tied to her family, but not as a hothouse society belle. She was more like an itinerant family coordinator. Her father, Bronson, founder of free-form progressive schools in Boston and Concord, Massachusetts, was never fully able to keep the family—his wife, Abigail, Louisa, and her three sisters—solvent and moved them frequently. They lived in a house, Hillside, in Concord, where Louisa would recall taking nature walks with Henry David Thoreau. For a while they lived in a communal village in Harvard called Fruitlands. (She wrote about their life there years later, in *Transcendental Wild Oats*.) They lived in New Hampshire and recurrently in Boston, in each place the Alcott girls spending much of their time trying to earn extra money to help their father. When Louisa was in her twenties, she published a novel, *Flower Fables* (her first novel, written at seventeen, would not be published for decades). And the next time her father announced a move, Louisa said no; she was staying in Boston to pursue her literary career, seamstressing on the side. Alone for the first time, she began to work on a series of stories called "Meg, Jo, Beth, and Amy," the characters who would become the March sisters of *Little Women*. Ultimately, when her publishers demanded, she would complete the novel in two and a half months. But for a time she put it aside.

One of her younger sisters had died suddenly at twenty-two. Her older sister had married. Louisa felt she had no choice but to move back to Concord, where the family had resettled, to help her mother. As the more levelheaded of the two remaining daughters, Louisa and her mother shared the endless duties of running Orchard House. (The March family in *Little Women* would live in a fantasy version of her childhood Hillside; Louisa May would write it seated in Orchard House).

For an aspiring writer, it was a grueling, at times unbearable life—baking, washing, mending, ironing, jobs that at the time could last for days. In 1858 she wrote to her married sister, "If I think of my woes, I fall into a vortex of debt, dishpans and despondency awful to see . . . so I say, every path has its puddle and I trust to play gaily as I can . . . in my puddle . . . while I wait for the lord to give me a lift."

For "economic salvation" she considered marriage. She considered it all of one day, coming to the same conclusion that Susan B. Anthony reached on behalf of an undecided niece: "Marriage. It is an all absorbing profession." Instead, she worked as a seamstress, a paid companion. She took teaching jobs at her father's school and argued with him about his plans to leave her the school (she didn't want it). As her mother aged, more of the housework fell to Louisa and her less-than-enthusiastic youngest sister. She had to get out. The Civil War was on, and she wrote in her diary: "November—30 years old. Decided I must go to Washington as a nurse, if I would find a place. Help is needed and I love nursing and MUST LET OUT MY PENT UP ENERGY in some way. I want new experiences. . . . So I've sent my name in if they will have me."

In Washington she worked diligently as a nurse-in-training at the Union Hotel Hospital, where she treated thousands of injuries, witnessed terrifying operations and many deaths. For a woman who'd spent most of her life indoors, it was an astonishing experience and she afterward reworked her letters home into a book called *Hospital Sketches* (1868).

She never really went "home" after the war. Living but not slaving in Concord, she became the editor of a children's magazine, *Merry's Museum*, and worked continuously for the suffrage movement. (She was the first woman to register to vote in Concord after Massachusetts passed its state suffrage law.) She wrote ten novels and two volumes of nonfiction. When her youngest sister died, she adopted her niece, Lulu, who'd been named for her, and took her to Boston, where she established a new family compound.

Louisa May Alcott never married because she could not envision the latter half of her life, like the first part, trapped in a house that needed cleaning. As she put it: "The loss of liberty . . . and self-respect is poorly repaid by the barren honor of being Mrs. instead of Miss."

Like Louisa May Alcott, Clara Barton, the youngest of five children, longed to escape from Massachusetts, once writing in her diary, "Have ye work, my brave countrymen, real work for me there? . . . Is there anything useful I can do?" She'd been working since age fifteen when, after tutoring her at home, the family sent her out as a teacher. For years she reported feeling nervous in these jobs, insecure, and always tired. She later worked to organize free schools in towns throughout New England—apparently still feeling very shy but not always quite so nervous. She was most proud of an experimental free school she had planned and opened in New Jersey. But when she learned that her male coworkers, even those beneath her in the hierarchy, were earning more than she was, she quit, "full of familiar uncertainty and queer sickness."

Through an acquaintance, Clara took a "real" job in the U.S. Patents Office in Washington—at just about the time wounded Civil War soldiers started appearing in the city. Although her only nursing experience had been the two years she spent tending a sick brother, she immediately began to organize relief efforts. Her quick, critical observation was that nurses were plentiful; supplies were short. She collected and advertised for food, blankets, and medicine and soon after founded an organization that would distribute goods to battle sites. The scheme was so efficiently executed that the U.S. Surgeon General granted her a pass to travel with army ambulances "for the purpose of distributing comforts for the sick and wounded, and nursing them."

She was one of the only women on the front lines of the Civil War, appearing as if on schedule at every major battle and making sure there was enough of everything to go around. After the war she spent years working to find soldiers still missing in action. She also took her first trip to Europe and while there met with members of the International Red Cross. Immediately she envisioned an American branch, an organization that would function like a Clara Barton during the Civil War: getting supplies and other assistance to disaster sites. Despite complex political opposition, she opened the first chapter of the American Red Cross in 1881 and began training recruits in emergency procedures and a new concept she had devised called "first-aid skills." Barton invented the first-aid kit. She wrote a

book called *The Women Who Went to the Field,* a Civil War study that included Louisa May Alcott. She was present at many Red Cross interven-
tions—fires, floods, tornados. As an older woman, she became one of the
first female diplomats in U.S. history and spent six months as a substitute
prison warden. She was the first woman ever to hold such a resolutely male
post. It was often said—and this was a real first—that she was "very popular among the prisoners."

Florence Nightingale's story had a far stranger and more ambiguous ending.
When the Crimean War ended, something in Florence, arguably the most
famous woman in England, seemed to snap.

Whether it was battle fatigue, psychosomatic or genuine illness—she'd
been exposed to hundreds of viruses—she retreated to bed, alone, refusing
all requests to appear or speak. The quarantine lasted months, until she was
named to a royal commission investigating health issues in the British
army. She was also commissioned to write a monograph on the health of
the British military in India. In 1860 she published *Notes on Nursing,* a
guide that is still in print, and used the rest of her Crimean funds to open
her own training hospital. But most of this activity, including her involvement in the Nightingale clinic, took place from her room. She communi-
cated through letters and rarely spoke.

By age forty she had done it all—reached her professional peak and
permanently won the war with her mother. It is hard to believe, but during the remaining fifty years of her life, Florence rarely left her flat. Now
and then she heard or gave lectures, attended openings for hospitals, and
had graduating students of the institute over for tea. But the majority of her
time she spent in bed with a malady even she could not cure.

I've always thought that Charlotte Perkins Gilman had Florence in
mind when she wrote her short story "The Yellow Wallpaper" (1892), the
tale of a woman confined to bedrest. (The diagnosis: nerves, neuritis, neu-
ralgia—the vague ailments ascribed to uppity women—a version of which
appeared on aspirin labels into the 1960s.) All day the woman stares at the
wallpaper, until one day its shapes and patterns—yellow flowers, loops, and

vines—start to undulate. Then one day a vine turns into a tiny struggling woman. Every day thereafter, she wakes to see tiny women crawling everywhere, trapped inside the yellow wallpaper, until the entire room is overtaken by a howling morass of fairy-size women.

Florence Nightingale is pictured in most history texts as a female crusader wearing a halo. Fair enough. She was a brilliant exemplar of what single women could accomplish despite intense opposition. But she is also a strange and bitter reminder of the high personal price such women paid.

AND NOW THE POOR DEAR THING

During the nineteenth century, many novels set out to map aspects of the spinster experience—*Cranford* (1853) by Elizabeth Gaskell, *The Mill on the Floss* (1860) by George Eliot, *The Last Chronicle of Barset* (1867) by Anthony Trollope, *Emma* (1816) by Jane Austen, which featured the classically inept Miss Bates, the ultimate spinster biddy, fluttering, talking out of turn, and babbling on at the sidelines. Miss Bates has a twittery cousin in Jane Osborne, the stuck-at-home daughter in *Vanity Fair* (1848) by William Makepeace Thackeray, and another relative in Miss Tonks, the schoolteacher in *Lady Audley's Secret* by Mary Elizabeth Braddon (1862).

But none of these books—and there are hundreds of them—"solve" the spinster's problem. Some of the characters walk through life oblivious, unaware that most people think them useless, afeminine, and dim-witted. Other spinsters have analyzed their social status and feel all the proper outrage, only what to do? They speak out in long angry monologues addressed either to mirrors or to parents who are powerless to help.

Very few novels propose alternatives. One entertaining exception is a British novel called *The Odd Women* (1898) by George Gissing. His story begins with a widowed doctor who, in the first paragraph, dies in a carriage accident. He leaves behind five daughters, none of whom has any known skills. He leaves them no money, and due to the sexist British inheritance laws, no house. They abandon the country estate that is no longer theirs and head for London. There they begin the downward spiral of so many single women of the time, both in life and fiction. Two sisters die. The youngest, prettiest, and least able to withstand it is sent out to do factory work while the older two talk a great deal about starting schools or perhaps just teaching in one. Yet they never do. They sit about the parlor of their hotel and, later, on the beds of shabbier rooming houses, and as months pass, their plans and their conversations make less and less sense. They're always drunk.

Then the three surviving sisters are reunited with an intense young woman they'd met years earlier. Her name is Rhoda Nunn, and she is hawkish-looking, unmarried, and proud, a spinster who considers her position a privilege. With an older friend of hers, Miss Barfoot, Rhoda has started a special school for single women; she teaches them how to "typewrite," and to take dictation. Recognizing that there is little she can do for the elder two, Rhoda persuades Monica, the youngest, to leave the factory and enroll at her school. But Monica is a poor, unfocused student and soon leaves to marry a much older man who has pursued—some might say stalked—her for months. Monica does not love him, but she knows she cannot support herself, that she has neither the will nor the talent to live in the world like Rhoda Nunn. The marriage is disastrous. The husband expects his young wife to wait on him. Monica is shocked by the presumption, uninterested and resentful. Watching it transpire, Rhoda again feels blessed.

That is, until Miss Barfoot introduces Rhoda to her nephew, Everard. He is deeply impressed with the solidity and devotion Rhoda brings to her work and, to Rhoda's amazement, he expresses romantic interest. For a long dreamy time Rhoda is enraptured by this attentive nephew and with the idea that a man should pursue her at all. It starts to seem that she might leave the school and marry Everard. Then Monica dies in childbirth and Rhoda, after agonizing contemplation, rejects Everard, relieved, it seems, to have that part of her life, that possibility, over and done with. "No man had ever made love to her," Gissing writes. "She derived satisfaction from this thought, using it to strengthen her life's purpose; having passed her thirtieth year, she might take it as a settled thing . . . and so shut the doors on every instinct tending to trouble her intellectual decisions."

Rhoda returns to the school and with the two reformed alcoholic sisters takes in Monica's child from the useless husband to claim as theirs. It makes sense. As she says, for women like herself, "the world is moving."

That meant the women who were known as "strong-minded." As *The Independent* observed in 1873, "A dozen years ago hardly one female could be found . . . who would openly acknowledge that she was strong-minded. . . . Now they not only acknowledge that they are such, but they glory in it." Investigative reporter Ida Tarbell added, "Four hundred years ago, a woman sought celibacy as an escape from sin. Today she adopts it to escape inferiority and servitude; superiority and freedom are her aim."

But even the strong-minded would find their own lives, their own gloried versions of an Old Maid's Hall, hard to sustain. Spread out among schools, settlements, and all receptive points between, single women struggled to keep up contact. Letters were very slow in arriving, and it was costly to travel. Holidays and birthdays passed without one's primary friends and relatives around to celebrate. Important news—of a move, an illness, sometimes of a death—arrived weeks, sometimes months, after the fact.

Losing a job could be traumatic. Aging single women found the hunt for work an exhausting, demoralizing process, and it was tiring to imagine reorganizing an unconventional life at age forty-plus. Some maintained the stamina for political work, living meagerly on small honoraria augmented by donations and article writing, but much about their lives seemed increasingly difficult. Serious politico-feminists traveled year-round, claiming no residence, their days spent on bad roads (in horse-drawn carriages or on wooden-seated trains) to reach provincial places that were often dangerous. Protestors sometimes broke up their speeches by hurling raw eggs, symbolic reminders of the speaker's presumably unfertilized ova.

"I do not feel like myself these times," wrote a teacher who was "staying on against my wishes" in Virginia, to a sister staying on against her own wishes in Ohio, 1875. "I dare not look at a map and the spaces between us and the impossibility of it so weakens me. I admit I have dropped into tears. . . . Will I ever see you? Or anyone?"

These separations, and other anxieties of spinster life, were most realistically expressed in a tiny genre of short fiction known as "spinster sto-

ries." Written in the mid-nineteenth century, these tales were often collected in year-end gift books, elaborately illustrated volumes of the year's
best literature, essays, and short fiction that made fancy and beloved
Christmas presents.

In these stories the spinster often appears as a wise, older aunt who one
day decides to talk of her life to a young niece. Usually, the niece is not
prepared to hear about it. My spinster aunt once fell in love? My spinster
aunt had a life outside this house? Of course, in the end the niece is forced
to reevaluate not only her views of her aged aunt (who isn't really as old as
she'd seemed) but her presumptions about women, marriage, what it might
really be like to live alone.

An interesting example of this genre is a story called "One Old Maid,"
from a Scribner's collection entitled *Handicapped* (1881), by Marian Har-
land. The story begins on New Year's Eve in the opulent dining room of a
mansion. There, beneath the chandeliers, we meet Juliana Scriba, a handsome middle-aged woman whose family has gathered for a private meal
that includes for the first time the fiancé of her daughter Emma. As the
guests debate their topic—"Is it nobler to live for others?"—the butler an-
nounces a Miss Boyle, "a tall meager lady . . . wrapped in a thick plaid
shawl, simpering and blinking." She enters, apologizing, declaring that
she's there but a moment and dare not sit. She was only passing and, but,
oh . . . Juliana, as if speaking to a servant, demands that "Co"—who is her
sister—sit down this instant!

Co, short for Corinne, sits and starts to talk. She talks for so long that
the entire table stares at her as she eats, her bonnet strings trailing around
on the plate. After applying a grandiose adjective to every food item, she
takes a "noble" orange and readies to leave. A butler hands her a large bas-
ket, and one son is instructed to see "his aunt" out with it. The fiancé is
shocked: Aunt? Sister to Juliana? *That?* He embarks on a long monologue
on the evils of celibacy, while the girls ask their mother, "How old is
Aunt Co? Forty? Fifty? Seventy-five?" Juliana defends Corinne, but it is
useless. They are all deep in discussion of the curse that befalls careless
women.

It's a long walk back to Co's, the original family homestead, miles it seems, all of it through snowy marsh. Corinne wishes out loud she'd worn her boots, but such is the weather of a spinster aunt. After what seems like an hour, she stops by a tiny house without lights, hears shrieking, and rushes her way to the back. Corinne hurries in to find a whalish woman jerking around on the floor. An impatient nurse, standing nearby, declares, "She has been this way the *whole time*." Corinne comforts "Lulu," the sprawling creature, announcing that "Sister" has come. Corinne and Lulu, as we've learned in a conversational aside between Juliana and her husband, are twins.

Meanwhile, back at Juliana's, there's another unexpected visitor, Aleck, a man once rejected by the busy, committed Corinne. As he explains, he has recently lost his wife and has come in search of his onetime love. Thrilled to learn that she's just left, he rushes out to her house (in a closed carriage, mind you). He enters rapidly, then stops cold as he sees an old woman rise from her chair. "Miss Corinne Boyle?"

"I don't wonder you ask, Aleck," Corrine says, faltering, "but I should have known you anywhere." Then she starts to sob. After a while, with her nose red and skin chalky white, they speak as old friends, although he cannot hide his disappointment and revulsion. His thoughts: "What a fool! What a sentimental simpleton he had been to forget that a woman must fade fast in a life like hers! Fade, and shrivel, and dry into hardness!"

For a while after he leaves, Corinne cries out to God at this unfairness. And yet as she calms down she reassures herself that God has guided her well in this life. Her ability to love, and receive love, was not to be within the realm of men; it is love born of commitment, honor, the keeping of a promise long ago made to a dying mother. She has kept her word and in return received unconditional love.

She has also upheld her end of one classical spinster formula: Divide a family of girls into wives and outcasts. The wives reign, and the outcasts, even if they chose their fate, as did Corinne, tell themselves elaborate religious stories about the rewards of their sacrifice. One recent example of this sisterly dichotomy occurs in *Marvin's Room*, by Scott McPherson (1992), a play first and then a movie starring Meryl Streep and Diane Keaton as the sisters. The sister who has remained at home all her life to care for ailing relatives is now ill herself with leukemia. After some persuasion, the prodigal, biker-chick sister returns home with her surly adolescent son. After many conflicts and awkward attempts at reconciliation, the sick one explains to the prodigal how she was able to stand her life as family nurse. It's because, simply, she has been unconditionally loved. And although she doesn't say this, she has been able to shut herself off from the world, avoid sex and the messiness of men in exchange for an unshakable sense of nunlike purpose. In the voice of the deluded martyr, she cries: "I've had so much love."

We are supposed to find this pathetic, and because it invokes such a profound denial of a fully lived life, we do. At the same time, she's had the love she claims to have wanted. In remaining true to her vow, so has Corinne. But the reader understands the spinster formula, the essential code. We are never allowed to consider her choice as anything less than insane.

True, sometimes spinsters themselves couldn't stand it at all and broke down. Jennie Gerhardt, heroine of the eponymous Theodore Dreiser novel (1911), finds herself dreading "before her [the] vista of lonely years. . . . Days and days in endless reiteration." But others were all too glad to avoid packing up the trousseau. For these women, an unusual degree of female freedom, work, caring for others, and the company of like-minded women represented a better solution to life than the role of wife. Even in the end.

The activist Frances Power Cobbe wrote in 1869, "Yes, the old maid will suffer a solitary old age as the bachelor must. It will go hard. But," she added, "she will find a woman ready to share it."

CHAPTER TWO

THE SINGLE STEPS OUT: BOWERY GALS, SHOPPIES, AND THE BOHEMIAN BACHELORETTE

I do love it—me makin' a spectacle 'o myself . . . but that's how it is now: [I'm] an American girl in her finery and telling the men "where d'you get off?"

—IRISH DOMESTIC TURNED "FREE WORKING GIRL," 1871

Here is the work-a-day fact: No one knows where you came from, no-body knows where you go.

—THE LONG DAY, BY DOROTHY RICHARDSON, 1905

. . . Your white collar girls? . . . I see them on buses, poor damned share-croppers in the Dust Bowl of business, putting up a fight in their pretty clothes and keeping their heeby-jeebies to themselves. There's something so courageous about it, it hurts me inside.

—KITTY, EN ROUTE TO WORK, KITTY FOYLE,

BY CHRISTOPHER MORLEY, 1939

A GAL'S LIFE

Picture a silent-movie set in the heart of Manhattan's old Lower East Side, scene one, twilight. We pan across the tenements and laundry lines and see what we expect to see: a tangle of peddler's carts, drunk, disheveled men, and large-bosomed women surrounded by animals and children who race like little Artful Dodgers in and out of the crowd. Making her way slowly through this mess is a girl. The camera picks her out, follows her, and slowly irises in to frame her face. Highlighted in her cinematic bubble, our girl twists a thinning gray scarf around her neck. Her face is chalky pale. Kohl liner has smudged to form half moons beneath her eyes. She looks ready to faint.

Back in the full shot that is her world, she limps along, past the garbage and the gangs of rude, hissing boys, and stops at last outside a windowless structure. Cut to the crumbly interior. The exhausted girl enters, then does what she's supposed to do and faints. Plaster drops like snow onto her face. Cue the villain.

Most likely she knows him, this man now staring down at her, assessing his options. (Clearly going for help will not be one of them.) He shakes her, slaps her a few times, then with a quick look around props her up against a wall and lifts her skirts. The rest we don't see, but we know that whatever went on it was her fault, *for she lives a depraved unnatural female life in a harsh, cold world that has depleted whatever slight moral fiber she had to start with.*

At about the time our spinster was canonized as an unfortunate social specimen, there appeared on the female landscape an even more unsettling single girl: the "factory maid" and her salacious cousin "the Bowery gal." These new single icons were identified and dissected in the penny press. They later became the heroines of cheap novels, live points of interest in city guidebooks as well as characters in early vaudeville. This depraved and unnatural female, the poor thing preyed on by horny landlords, would become a staple of the new aesthetic form known as melodrama. She was born to fade to black.

The Bowery and factory gals were immigrants, part of the European exodus that had begun during the 1820s and increased radically every fifteen years thereafter. (In 1830, for example, there were an estimated 18,000 new Americans—Germans, Italians, Poles, Scots, Irish, Greeks. By 1845, the number stood at roughly 250,000.) As one commentator put it, Europe had "vomited."

And it spit up increasingly undesirable transplants, meaning eastern European Jews and unwed women.* Like many middle-class spinsters, these women were often dangerously poor and thought to have psychological problems stemming from their presumed unwanted status. That was about all they had in common with the average spinster. According to all reports and dramatizations, foreign girls were crude, illiterate, and extremely rude in what accented English they possessed. They spoke back to men. They walked the streets as they chose, unescorted and, as we shall see, improperly dressed. In the views of one nineteenth-century British visitor, the American working girl presented a moral calamity that, considering the temptations of New York, could prove even more disastrous than the English model. As he wrote in 1870, "They are neither fitted for wives by a due regard for the feelings and wishes of their husbands, nor a knowledge of the simple rudiments of housekeeping . . . one of their common remarks to each other when speaking of [men] . . . is that they would like to see a man who would [not] boss them."

That, at least, was the communal fantasy. In truth, many of these girls, especially the newly arrived, lived quietly with their families. The emphasis was on work, usually "out work," freelance piece sewing that brought in pennies—*if* the sewn pieces fit those in some unseen larger batch; *if* the home workers were not undercut by aggressive family groups equipped with sewing machines; and if everyone stayed healthy and could switch off during the night to meet deadlines.

By 1860, single working women formed one quarter of the total U.S. workforce and not only in home-based seamstressing. When they'd been

* The majority of applicants turned back at Ellis Island were unable to prove that they had waiting relatives. Either that, or they had physical problems (usually eye trouble) and/or mental disorders. Being female and single—and especially if there were no waiting relatives—was at times as incriminating as rheumy eyes. Many, many lone female travelers were sent back.

around a while, girls fourteen years and up might find work in factories; others—usually the Irish, Germans, and Scandinavians—worked as maids. Whatever they did, they returned home after twelve-hour work-days, to a series of mandatory female chores. At the end of the week these girls were further expected to turn over all outside earnings to par-ents, pay envelope unopened. (The practice was never enforced among boys.) Worse—although girls argued the point—was getting by on your own.

For her book *City of Women*, scholar and urban detective Christine Stansell studied the New York City census for 1855 and found that of 400 single women surveyed, 224 lived on their own, somehow stretching three to four dollars per week to finance a tiny space in a boardinghouse or a bed in a dorm or, worse, an almshouse, what would look to us like a homeless shelter. In that same year it was estimated that close to 500 single women and young girls arrived in New York City every week, not only Europeans but Asians and "country girls" who'd run off from Upstate New York or Pennsylvania farms.

Alone, unsure what to do, some became "learners," a misleading term for slavelike seamstresses who worked fifteen hours a day, six days a week, receiving in exchange only meals on the days they worked. To pay rent somewhere and to feed themselves on Sundays, learners had no choice but to double as prostitutes. Others were able to bypass "learning" and work for a few dollars a week in sweatshops, small makeshift factories hidden within tenement houses, but very few got by without occasional hooking. Others made their way up to the big shops—the factories, where they worked as bookbinders, fancy-hat or artificial-flower makers (good jobs, relatively speaking), or as inside seamstresses, cigar makers, shoe manufacturers, but-ton or box makers.

Like the tenement sweatshop, the factory was a workplace nightmare, only bigger. In a space the size of a gymnasium, hundreds of women crowded almost on top of one another around tables or hulking machinery. They worked at their manual tasks for hours with only minutes-long breaks. The air seemed to be clotted, and the noise—like that of an indoor construction site—routinely led to partial hearing loss within a year. Many workers had scars on their hands and faces and permanent dye stain on their fingers.

One Christian organization published an end-of-the-year volume on women in the city, 1877. In language that had clearly been translated by an editor into readable English, one girl described her first view of the factory: "I felt within me a deep and dark revulsion at the grim brick walls and the innumerable dirty windows and rusted fire escapes. It looked a ruin. The impulse I had was to run away, but there was a fascination with it, too."

For a glimpse inside, let's look at the once scandalous and banned novel *Sister Carrie* by Theodore Dreiser (1900). Here we follow Carrie on her first day of work as an ill-equipped new factory operative in Chicago:

> Carrie got so [anxious] . . . that she could scarcely sit still. Her legs began to tire and she felt as if she would give anything to stand up and stretch. Would noon never come? It seemed as if she had worked an entire day already. She was not hungry at all, but weak, and her eyes were tired straining at . . . one small point . . . her hands began to ache at the wrists and then in the fingers, and toward the last she seemed a mass of dull complaining muscles, fixed in an eternal position and performing a single mechanical movement which became more and more distasteful until at last it became absolutely nauseating.

Women staged "sit-downs" and actually went on strike—for better pay, windows, some form of toilet facilities, regular breaks—as early as 1825, but with little success. The only organized labor power lay in the male unions, and these groups, run like fraternal orders, excluded females. In the idealized social scheme, women were supposed to quit their paid jobs and go back to the home, resurrecting some shred of the former preindustrial order. (In fact, the only union discussions of working women early on concerned prostitution.) Working women knew where they stood—and that was alone. During their first major strikes leaders declined all advice offered by men.

But as much as the factories were filthy and dangerous, they offered girls something unavailable anywhere else, and that was companionship, the social connections that might lead to some small life beyond the family or the tiny room. On many floors in the needle trades, in the book binderies and cigar lofts, girls sang as they worked (a favorite: "The Fatal Wedding"). They shouted the latest gossip above the noise. A heavily grease-stained volume, *The Lucky Dreambook*, made its way around and girls recorded their wishes. And many read, or learned to read, from "yellowbacks," early romance novels with titles like *Woven on Fate's Loom* or *Lost in a Fearful Fate's Abyss*.

The factory served as an unintentional means of assimilation. Irish, Jewish, Italian, Hungarian, Greek girls—well, some of them, anyway—learned to work together, the older girls offering linguistic corrections and lessons in the sartorial tricks that could make one look like an American. Ignoring management, girls ran secret contests and lotteries and held parties on their breaks for almost every occasion. The last survivor of the horrific Triangle Shirtwaist fire in 1911 recalled recently that when the fire broke out on floor six, the girls there had just lit the candles on a cake—a coworker was getting engaged! Quickly they scattered; the survivor, who'd somehow make her way to a staircase, looked around for her engaged friend and saw her standing by a window. When she looked away and then back, the girl was gone; like hundreds of others, she had jumped.

There was only one decent thing to be said for factory life: There were set hours. The workday started, you rang in ("punched in"), and you rang out. You were, in the words of one domestic who knew no such luck, an "independent." Life for the domestic, usually an Irish girl—74 percent of all Irish girls in 1855 and an even higher percentage in 1870 worked as maids—was erratic. Their lists of tasks were long and often incomprehensible, involving both heavy labor and the care of clocks and Victorian music boxes and sculptures and various other precious objects they'd never before even seen. Newly stamped with her True Woman status, the wife, said one laboring girl, seemed never "to know what she wants done and how does she want it done? So she changes it 'round all the time and it's you who gets the shriek, like a bloody animal, if you're wrong in figuring what she wanted."

Added another girl, nineteen: "I would always rather work with a man. They know what they want done and you do it."

Yet the True Woman had a hard time comprehending why such a girl, known among employers as a "Bridget," would not be grateful. As Catherine Beecher herself wrote: "We are continually harrowed with tales of the sufferings of distressed needlewomen and yet women will encounter these chances of ruin and starvation rather than make up their mind to permanent domestic service. Now what is the matter with domestic service?"

One Bridget explained: "Your life is not your own unless she says it is. She will always think of some other trifle task."

This barely concealed hostility made wives suspicious of their Bridgets and far more likely to watch them closely for any change in attitude and appearance. Even observers like Catherine Beecher picked up on the growing tendency of maids to leave work in fancy clothes. And reports filtered back that such and such a girl had been seen down the street with a man. In England there had been a brief fad among newly prosperous matrons to have their servants look prosperous, too. But here, in the States, newly monied women were often insecure; a servant who put on airs was likely to be disciplined. No fancy clothes. Not a hint of cosmetics. No men picking her up from the kitchen door. "Hah!" one girl told a female reformer: "She is daft. What man would I want to have come to pick me up here anyways? Why would I want to have him see me here? To think that the best I can do is work in someone's kitchen?"

Employers complained about the "servant problem" and the girls quit and went looking for a better place, but the situation never seemed to improve. In 1863 reformer Virginia Penny published the first edition of *Employments of Women,* for decades the most detailed listing of every job available to women, complete with technical workplace advice. (For example, in factories, "women should not wear hoops, as they check the progress of all whom they meet, in narrow passes and between machinery.") About "serving girls" she agreed, they are "generally and unhesitatingly denounced, even in their presence, as pests and curses."

For the average working girl, the logical conclusion to life was still in marriage, usually arranged or at least encouraged by the available relatives. If there was no immediate male candidate, elders of the community turned to the "homeland" or "exile" organizations that helped with the perplexing details of American life, including housing protocol, insurance, written English, and various legal matters. Quickly, however, many girls came to view the community's Landsmanshaft balls, with their predictable collection of boys, or the yearly Oktoberfest outing the way an American mall rat might react to sitting through a four-hour plenary session of the Kiwanis Club. Once a girl had "got out" a bit, seen even a tiny slice of the city, its elaborate, romantic store windows, the neat pretty clothes on the shop girls, once she had read the sexy novels at work, sung the songs, she felt like doing something . . . new. One Grand Street sign put it this way:

WOMEN, WANT! PLEASE, PLEASE WANT—BEGIN TO WANT!

ALL THE NEWS THAT FIT HER (AND SOME THAT DIDN'T)

The early New York press concerned itself largely with business. Editors and publishers were there to cover an international seaport, a vast manufacturing sector, the hub of the nation's transportation systems and its highest financial institutions. The papers they put out reflected that solemn responsibility: *The Commercial Advertiser, Mercantile Adviser,* and, among many others, *The Journal of Commerce.* Other less illustrious papers covered topics of more general interest: riots, fires, strikes, sex scandals, murders in seafront "bawdy houses," and the discoveries of badly mutilated dead prostitutes.

There were hundreds of papers in any given year, including by the mid-nineteenth century the *New York Times* and the *New York Post.* But for the purpose of identifying, covering, and ultimately mythologizing the single working girl, there was the penny press.

The term *penny press* suggests the kind of tabloid many of us try very hard not to read while standing in line at the supermarket. But these were in many instances full, well-edited papers best known for introducing and developing the urban sketch—that unlikely slice-of-life adventure that would much later come to be known as the human interest story. In these personal, chatty communiqués, writers acting as cultural explorers and translators introduced the latest in unfamiliar city types—single working girls, for example—to a curious and nervous public.

The penny press dates to 1833, when Benjamin Day bought the *New York Sun* and put in place an iron-cast steam-powered press so fast and so cheap to run that he upped his print run by 100 percent and cut his price to a penny. He also hired newsboys, like those in England, to hawk papers on the street—shrieking and badgering passersby, as if the Messiah had arrived (or a beautiful lone girl had been murdered) and only the *Sun* had the story.

The penny daily came into its own a few years later with the launch of the *New York Tribune*, a daily (including a more in-depth weekly version) that was founded and edited by Horace Greeley. Greeley was in all respects a public figure: a genuine intellectual, a sometime politician, a friend of Abraham Lincoln, a vehement abolitionist, and a man with an interest in just about everything from single women and their economic lives (feminist writer Margaret Fuller was a Boston correspondent) to world politics (Karl Marx covered London). He refused to run sensational police news or "objectionable medical advice," and he introduced by-lines for reporters. He shared the journalistic spotlight with James Gordon Bennett of the *New York Herald*, a second-generation journalist with the sensibilities of a P. T. Barnum. He personally financed Henry Morton Stanley's trip to Africa to find the lost missionary Dr. Livingstone and introduced polo as a sport to the United States, doing most of this while running the newspaper from abroad in Paris.

But the two men at least had one idea in common: Take the urban sketch—the man-about-town exposés, the true tales of low life, the unknown lone girl included—and make it into a regular news beat. As writer Hutchins Hapgood had noted sardonically just years before, ". . . the curiosity of well-to-do and so-called respectable people leads them to [under]go any physical, esthetic or moral discomfort in the search for truth and human nature . . . [especially] 'low life.' "

Here was the first mass-media presentation of the single woman. There were many unexpected correspondents out in the field.

In every newspaper office, hundreds of "true-and-shocking-tales" flew, uninvited, over the transom. Many of these unsolicited works came from middle-class wives who, quoting one, "have taken it upon ourselves to go out upon visits [to the poor] and to be of good use in recording what we have found." What they found were women of the tenements boiling potatoes and cabbage (our brave visitors swooned but did not, we are assured, faint from the stench). They typically encountered half-dressed children, husbands who read or drank without speaking, and seated off to the side, the infamous lone girl sewing and accidentally, repeatedly, stabbing herself with the needle.

Along with the wives there were many church ladies out on the beat, assisting the poor and in the process seeking conversions to their faiths. In their missives, the air is always damp, vaporous, and reeking of "imminent death." There is a lot of coughing. Swearing. Children shriek. The self-styled missionaries worry that the lone girl, seventeen, a seamstress, a factory lass, will not be able to manage the children once the woman on the bed has converted to the faith and died, coughing. William Dean Howells satirizes the dramatic pretense of these reports in his novel *The Minister's Charge* (1902). Here the niece of a devoted visiting woman tells a friend of her aunt's good works. Every day, it seems, this aunt "carries bouquets of flowers to the deserving poor." "Why?" asks the friend. Says the niece, "They prevent crime."

Other chronicles arrived from the young male aristocrats who invented American "slumming"—drinking, smoking opium, and mixing with prostitutes whenever possible. Such dissolute rich boys were not likely to become reporters, in the sense that they were not likely to sit at a desk every day and crank out copy. But some wrote up their experiences in conversational essays; real reporters borrowed from them.

Many reporters, all of them men, did not regard themselves as permanent, serious journalists. Like "actor," "journalist" was not yet deemed quite a respectable profession. Despite the influence of mighty editors like Horace Greeley, staff reporters imagined that they were on the job to get in shape for writing their future books. Articles were like warmups, a means by which to hone one's talent at crafting vignettes or eliciting (or inventing) the biting quote. And it was handy to have so much material to draw on: these fussy Christian women tracking seamstresses and factory waifs; the uptown cavaliers frequenting the top-notch whorehouses and concert saloons. On daily deadlines, one had so little time to get out and just *look*; here was a way to collect exotic mise-en-scènes and enhance dull and ordinary reportage writing.

The frequent subject of these hybrid narratives was the lone girl, preferably in the form of the beautiful, suffering young worker—the industrial-era Sleeping Beauty. In story after story, writers played out the tragic prophesy of her life, whether or not they'd ever actually met her. Here is a prime example from one Edgar J. Fawcett, "faithful correspondent," writing beneath his beefy photo in an 1869 issue of *Arena* magazine:

> What wonder . . . beneath the onus of her torments . . . that their morals, like their clothes and fingers, are sadly stained? Haggard and jaded, they are . . . robbed of even the physical chance to seek ease through sin . . . [desirable only to] a Quasimodo of the slums. How should it concern You, Mrs. Fine Lady, to care that girls of the same age of your Carrie and Fannie are starving . . . walking miles to work in direst weather in thinnest tattered shawls."

That's not to suggest that all stories on the working girl were moralistic or sex-drenched inventions. The major penny presses ran many serious exposés of factory and immigrant life, and a young woman's unsteady, often terrorizing, experiences within. The author was usually George G. Foster, the so-called Dickens of New York City and the *Tribune*'s onetime "city items editor." A self-styled urban ethnographer, he'd written a small library of hidden New York titles including *New York by Gaslight* and *New York Naked*. He'd written a novel, *New York Above Ground and Underground*, and he'd collected his works under the title *New York in Slices*. His following was huge and included many men who used his books as clandestine guides to the whorish New York. But his editors recognized in him a real reporter.

In one long 1845 series, "Labor in New York," he found young female cigar makers who worked twelve-hour shifts standing, passing the time by singing "ribald drinking tunes," each "courteous" to the others "when it came time for her to try for a harmony." He contributed to investigative series, including the famed "Dens of Death," a three-month extravaganza in 1850, and proposed or influenced many others, such as "Hot Corn: Life Scenes in New York" by Solon Robinson, the agricultural editor. Not that this was an agricultural story, per se. The corn girls, many about fourteen, many black, were street vendors who sold roasted corncobs, as popular then as Italian ices and huge pretzels are now. Their famed cry—"Hot corn, hot corn, here's your lily white hot corn, hot corn all hot, just come out of the boiling pot"—was believed to be less a fast-food pitch than a sexual come-on. (Perhaps that's why the ubiquitous "corn girl" vanished in film to be replaced by a pure and virginal Lillian Gish type selling pencils, apples, or matches, none of which make a big appearance in the records.) Like Foster, Robinson later extended his piece into a popular book and *Hot Corn* even now stands as a compendium of eccentric lone-female types in old New York City. (Its subtitle: *Including the Story of Little Katy, Madalina, the Rag Picker's Daughter, Wild Maggie &c.*)

Its success—two thousand copies sold in 1854—encouraged penny-press lords to recognize a reader who had even more interest in this female figure than the average male reader. That was the female figure herself.

IN WHICH THE TIRED HUDDLED MASSES FIX THEIR HAIR

The average immigrant working girl lived in two distinct worlds—the world outside and the unavoidable one inside. Reconciling the two demanded a huge amount of mental energy. Girls were under the strictest family scrutiny. And even those who lived in boardinghouses confronted questions: Where had she been and with whom had she spoken? Just who was that man walking up and back across the way? What girls did she know at work, and "what" were they? (German? Jew? Irish? Swede? Slut?)

Anzia Yezierska, a Polish immigrant who wrote stories in Yiddish about ghetto life, focused much of her fiction on the tension between frightened, old-world parents and their newly American daughters. In *The Bread Givers*, a novel subtitled "A Struggle Between a Father of the Old World and a Daughter of the New," young women argue repeatedly with their fathers about the right to leave the house on their own. "Don't you know what's out there?" one typically bellows. "HOW can I know anything?" replies the girl. In "Fat of the Land," a short story, a young woman laments the embarrassment she feels when with her mother: "God knows how hard I tried to civilize her so as not to have to blush with shame when I take her anywhere. I dressed her in the most stylish Paris models, but Delancey Street sticks out from every inch of her. Whenever she opens her mouth, I'm done for."

Yezierska, who'd gone to Hollywood to work as scenarist on the film version of her story collection *Hungry Hearts*, was known as "the queen of the ghetto" or "the immigrant Cinderella." She always returned to the Lower East Side and somehow managed to live there in a way unimaginable for most immigrant women. She married twice and had a child, but unable to live a constricted wife's life, she left the child with her husband and lived alone.

Her gift lay in detailing the generational assimilationist battle but also in revealing the underlying ambivalence felt on all sides. It was never as simple as girls begging to leave and frightened parents shrieking NO! While most immigrant parents feared America and what was "out there," they also wanted their children to fit in, to make a good life, to marry, and, while keeping the faith and traditions, to do what was needed to thrive. Many new arrivals were urged to bury the wigs, lose the cloggish thick-laced shoes, the shawls and kerchiefs, plus any other article of clothing that reeked of the homeland. One man, age thirty, wrote to a late-arriving cousin, then seventeen: "Don't take your dresses. Just one to wear. . . . If you try to wear them here, we will not let you wear them."

Ultimately, however, it was not that difficult for the young single girl to balance out these demands. That's because it was impossible to ignore what one called "the Americanist way." Whatever their inherited ambivalence, young women learned to "want." They wanted to "put on style," and they were willing to spend money earmarked for their families to do so.

Wrote one factory girl in 1906, "Some of the women blame me very much because I spend so much money on clothes. . . . but a girl must have clothes if she is to go into society at Ulmer Park or Coney Island or the theater."

One Sophie Abrams recalls her first real day in America as the day her aunt took her shopping: "She bought me a shirtwaist . . . a shirt, a blue print with red buttons and a hat like I never seen. I took my old brown dress and shawl and threw them away! I know it sounds foolish, we being so poor, but I didn't care. . . . when I looked in the mirror, I said, 'Boy, Sophie, look at you now . . . just like an American.' "

The daily press continued to cover the working girl as the terrorized figure at the heart of melodramatic sex plots and/or the victim of workplace or street abuse. But from time to time editors addressed single women as readers with questions. Following the example set by the new women's magazines, papers launched personal-advice columns. By 1900, even the *Jewish Daily Forward* ran a Q-and-A called the Bintel Brief. Some sample questions: "Is it a sin to wear facial powder?" (answer unrecorded) and "Does facial hair make a bad impression?" (It does.) And over and over one read, "IS there anything I can do to hide the marks on my forehead?"

To look an absolute American was not solely a matter of dress. As many a heart-sinking magazine piece declared, fair, untainted skin alone identified the native girl. And many, many immigrants had arrived with noticeable blemishes. Often these were smallpox scars or acne caused by poor diet, stress, delayed adolescence. Whatever the cause, facial blemishes were widely attributed to syphilis, a disease often diagnosed by the appearance of red splotches. Dermatology did not exist yet as a medical specialty, and so a girl looking to have her skin healed had to wait to see the doctors on duty at the syphilis clinic. And any female seen entering or leaving a syphilis clinic was presumed to be a whore.

Some refused the humiliation and tried to treat themselves. (Not that so many who saw VD doctors got "well.") It was on matters just like these that young women turned en masse to the advice columns. They learned, in this case, that the "fairest skin belongs to people in the earliest stages of consumption or [to] those of a scrofulous nature," though there were ways to emulate a native glow. According to one story, the most efficient means was to starve oneself, thus "securing the purity of the blood." Rest was important, cold breezes, running quickly around, then sitting and breathing until one felt dizzy. If none of that worked, girls were advised to track down a massive beauty volume called *The Ugly Girl Papers* by Susan C. Power (1875), a dense collection of beauty advice that had a small-type table of contents four pages long.

From this a girl learned that even "the worst face may be softened by wearing a mask of quilted cotton wet in cold water at night. Distilled water." If that was not possible, there was advice on the clever usage of "carbonate of Ammonia and powdered charcoal . . . lettuce as a cosmetic . . . the secretive ways of arsenic," and, should such materials prove difficult to obtain, a reader could still study "how to acquire sloping shoulders . . . how to use red hair . . . [and] the means to imitate the serpentine glide of the Creole."

The average girl, the one who barely spoke English, might have sought out the less exotic but no less precise *Young Ladies' Counsellor: On the Outlines and Illustrations of the Sphere, Duties and Proper Appearance of the Young Woman*. Others experimented.

One of their best experiments was in "banging," a style that caught on like the shag. "One of the first things we learned," wrote an anonymous woman "of business," "was our way in the art of banging. We let our hair cover our foreheads in a small quick cut that would of necessity keep hid any flaring." Once a girl was banged, all the sashes and ribbons and other fancy accouterments made better sense. Wrote one memoirist years later, banging was "the second best" thing that one could get to "a nose job."

Whatever they tried, girls had to be clever and stylish on a pittance, and from the extant illustrations it seems a few at least succeeded. Anzia Yezierska made this point in *The Bread Givers*: "It took ten cents worth of pink paper roses purchased from a pushcart on Hester Street to . . . look like a lady from Fifth Ave."

THE BOWERY BABE

Before we meet this uniquely decked-out single archetype, a few words about the world she inhabited. Historian Kathy Peiss has called the early industrial era the cultural age of "commercial leisure." Huge public entertainment venues—Coney Island, dance halls, theaters—opened to the working classes at just the moment the working classes were discovering the concept of "fun."

Everyone secretly longed to see what was out there. Many girls had spent their childhoods walking the neighborhood, peeking out at the world from behind packages and bundles of fabric they were bringing home for their mothers. At seventeen or at twenty-one, they were ready to go out. One young girl, nineteen, told the *Herald*: "All the waiting to go out and see people, to be brave enough to do it, to walk outside. Yes, we all heard about it; I don't think any of us even imagined we would do it—go to a dance with two girls from the floor? . . . It was a very long time to tell mother. Mother did not have many pleasures in her life. . . . I was very worried of how I would dress."

The only drawback was that these adventures and outings cost money. Girls never had enough. They didn't make it, and what they made they "handed over." Boys had the cash, and the crude equation came down to this: Girls who wanted to go out, who finally got up the nerve, understood that they'd be "treated." The boy would pay her way. If this was not the first "treat"—if she'd walked out with him before, accepted ice cream or drinks, or gone with him to a park or a play—he'd expect some form of sex in return. And often he just took it. The girl who experienced these pleasures, this slight sense of freedom, also ran the risk of the murky occurrence now known as date rape.

The most infamous "treating" episode concerned Lanah Sawyer, a young woman who accepted the offer of treats—ice cream and a walk around the Battery—from a refined professional man who called himself "lawyer Smith." His name was in fact Harry Bedlow, widely known to others as a "rascal" and "rake." Afterward, he offered to walk Sawyer home and lured her instead into a bawdy house, where he raped her. At his trial, Bed-low was found not guilty in fifteen minutes. Despite the minor riot that fol-lowed—and some of the rioters were working-class men—the general consensus was that both had played their parts in the script. He had taken her out, treated her, bought her trifles, then taken what he deserved in re-turn. In the "commercial culture of leisure" rape (and acquittal) would be-come a recurrent motif.

In the "old" countries, girls had moved seamlessly from the father's house, perhaps briefly to an employer's, and then to the husband's. Usually the family knew the fiancé and his parents; marriages were often arranged. In the new world, and in its odd new single sector, girls would soon wan-der off in gangs to the Bowery, to the crowds and dance halls, so that their families could not possibly oversee whom they met or what they did. And men in New York City seemed less reliable than they had back home; they moved on—to other women, to other jobs outside the city.

As Christine Stansell wrote, in *City of Women,* "As people moved around . . . from the Old World to the New . . . and from country to city . . . and [amidst] the mobile and anonymous circumstances of the city . . . methods of ensuring male responsibility weakened."

The most extreme example of this breakdown was the Alma Sands case. Sands was a Quaker girl who lived with her parents and took an in-terest in the family's boarder, one Eli Weeks. The two slept together—not unusual in certain Old Country courtship systems; in fact, it was viewed as a sign of the couple's seriousness and especially the commitment of the prospective bridegroom. Then, on the night before she was supposed to marry Eli Weeks, Alma Sands turned up dead. After weeks of wild public speculation, a jury indicted Weeks, describing him as a man who under-stood the depth of his commitment—an engagement—and in "fury" at "his unbearable promises" took unique, punishing measures to break free.

The Sands murder evoked a response similar to the hysteria surround-ing the 1969 Manson murders. Everyone talked about it in gory detail and traded in rumors about witchcraft and satanic practices. Hundreds lined up to see the house where it occurred and, later, to see the girl's shrouded body. Mothers, in particular, dragged their daughters to make a point that was sadly never less than confusing: Know and trust the man, my dear, although it's hard now to ever know or trust the man. In cartoons a joking case was made for marrying one's brother. Although who was to say how city life had changed one's brother?

In the early days of working-girl life, most avoided the Bowery and instead gathered in groups of four or five and, arms linked, headed to Broadway. In an 1863 guidebook, *Miller's New York as It Is, or a Stranger's Guidebook*, the authors made the distinction: "To denizens of New York, society is usually known under the generic divisions of Broadway and the Bowery." Broadway was the street—the golden thoroughfare of theaters and their wealthy clientele in furs and silks. For a working girl, there was little else to do but look. To hook up, to have a real time out, meant turning around and heading back to the Bowery, and this did not seem—not at first, anyway—to be an option.

We hear the word Bowery—a long two-way boulevard running from Manhattan's East Village into Chinatown—and light on phrases such as "skid row" or perhaps "junkie bum." But back then it was a *scene*. At sundown every day, this hub of the butcher's trade became the site of a daring all-night party. Couples crowded for miles beneath the elevated train, or El, whose tracks cast slatted lantern strips across the gaudy attractions— the famed Bowery Theater, freak shows, oyster houses, hundreds of eateries and food carts, some selling the first mass-produced ice cream, and the concert saloons (*saloon* was a takeoff on the word *salon*); these were for men only. In the average concert saloon, "waiter girls" were often topless and there were bedrooms at the back.

Reigning over it all was a bunch of Irish boys, former gang members or pals who'd once worked together on the city's famed volunteer fire crews. Now they worked mostly as journeymen and laborers. At least during the daylight hours. At night they came out dressed to rule. This was hostile male turf; girls were never entirely safe, but to some extent Bowery boys viewed the single girl as a compatriot—usually Irish and always working-class—and as such entitled to some brotherly protection. (Again, not that she was immune from brotherly advance and, sometimes, attack.) Raconteur and socialite Abram Dayton, a scion of the elite Knickerbocker clan, recalled that he'd gone down to the Bowery and easily slummed his way into numerous quick-sex encounters. But after the rise of the factory culture, with its rituals of the Friday-night stroll, he warned that "the Broadway exquisite who ventured 'within the pale,' was compelled to be . . . guarded in his advances . . . any approach . . . wither by work or look was certain to be visited by instant punishment."

The Bowery boys, known in their self-created legend as "the b'hoys" (thus making the girls they kept around "the g'hals"), may be viewed as a first modern peer group. It was a time of union instability, so they were not organized as fellow laborers. They had no other political or religious affiliations. But they were linked, generally speaking, as ethnic laborers, an underclass only too aware of the distinctions between Broadway and the Bowery. If they shared no political or union line, they had a sensibility, a posture, a distinct manner of speech and a unique form of dress that marked them as members of an unofficial social club.

The b'hoy, from what's described, wore his hair in a high combination of pompadour and ducktail. Abram Dayton recalled seeing "black straight broad-brimmed hat[s] . . . worn with a pitch forward . . . large shirt collar[s] turned down and loosely fastened . . . so as to expose the full proportions of a thick, brawny neck; a black frock coat . . . a flashy satin or velvet vest . . . pantaloons," all worn with a lot of jewelry. The final image suggests fifties hoods dressed in drag. Low-life chroniclers characterized the b'hoys as a tough and defensive lot; still, they were so devoted to their "airs," to their internal code of politesse, that they seemed posed there on the street kind of gallant.

The girls thought so.

As I've said, few girls made their way to the Bowery—not at first. (Even the ones who went to gape at Broadway were usually home by eight, telling wholesome lies to parents who could not begin to understand this new scheme.) The bold ones who "walked out" were usually, like the b'hoys, transplanted Irish—tough, independent, a bit hotheaded. An estimated eight out of ten young Irish girls had come, some alone, to the United States as family scouts. They sent for their relatives, as many as they could, using the pay they made as domestics.

Friday nights were a release, and all over the "east end" one might view "a continuous procession," as George G. Foster wrote, "which loses itself gradually in the innumerable side streets leading . . . into the unknown regions of Proletarianism." The girls busily losing themselves had dressed ecstatically. Using magazine illustrations, inexpensive patterns, or improvisation, the Bowery gals put their seamstressing skills to work and made dresses that paid homage to uptown fashions. Then, as if the dress was a cake, they decorated it. They loved notions: fancy buttons, lots of lace, ribbons, bows, fake-silk sashes, any small inexpensive item they could afford. One observer reported that these had no "particular degree of correspondence or relationship in color—indeed [it was common to] see . . . startling contrasts . . . a light pink contrasting with a deep blue, a bright yellow with a brighter red, and a green with a dashing purple or maroon."

The Bowery girl declared her independence from proper female decorum by appearing in public without a hat. All good women wore hats. The only exceptions were prostitutes, who needed open faces to make eye contact with prospective johns. Proper women went further and trimmed their expensive hats with veils and, below, wore heavy clothing to cover every imaginable body part. Skirts were worn so long for a while that it was a class marker, a sign of breeding, to have a strip of mud on one's hem. (It meant that one had been out, appropriately dressed, promenading, stepping into and out of a coach.)

Excluding the reform set, the suffragists, the bohemians, and the "aberrant" (for example, the Lucy Stoners, women who fought to keep their names after marriage), prominent women went out for walks, or promenades, at appointed hours. They shopped, had their lunches and tea dates, then, as if returning from an afternoon shore leave, scurried home quickly with muddy hems. (That is, unless they had a planned assignation; certain madams in the best, least suspicious of brownstones catered exclusively to upper-class women and their lovers.) Occasionally, through the veil of her hat, a woman caught a glimpse of a g'hal, known to her as a servant, wearing . . . the Lord knew what.

As one remarked, "The washerwoman's . . . attire is now like that of the merchant's wife . . . and the blackboot's daughter wears a bonnet made like that of the empress of the French."

The true Bowery g'hal liked to look at least as outlandish as her evening's companion, the b'hoy, who had a very clear idea of how his date should appear. Those in the Bowery fraternity, it may fairly be said, worshipped themselves. They spent much of their time watching plays and theatricals devoted to their own exploits as firefighting heroes and rulers supreme of the boulevard. Many of these lengthy epics, performed at the Bowery Theater, concerned a legendary firefighting hero called Mose, a John Henry/Paul Bunyan type who could walk through flames and had with him at all times his proportionately sized woman, Lize. Every Bowery girl wanted to be a beloved, tough-looking Lize. Every "reporter" out on the Bowery hoped to find one.

"Her very walk has a swing of mischief and defiance in it," wrote George G. Foster of the Bowery girl; Abram Dayton noted, "Her gait and swing were studied imitations of her lord and master, and she trips by the side of her beau ideal with an air which plainly says, 'I know no fear and I ask no favor.' "

One less sympathetic writer characterized the g'hal's this way: "The Bowery Girl, the 'cruiser,' . . . is taught early on that 'the world is graft.' . . . She knows that she must take care of herself . . . she must be shrewd and rely upon herself alone. She drinks very little, saves her money for clothes. Then, when she is gaily attired, she goes . . . and 'grafts' in various ways."

GETTING HOOKED

No matter how comfortable she felt out promenading, the Bowery girl, like any woman on the streets, was likely to be viewed as a "vagabond," a potential prostitute dressed not for an evening out but for work. The associations between prostitution and lone women were so deeply embedded in the culture that women themselves often assumed that their peers, other gals they happened to pass on the street, were on the make. Even a girl stuck at home, guarded by a tyrannical father, could easily adopt that view based on the stories she read. Novels and magazines were filled with tales of prostitutional woe; periodicals seemed to run entire tales-of-woe sections. Here, from a newspaper account, is the testimony of one landlady who'd lost a tenant to the streets:

> I seen her. 'A tiltin' off her head, to sees up and back on the street . . . this girl, 'corse, she'd 'a lived in my old house. I felt turrible about her leaving . . . a house that she know'd was decent and where she could manage to live within her means . . . she was good when she came to this house. When I seen her that day I tried to get her to come. Coffee. She looked almost grateful . . . but she saw a man . . . and turned on me and raced to do what she would.

In fact, it was extremely difficult to assess who was a real sex professional. During the nineteenth century and on into the twentieth, prostitution fell under the criminal heading of "vagrancy." Vagrancy, as then defined, meant loitering—standing or else walking up and back along a stretch of sidewalk. (Mothers, waiting to cross streets, were anxious to keep their girls moving lest they seem "loitery.") Vagrancy arrests more than doubled between 1850 and 1860, but how many of these related to prostitution and how many were the result of more girls simply out on the street, it's hard to say.

Like other cities, New York had a long tradition of hysterical estimates. In 1832 the evangelical Magdalene Society wrote in its annual report: "We have satisfactorily ascertained the fact that the numbers of females in this city, who abandon themselves to prostitution is not less than 10,000!" Throughout the mid-nineteenth century the Ladies' Industrial Association, an early union, with almost all the city papers concurring, would claim that poor girls were turning in desperation to the street or low houses at rates approaching, roughly, 50,000 to 100,000 per year. The Justice Department predicted that by 1910 the figures would rise to 200,000 nationwide, and New York City, of course, would hold its own.

The obvious fact was that no one could live on two dollars a week— the typical salary—or even on a generous raise to four dollars or, if she was very lucky, seven. In 1870 the *Herald* estimated that 5 to10 percent of all young working women made extra money by hooking, treating it as an adjunct to their jobs, although most sources, the *Herald* included, believed that the majority did not take it up as a career. But so hopeful a conclusion was open to ongoing debate.

In *The Women of New York, or Social Life in the Great City* (1870, "with numerous engravings"), George Ellington, wealthy man-about-town and writer, told the whole story, cold. In a chapter entitled "Women of Pleasure," he ran through what a girl could earn for sex in all kinds of situations. On the street, if she survived, she could make per session what a factory girl made during a week, roughly three to four dollars. In the "disorderly" houses, usually down by the seaport, arrangements were made on the spot, while at the merely down-at-the-heels parlor houses, pay ran at ten dollars a week and at the cleaner ones reached twenty to twenty-five. More respectable parlor houses paid live-in girls up to seventy dollars a week. At the elite houses the women— white women, usually actresses, showgirls, other out-of-work performers—started at two hundred per week and were known in some cases to marry their clients.

Prostitution was a major slice of the underground economy, a fact well known to politicians and the police, who accepted regular payoffs. Many landlords preferred hookers over working-class tenants because they obviously made much more money. (And under common law, owners were not regarded as accessories to a criminal act that happened to take place on their properties.) For a percentage, theater owners allowed prostitutes to see clients in the third-tier balcony. Several of the city's most exclusive bordellos were run out of luxurious brownstones owned by the Catholic church.

As hierarchical, almost organized as this sounds, there was a randomness to sex work. Women never knew exactly when they'd need to go out there, and many were so terrified by the prospect that they postponed it as long as possible. Here is a recounting of a first time out, an act of enormous desperation, taken from a novel called *The G'Hals of New York* by Ned Buntline (1850). The story: Mary and Susan, the oldest of several orphaned sisters, are broke and about to be evicted. As a last resort, Mary has miserably agreed to an assignation. It's dusk when she leaves. Susan waits. And waits.

> The wind swept hoarsely, in loud wild wailings, up against the windows, as if they were moaning over the sacrifice her sister had that night made . . . to shield her sisters from absolute want and death . . . Mary, out on such a cold and fearful night on such a horrid mission . . . [Susan's] dreamy fantasies ran . . . the body of a girl, half naked, stark and cold . . . A girl who had gone forth from that very house on Essex Street. . . . the clock struck four and Susan's heart began to throb heavily and painfully. . . . Mary had not come home. . . . [but] the door swung back and Mary, her face flushed and haggard, her eyes fearfully wild and brilliant, and half-glaring like a maniac's came whirling into the chamber— stretching out her right hand in which she clutched a number of bank notes [and] muttered in a hoarse deep toned voice: " 'Tis here, the price of infamy—money! Money! We'll gorge on't. Ha! Ha! Ha! Ha!"

ONE VERY LONG DAY

There are few extant records of the working girl's life, whether she spent it working in a brothel, a factory, or both. Because of language barriers, illiteracy, or all-out exhaustion, very few of the earliest single girls took many notes.

It's a real discovery, then, to come across *The Long Day* (1905), a vivid diary reworked in prose form by a young woman named Dorothy Richardson. Her story begins on a train as she travels from rural Pennsylvania to New York City, where she arrives "an unskilled, friendless, almost penniless girl of 18 . . . a stranger in a strange city." There is but one thought in her head, which she repeats like a mantra: "work or starve, work or starve."

Some selections:

DAY ONE, 6 A.M.: I had written the YWCA some weeks before as to respectable cheap boarding houses. . . . Was this it? . . . I jumped out of bed . . . there was a little puddle of water in the middle of the floor under the skylight, and the drip had brushed against . . . my shirtwaist and soaked into the soles of my only pair of shoes.

MEET THE NEIGHBORS: Breakfast consisted of heterogeneous little dabs of things . . . [I turned] my observations . . . to the people at my table . . . an old woman [who had] difficulty in making food reach the mouth . . . a little fidgety stupid-looking and very ugly woman . . . and a young girl who seemed to be dancing in her seat beside me.

HAVE YE WORK?: Advertisements for cigar and cigarette workers were numerous, accordingly I applied to the foreman of a factory at Avenue A who wanted "bunch makers." He cut me off, asking to see my working card; when I looked at him blankly, he strode away in disgust. Nothing daunted me for I meant to be very energetic and brave. . . . I went to the next factory. They wanted labelers . . . this sounded easy . . . I approached the foreman. . . . He asked for my experience. "Sorry we're not running a Kindergarten here."

DAY TWO: "Girls wanted to learn binding and folding—paid while learning!" The address took me to Brooklyn Bridge and down a strange dark thoroughfare . . . zigzag alleys wrigg[ling] through a great bridge arch into a world of book-binderies. . . . Supervisor civil. He did not need girls until Monday, but he told me to come back then and bring a bone paper cutter. Might find something better.

DAY THREE: I found it! Salesladies—experience not necessary— Brooklyn. Lindbloom's. After much dickering, Mr. L. and wife decided I'd do on $3 a week—working from seven until nine in the evening, Saturdays until midnight . . . if I must Work and Starve, I should not do it in Lindbloom's."

In the meantime—day four—the landlady has revealed herself as a religious nut, spying on girls, entering and searching rooms. Our protagonist flees.

TOO DEAD TIRED TO MIND: I had a chance with the janitress of a fourteenth street lodging house. She had a cleft palate, and all I could understand was [it would cost] one dollar a week with light housekeeping . . . bedtime arrived. I moved closer to the most . . . mutilated cook-stove that ever cheered the heart of a . . . "light housekeeper." . . . Its little body [was] cracked and rust-eaten—a bright merry little cripple of a stove. . . . On its front . . . in broken letters [it said] "Little Lottie." . . . Straightaway, Little Lottie gave me an inspiring example of courage and fortitude. Still precaution prompted me . . . to drag my mother's trunk against the door . . . this was the first journey it had made since it carried her bridal finery to and from the Philadelphia Centennial.

NEW MANTRA: How different it all was in reality from what I had imagined it would be!

BOXED IN: The office of E. Springer & Co. was in pleasant contrast . . . A portly young man who sat behind a glass partition acknowledged my entrance by glancing up. . . . The man opened the glass door. . . . Possibly he had seen my chin quiver . . . and knew that I was ready to cry. . . . The foreman sent word that No. 105 had not rung up that morning, and that I could have her key. The pay was $3 a week to learners, but Miss Price, the superintendent, thought I could learn in a week's time . . . the portly gentleman gave me the key, showed me how to "ring up," in the register. . . . henceforth I should be known as "105."

FIRST DAY OF WORK: Sickly gas jet, and in its flicker a horde of loud-mouthed girls were making frantic efforts to insert their keys into the time-register. . . . Everyone was late. . . . I was pushed and punched unmercifully by the crowding elbows, until I found my-self squeezed tight against the wall . . . thread[ing] a narrow pas-sageway in and out the stamping, throbbing machinery. . . . By the light that filtered through the grimy windows, I got vague con-fused glimpses of girl faces shining like stars out of this dark, fear-ful chaos of revolving belts and wheels . . . through the ramparts of machinery, we entered . . . Phoebe, a tall girl in tortoise earrings and curl papers, was assigned to "learn" me.

WHAT PHOEBE SAYS: "No apron! . . . Turn your skirt! The ladies I'm used to working with likes to walk home looking decent and re-spectable, no difference what they're like other times."

WHAT PHOEBE SAYS TO ANY REMARK, MADE BY ANYONE: "HOT A-I-R!"

WHAT THEY DO: . . . paste slippery strips of muslin over the corners of the rough brown boxes that were piled high about us in frail, tottering towers reaching to the ceiling.

AFTER DOING IT FIVE MINUTES: shoving and shifting and lifting. In order that we not be walled in completely by our cumbersome ma-terials, every few minutes we bore tottering piles across the floor to the "strippers."

TEN HOURS LATER: Dead tired. The awful noise and confusion, the terrific heat [and] foul smell of the glue, and the agony of breaking ankles and blistered hands seemed almost unendurable.

NUMBER 105 ARRIVES HOME: I stopped myself dead. An older woman said, "Youse didn't live there, too?" I stood before the mass of red embers . . . dazed . . . stupefied . . . and watched the firemen pour

their quenching streams upon the ashes of my lodging house. . . .
Nobody knew anything definite. "Five, ten dead."

IN A WOMEN'S SHELTER: Whatever is going to become of me? Why
in the name of all common sense, had I ever come to New York
City? Why was I not content to remain a country school-m'am?

Henrietta, a religious, industrious coworker, hears the story and offers
our girl a room. Other workers advise against it; they say Henrietta is
strange, not as she seems. But our heroine decides that they, as lazy dopey
girls, resent Henrietta for her excellent work habits. Later, walking
"home," our girl begins to suspect that Henrietta does indeed have things
to hide. Her house, far to the other side of town, is a squalid firetrap. And
there's a man waiting for them in the room. A religious friend, says Henrietta, though the pious man is . . . drinking. Our heroine feels as if she's
wandered into an opium den and, terrified, finds that she can barely speak.
Henrietta and the pious drinking man go out on an "errand," leaving our
nervous heroine alone to look under the bed, in the closet—where she
finds liquor—and finally out the window, where she sees Henrietta walking back now with *two* men.

Panicked, she flees and in her rush trips over an old woman lying half
asleep on the stairs. The woman says she lives there (on the stairs, at
least) and sympathizes with the story. In her view, Henrietta is indeed a
drunk, a religious nut, and a whore. The old woman and our heroine, "two
strange compatriots," decide to leave the building in search of food, shelter, anything more comforting than where they are. For hours they wander the city, at last reaching Bleecker Street, where they find an all-night
cafeteria willing to accept such shabby females. Our heroine uneasily spies
a mirror.

THE GIRL AND THE LOOKING GLASS: Truly I was a sorry-looking ob-
ject. Had not been well washed or combed since the last morning . . . I had forgotten my gloves, a brand-new pair, too; my
handkerchief, and most needful of all else, my ribbon stock collar,

without which my neck rose horribly long and thin above my
dusty jacket. . . . I began to feel for the first time what was for me
at least the quintessence of poverty—the absolute impossibility of
personal cleanliness and of decent raiment. . . . I was combing my
heavy hair using a small side comb I wore to keep it up.

Soon after publishing *The Long Day,* Dorothy Richardson was revealed
to have worked six years as a reporter and freelancer for the *Herald,* which
had serialized her book. But she defended herself. As she publicly explained, she had indeed come to New York years before and, for years after,
had worked in factories, laundries, and as she put it, "worse by far." She
worked her way out, thanks to a friend she'd met in a boardinghouse. With
this woman's help, Richardson got a job in a store and worked her way up
to the near-exalted position of coffee-machine demonstrator.

She liked writing and sent in stories about her life to magazines and
papers; eventually she landed a job writing society announcements at the
Herald. She took on the massive task of "writing my life" without a firm assignment. On her own time, she went back to the factories, undercover, re-
visiting and "bringing more up to date" the scenes she had witnessed years
before. Her story was part autobiography, part investigative reporting, and
the end result, she believed, a truthful portrait.

Not everyone believed her story—not the train ride or the crummy
houses and the fire, which was in particular an obvious plot point in melodramatic narratives. As additional evidence of deceit, many cited her
middle-class disdain for factory colleagues. As she wrote, "Most girls could
not work properly. They did not know how to work . . . there was something imbecilic in them. . . . They were female creatures doomed from their
mothers' wombs. Physically, mentally, morally doomed." She further noted
an excess of bulging foreheads, eyes placed too close together, outsized
noses, and as "kind words butter no parsnips," she was quick to point out
how many seemed headed for the Tenderloin, an area west of Sixth Avenue stretching up to Thirty-fourth Street and rapidly becoming the city's
hub of prostitution.

In 1900, one in five American women worked, together accounting for

18 percent of the country's labor force. (It's unclear if that figure included underaged workers; another common statistic claimed that 40 percent of all unwed daughters fourteen or older worked outside the home.) In 1910, in New York City alone, 34 percent of all women went to work every day. And many worked in the way Dorothy Richardson described. Regardless of how she collected her data—and I believe her explanation—her account stands among the most vivid and chilling records we have of the single-girl working life.

THE GIRL BEHIND THE COUNTER

During the mid-nineteenth century, *Arena* magazine published one of many stories extolling the miracles of the Boston factory system and its 60,000 inhabitants, with special emphasis on the famed "Lowell girls." Compared with the 600,000 slaves of the disparate, confused New York system, the Lowell enterprise sounded like girls' camp. The girls had their own dorms or cabins. They took classes, and they were so grateful, so content, that they published a newspaper, the *Lowell Offering*, filled with essays, poems, and songs. Of course the most memorable Lowell anthem was the one girls enthusiastically performed when on strike. Dressed in white muslins and boaters, they'd walk hours singing, *"Oh, isn't it a shame . . . that such a pretty girl as I, should be locked inside a factory and left alone to die! Oh, I will not be a slave! I will not be a slave!"*

It was clear that management had never spent much time on "the campus." Lowell dorms held ten or twelve girls to a small room, three or four sharing beds. The so-called classes met sporadically and covered rote topics of etiquette. But the details didn't matter. The owners had found a way to keep their business and their employees locked in one place—a feat impossible to accomplish in New York City.

Getting to the point, however, the *Arena* author noted that New York did indeed have its advantages. "With fewer class markers," he wrote, New Yorkers were "sometime[s] likely to strike 'a middle ground' . . . create . . . a class between. . . . Not the wretches of factories and sweatshops . . . nor the poor but morally upstanding widow. We shall see if this new type—the girl of the great shops—fares better than her predecessors."

A new type, perhaps *an entire social class,* of working woman! They quickly became known as Shop Girls, or Shoppies: young, white, usually American-born, and thus ideal candidates to stand behind a counter and sell dry goods, which meant, for a female employee, to fetch them and show them to wealthy customers. In exchange for these efforts, the shop girl received little more than her factory cousins. But the view from her place at the counter was a world away from Ludlow and Grand and Delancey Streets.

The mid-to-late nineteenth century stands out as the World's Fair age of high-end retailing. Palatial stores, among them Siegel-Cooper, A. T. Stewart, Lord & Taylor, B. Altman, and Arnold Constable, sold extensive merchandise from around the globe in settings that might have vied for the title Most Exotic *and* Most Bizarre. Every store had live orchestras, waterfalls, a Persian- or Japanese- or Dutch-themed tearoom, and alternating special attractions—tableaux vivants, ice-skating rinks, carousels. Sometimes there was a stocked pond and, in more than one establishment, live strolling peacocks. The *King's Handbook of New York,* 1893, asked, "What are the Parisian Boulevards or even Regent Street to this magnificent panorama of mercantile display?" My favorite description comes from the philosopher Walter Benjamin, who called the department store "both a landscape and a room."

Together, these grand department stores formed "Ladies' Mile," a stretch of Broadway and Sixth Avenue, beginning at Ninth Street with Stewart's and ending at Twenty-third Street with Stern Brothers. The ladies themselves arrived in shifts. The morning crew, usually with maids in tow, came determined to shop. They stayed on and were joined by hundreds of others for lunch, some of whom might stay around for the elaborate late-afternoon tea service. The daily promenade had expanded to fill all the time available.

For the girls who staffed the enterprise, however, life was far from glamorous. The standard-issue shop uniform—a bust-hugging shirtwaist and a long cinched skirt—was so tight that even standing still in it required effort. And salesgirls often stood in the same place for six hours at a stretch without moving. For this they earned between five and seven dollars a week, depending on how long they'd been there and how good a record they'd kept (attitude, neatness, sales). Less visible—and less well paid at three dollars per week—were the wrappers and stock girls who moved on ladders for hour upon hour at the back. Cash girls, or runners, most of them very young, received two dollars a week. In all jobs, but especially those at the counter, girls were instructed to control their facial expressions. There was a point in a transaction at which she smiled; at other times, she was impassive.

This seeming robotic quality led customers to believe that sales staff, like factory workers, were inherently dumb. If not, so the reasoning went, why would they be standing there in the first place? The answer was that they'd be standing there, or standing someplace else, but that they would, given the situation, have to stand somewhere, doing something they did not want to do. As the reformist Clara E. Laughlin wrote in a fascinating book, *The Work-a-Day Girl: A Study of Some Present-Day Conditions* (1913): "The average girl has no idea what she wants to do . . . except that she wants to . . . and must . . . earn money . . . the majority of girls drift in[to] this or that because they have a friend . . . the notion of the number and variety of possible employments is usually limited by what they know of the occupations of their acquaintances."

That was true. And friends who got there first put it bluntly: Find a tolerable place, and please, don't ask us what we really think or what we've already begun to figure out. For example, veteran shop girls knew that ten years before, men alone had done their jobs. Sales positions opened to women only as companies had grown, departments had spidered, and men had moved into the new managerial jobs. And they also knew that when men held the sales jobs, the work itself had been more interesting. As sales clerks, men had aggressively sold and developed relationships with customers; women, forbidden these exchanges, took a first step into what we'd call "the pink-collar ghetto." As one manager explained, "Female salespersons do not urge the customer to buy . . . they simply ask the customer what he or she wants, and make a record of the sale."

As she did this, bosses and floorwalkers, that is, male department managers, watched and judged her constantly. Had she made any slips? Was there a hint of rudeness in the voice, self-defense or disagreement? Had she been deliberately slow? Was her posture "slagging," and did she seem evidently tired or exasperated when a customer asked to see that fifteenth variation on a scarf?

One shop girl, nineteen, described her practiced stoicism to a social worker:

> Sometime I do admit I would like nothing more than to leap across my counter and topple on that girl, no older than me . . . smack her face the way it never smiles and demands you show it this and this. It's not right. One day a girl came in. She had a feather in her hat and a fur, a little thing who told me I had better accustom me t'a call her "m'am," and I thought, I will jump across and I will break her face up, smug pup's nose. . . . [still] I was always smiling, smiling, yes, yes.

But she had problems far worse than uppity customers. By as late as 1890, some stores still provided no benches or perhaps had just one (hard, small) bench for girls to sit on during breaks, that is, if breaks had been established as a custom. Many girls ate their lunches—pickles, rolls, and tea—standing up. Much worse, many of the best stores had no employee bathrooms (workers were encouraged to take care of personal maintenance matters before leaving home in the morning; it was "their business"). Mary Gay Humphreys, a journalist and reformer who took the working girl as her subject, regularly escorted small parades of girls to her apartment house to "use facilities."

Humphreys combined a reformer's intensity with genuine skill as a journalist. She listened and reported as opposed to moralizing or operatically exaggerating the gal's life. She banished the slangy linguistic back bends that made the working type, especially the factory girl, seem so alien. It was common to read about girls who, asked about, say, a boyfriend, replied: "He's 'n me 'a go 'a wooken a bit—not w-h-a-t you say?" These pidgin dialects, whether Irish-Yiddish or Italian-Scottish, made the girl seem not only alien but mentally feeble. Humphreys's pieces, printed in a variety of newspapers and magazines, were so immediate that it's easy even now to imagine standing there, five hours into the workday and desperate to pee but unable, according to store policy, to move an inch. As she wrote: "Because the immediate surroundings are . . . hospitable, there is little comprehension of what a girl must get through on the average day, standing behind a counter for hours, back aching, waiting on rude bargain-hunting women. . . . and then the management . . ."

Humphreys was the first journalist to record the practice of "treating" as it occurred in the store. In one story, she quotes a young woman who'd been drawn into conversation with her boss. Between puffs on a cigar, he told her, "You got the look, get a man, go out with him and let him pay. Don't wear this shirt again. It is filthy, a disgrace." (No surprise, as it was likely her only one.) After similar encounters, many girls walked into the back—provided there was no one to see—and started crying. As one of them told Humphreys, she understood the barter concept but the terms of this one "startled" her. "If they expect this or that for an ice cream, what can they want for a hand-stitched shirt?" Some took the boss's advice and attempted to find male help they could emotionally afford. Others didn't think about it in such specific terms and just went out.

This was the age of the great "rackets," huge public balls that had started as a youthful response to the dull extended-family dance. Anyone could go—invitations replicated like chain mail throughout the factories and stores—and as George G. Foster wrote, everyone went, "the folding girls and seamstresses, the milliner's apprentices, the shopgirls . . . all unmarried womanhood." Sometimes there were six balls on one night for them to choose from and a selection of venues. By 1890, thousands of dance halls stretched south from Houston to Canal Street and across the city from the Hudson River to Avenue B.

Shoppies traveled in groups—"lady friends" they called one another—and they were said to like the wild dancing or "rubbering." Some of them even "spieled," a notorious dance in which a couple twirled or whipped their way across the floor until someone either fainted or fell. (No one said it outright, but dancers were thought to faint or fall at the point of orgasm. It was perhaps this bit of gossip that inspired one senator to proclaim, "Rome's downfall was due in part to the degenerate nature of its dances, and I only hope that we will not suffer the same result.") Some, however, found the smoke and the sweat too much after a long day spent saying "Yes, ma'am." They were happier heading back to their rooms for quiet dinners, reading, and, as always on so minuscule a weekly budget, the mending. (There were other means for attaining new shirtwaists: making a new one, or cleverly reinvigorating the sagging gray one using bleach.)

Some nights after curfew—and all rooming houses had 9 or 10 P.M. curfews—three or four girls would crawl through the dark to an appointed room. Someone brought chocolate to melt on the hot plate, someone brought a robe to stuff beneath the door to block the smell. Settled in, they reviewed the current themes: How much longer can we stand working at Stewart's? Waitressing, do you get wages *and* a tip? And—the eternal question—whom should I marry and how soon? According to the few diary entries on such secret soirées, the conversation often centered on whom *not* to marry. Or on why to marry at all. The papers were filled with murderous stories straight out of the courts. In *City of Women*, Christine Stansell dug up many disturbing examples, ones any working girl might have read for herself: "Mrs. Towney met her death over a turkey. Incensed about the way she had prepared the fowl as about the money she had spent on it, her husband set about beating her, interspersing his blows with sarcastic reproaches 'you made great preparations, didn't you?' "

Another man murdered his wife for taking four shillings out of his pocket. As he explained: "I will serve blows to any damn whore who dares rob me."

But enough of that. The conversation took a turn to cosmetics (eyebrows and how to make two out of what was often the one) and, more significant, clothing. Shoppies did not share the usual sartorial goals of the working class: urging wide feet into slim American slippers and attempting to master the impossible corset. They had other concerns. A working shop girl typically traveled some distance to and from work, in all kinds of weather, then spent an average of ten to twelve hours on her feet. From all descriptions, her uniform by day's end was like a straightjacket. Many otherwise apolitical girls became adherents of dress reform.

The ideal, as one sympathetic writer explained, was to design for girls "a loosely arrayed garment that allows for easy movement but does not in any way excite the male libido." There were all sorts of proposals. Many called for a kind of loose-fitting long-sleeved overall that would come with an attachable skirt to hide the pants and, sometimes, a "bodice vest" to hide the upper portion, or bib, of the overall. And there were plans for jumpers, long or short, to be worn with "broadened," meaning wider, less constricting, shirtwaists. There's no record detailing whether or not anyone actually executed these designs, if anyone ever wore them, or if anyone was bodily removed from a store as a result.

Rather, it seems, there were scattered instances of rebellion. In 1907 four hundred New York shop girls signed up for the Rainy Day Club, a citywide movement of working women who demanded the right to wear shorter skirts, raincoats, and rubber boots to and from work when it rained. The idea dated to the Civil War, when women had replaced men in many difficult jobs and found themselves essentially disabled inside their clothes. They had admired the nurses they saw out around the city; they dressed so sensibly—rain boots in bad weather and, always, shorter hems. (Nurses, like shop girls, could not afford the status symbol of the muddy hem.) The Rainy Day Clubs published pamphlets advising girls to shorten hems by four inches and to wear galoshes when it rained.

Official reactions varied. Some stores forbade all galoshes or demanded that on wet days girls arrive very early, long before any customers, so that they could remove their galoshes in the entryway and walk on store floors in workplace shoes. Some store managers let it filter down through the floorwalkers and buyers that these shoes—especially if skirts were an inch or two higher—would have to be "decent." Most took no official position on the skirts, considering that most girls remained half visible behind a counter and rarely ventured onto the floors.

The nasty response came in the press. By demanding certain rights, shoppies were said to have put on "ludicrous airs," to loudly have proclaimed themselves a "better class of girl deserving of higher things," when in fact they were mere "independent strutting figments that wither[ed]" as they arrived back at their "shabby" homes. While playing the role of fine shop girl, such deluded female creatures were unbearable. "The American woman is vulgar," wrote Hutchins Hapgood, in *Types from City Streets*. "[and] some of our most vulgar women are our salesladies. . . . They demand what is their 'due.'. . . They read the society columns and [the magazine] *The Smart Set*."

Others accused the girl of acting up like her lewd cousin, the factory gal. Shoppies were frequently said to dance on their breaks and, according to many magazine reports, were "known to sing at any opportunity." A twelve-paragraph letter in *Harper's* magazine added to the indictment. "She sings, it is true, and she may also be found casually . . . strutting—talking out of turn—flirting, singing, dancing in the streets . . . I have heard the most vile language tossed between them . . . such that would make me . . . run in shame."

Employers complained of "blue Mondays," hangover days when the girl who'd been out "rubbering" could be observed leaning as opposed to standing. If blue Mondays became widespread, management deployed the store detectives to gather intelligence about the offenders. (Chances were that management had already gathered basic family information on its girls; they kept track not only of a girl's "books," or sales records, but of her outside reputation.) As long as a girl kept up her "books," much of what she did outside could be overlooked, provided she brought no "ill-repute" to the store or began to look "mangy." Borderline girls, those with good but occasionally erratic books, might be permitted a blue Monday or two. But they would not receive raises and they might suddenly be transferred to less desirable counters, and they would know exactly why. Nonperformers who "rubbered" too intensely and rolled in Mondays looking "shot" would be fired. As one girl told Hutchins Hapgood: "I do my work, they know that. When I no longer can 'deliver the goods,' they will fire me, of course. That's my risk. In the mean time, however, I can do whatever I please, and they won't say a word."

The fact was, after all, that they were girls—85 percent of the store populations, circa 1900, were single, and most were under twenty-one.

They were less faux ladies or incipient radicals than they were ordinary late adolescents. They liked to dance, whether on the streets, out at rackets, or in the store salons management eventually opened for the "tired, deserving female employee" on her breaks. In almost all photos of these salons—and there were numerous for release to the press—we see crowds of long-skirted girls waltzing with one another to a gramophone.

In secret they fashioned a subterranean girl culture within the store. Twice a month word went out through all departments that it was "fairy day." On fairy day, two girls were chosen as the fairy queens and endowed with the right to "perform all mischief," while their colleagues covered up their every act. Typical fairy business included sending unsigned mash notes to bosses and surrounding male floorwalkers in a flirtatious group while the fairy attached a silly tag to his back. By the greatest of horrific mistakes, a fairy queen might spray a parfum *français* into the face of an obnoxious client. Regular store social life, however, took the more traditional form of a club.

Almost every department had a club running its own special activities, from dances and parties to what we'd call self-help groups. One store had a very active "foot mould social club" and, on a different floor, a "fine linens sistership and social organization." Mostly, the clubs tried to alleviate the dreariness of store life. Every member, for example, had, in addition to a fairy day, an "un-birthday." On this day, the anointed gathered with her pals to slice up what was called a "Halloween cake," a mountainous lopsided confection that had baked within it two tiny objects: a ring that signified marriage and a thimble forecasting spinsterhood. The results, turned up in slices, were published in the club's private newsletter and sometimes in the larger storewide newsletters shop-girl clubs put out each month.

At Siegel-Cooper the house organ was called *Thought and Work*, a compendium of intrastore courtships, marriages, makeup tips, and celebrations of various departments within the store. Say the subject was leading salesladies. Twenty or so girls would be featured, as if in a theater program, delicate wreaths etched in around their faces, their area of expertise ("fine linens," "ladies' shoes," "artificial flowers") spelled below the photograph in fancy script. Eventually management decided that *Thought and Work*

contained too little about work—and, for that matter, no thought at all—
and discontinued it.

Occasionally the clubs exhibited nascent hints of feminism, or at least
signs of independent thinking. In 1910, for example, the Siegel-Cooper
Bachelor Girl Social Club organized a celebration of Washington's Birthday "without even inviting men." Instantly they were denounced by male
employees as man haters. Replied the bachelor girls: "No, we are not married, neither are we men haters, but we believe in women's rights and we
enjoy our independence and our freedom. Notwithstanding that if a fair
offer came our way we might not [sic] consider it."

Wealthy matrons found such beings coarse and undesirable in all ways,
but their daughters were often intrigued. Trapped in a life of calling cards,
formal teas, and chaperoned balls, young society girls craved some small
measure of freedom before the inevitable wedding. Not that one would be so
low as to actually *work*, but they had heard of these dances—the rackets—
and there was something, why, it went without saying, *monstrous* in it all,
yet still compelling.

"Slumming" even then had its magnetic lure, but it was rare to stum-
ble upon the ideal circumstances for actually doing it. Rackets presented
the perfect opportunity to anonymously and briefly indulge in—or at least
watch—rowdy downtown behavior. Of course the girls under investigation
were very "low," headed for a life one could not begin to contemplate. Yet
in the heat of a spiel, they seemed powerful—daring girls, brave, and perhaps even the tiniest bit enviable. Some of these same well-bred young
ladies felt a secret fascination with stage stars. They would not, even for a
laugh, stand among the "matinee girls," the back-door fixtures who waited
every day for their current idols to exit. But they were drawn to actresses,
who throughout the nineteenth century had set the leading fashion trends.
(Serious dramatic actresses were expected to supply their own costumes,
and part of the thrill of theatergoing lay in the anticipation of seeing what
they wore.) Actresses were also considered somewhat disreputable.

Out on her own, slumming with her beaux, the upper-class girl went
to the shows. Actresses were interesting, but more immediately thrilling
were the sequined chorus girls and the showgirls, curvaceous balletic things

who appeared entr'acte to show new fashions. And everyone had a secret fascination with the Ziegfeld Follies girls and, most important, with Ziegfeld's famed Floradora sextette. All six of these special stars, super-models of their day, would marry millionaires.

In part, the allure of the working girl—like that of a low actress—derived from how much the mere idea of such a person upset one's mother. Whether a shop girl or a showgirl, she was the exemplar of everything a daughter should not be—and should not even be exposed to. A great many mothers found these young working women personally threatening. If factory girls were thought to be whores with day jobs, then shoppies were believed to be mistresses in waiting. They spent their days surrounded by beautiful things and were encouraged to have men buy them clothes. If the girl was pretty, smart, and ambitious, she might walk out after work with a man, a husband, she'd sold a hat to. They would very likely "treat" each other in all sorts of ways.

One of the era's most popular plays was called *Only a Shopgirl* (1902) by Claire Wellesley Sterling. Posters show a wealthy fur-clad wife bursting into a dim boardinghouse room. She points one manicured finger at a shirtwaisted girl named Hulda. Hulda stares back defiantly, her smaller siblings gathered around her in terror. "YOU," shouts the woman, "are nothing but a low shop girl!" Says Hulda: "Better a low shop girl than a fashionable idler as heaven is above hell!" The play was produced throughout the teens and the themes reworked in several silent films until its class love triangle gradually entered the standard melodramatic lexicon.

For all their efforts, the fairy days, dances, and clubs, shop girls were unable to resolve their most basic problem: They were shop girls. And no matter what they did on weekends, the workdays were still long and depressing, and once or twice a month they took department inventory, at no extra pay. One plant observer, or investigator, captured the unavoidable results during a 1909 study of twenty stores. Here is his report on one set of counter girls:

> I have been watching three misses . . . for three days now. The first is most instructive. . . . she wears a fixed smile on her made-up face, and it never varies, no matter to whom she speaks . . . [First]

she is either frowning or her face, like that of the others, is devoid of any expression. When a customer approaches, she immediately assumes her hard forced smile. . . . As they leave, it amazes how quickly it departs . . . I've never seen such calculation given to the timing of a smile. . . . The others make less drastic of an effort. . . . I have had the impression that one or both is lost in thought or asleep while standing.

But occasionally one read of a shoppie who, despite the physical rigors of work, the snotty clients, the pimpish bosses, seems to have done more than plot fantastic diversions; she'd made for herself a good life. One 1905 magazine story, "After Shop Hours—What?" follows "Bess," an admirable, organized shop girl, as she describes what she does with her free time, each activity accompanied by small, if unfortunately blurry, engravings. As Bess was only too happy to explain:

MONDAY: Dine out or have chafing dish supper with one of the girls. To bed at 9:30.

TUESDAY: Read with one of my men friends (in parlour), novel or any book we choose. I do my week's mending or fancy work while he reads. Sometimes we sing duets. To bed at 9:30.

WEDNESDAY: Dancing class. To bed at 10.

THURSDAY: Have someone to dinner. Sew or read or play games. To bed at 9:30.

FRIDAY: Two of my girlfriends and I have our fairy tale readings for settlement children every other Friday. Other Fridays we go out to a lecture or to something of the sort. To bed at 10.

SATURDAY: To theater or opera or dance and to bed any old time.

SUNDAY: Sleep. Every other Sunday is the Good Time Friendly Club. We have cake and tea and a sociable time. Others, I go for a walk with some of the men and the girls. To bed early.

The editors of this story made it clear that Bess was lucky. Most working girls were so anxious or so tired they did not get much from their time off, not even much-needed sleep. As more young women took jobs— nearly 60 percent of all New York City women, aged sixteen to twenty, worked during the early 1900s—a new set of reformers stepped in to help the workplace advocates. If Mary Gay Humphreys was concerned with underage cash runners, rest facilities, and horny floorwalkers, others now wondered how this girl might organize a "meaningful well thought out and rounded" life.

These were the words of Grace Dodge, a wealthy, socially conscious woman who "for them alone" opened the first YWCA, on Fifteenth Street. (She meant well, but given the time and place, "them" meant only white non-Jewish women with references and provably good reputations.) She also inaugurated a more inclusive network of clubs meant, and I quote from the cover of her popular book, *A Bundle of Letters to Busy Girls* (1887): "[to help] those girls who have not time or inclination to think and study about the many important things which make up life and living." Dodge feared girls "had not time for the higher things." She seems also to have believed they had not time for lower things. At weekly meetings, many held in her downtown apartment, she covered everything, for example: attending work with one's menstrual period and "the disposal of rags." Another: the importance of bowel movements and whether it was acceptable to move one's bowels at work. She discussed clothing, hair, correspondence, and she expressed her belief that far more enjoyable than a racket, a wild dance, was a pleasant tea or reading party. Not all present agreed.

In fact, her "girls" increasingly agreed about very little. And the conflicts among club members became harder for Dodge and the growing number of her imitators to ignore. The better-attired, better-spoken women resented the presence of the immigrant girls Dodge had deliberately sought out and invited. Periodic attempts at unification ended in mild chaos, chair rattling, factions marching out as the "other side" spoke. One famous mêlée broke out over Dodge's suggestion that club members wear badges. One young woman is reported to have shouted above the others: "Why should we want to tell everyone who rides in the streetcar with us that we are nothing more than ragged working girls who spend their entire evenings in a club hearing a lecture that is good for us? . . . Is it necessary to . . . advertise our status as working girls when that status . . . is as quickly recognized as that of the wealthy one?"

The clubs split up, despite Dodge's insistence that girls, together, had so much to learn! Factory girls increasingly had their own very serious concerns—unionization, strike coordination, and the ongoing campaigns for workplace improvements. Shop girls continued, in the words of Mary Gay Humphreys, to "come in at night, nervous and tired, to be confronted by the problem of food, clothes, rent . . . of forever providing for bare material necessities." But the shop girls, better dressed, more articulate, had at least a few options.

Store life was not as it would be in the movies: a fun, ducky universe populated by adorable girls like Louise Brooks and Clara Bow, whose signature film, It (1927), among many others, was set in a big store (a fishbowl universe perfect for the stationary camera). But real-life shoppies, like their movieland counterparts, had a pretty good chance of finding the exit. That most often meant marriage—but not always. Many girls, supporting themselves, sending money home, would continue to work and live singly. And the more intelligent and ambitious among them might land a very different kind of job.

Some of these young women, often much to their surprise, became teachers. Public education had been compulsory since the 1860s, and as urban life overtook rural, more families, less in need of farmhands, complied with the law. At the turn of the century there were more schools than ever before, more students, and a constant demand for young teachers. Although very few young working women had secondary degrees, many had high school diplomas. (In fact, 60 percent of all high school graduates in 1880 were women.) Because they'd finished high school, and because teaching was associated with child care, many who'd never even contemplated teaching got the job. As early as 1910, 98 percent of all teachers, at all levels of the public-school system, were women.

But many, many more headed into what was known, with a slight hint of exotica, as "the world of business."

True, there was never the slightest trace of exotica once you got there. But it was better. Better pay. Better people to mix it up with. "Aren't we all women in business now and more of us as the years pass?" asked film star Mary Pickford in a 1911 movie magazine. Without mentioning her salary, she exulted, "We are all working girls, and I am ever so proud to be among you!"

I AM A TYPEWRITER

In the original single work schematic, office work was about as good as it got. The pay could start as high as ten dollars per week. The work did not require hours of militaristic standing, and the men did not seem as ungentlemanly as they had back in ladies' shoes. Even the jobs themselves sounded better: sorting "clerk" or file "chief," positions requiring some rushing around, some work seated at one's own desk. There was the "typewriter," the original name for both the machine and its operator. Above them all, to be had through promotion, was the secretary, and best of all, the personal secretary. The boss chose her above all others, allowing her to move freely within the inner sanctum of the business (except at luncheons), and trusting her to be highly skilled and discreet in all matters, including who it was the boss actually took to lunch.

As newly self-defined professionals, young women worked to master their jobs, and worked, too, to overlook the feeling that these tasks were as tiresome as the ones they'd performed in stores. Typewriters began their day by grooming their machines, a process that, in photos, suggests a row of well-dressed young women picking inky nits off large black armadillos. Others ran letter presses, primitive copying devices that required inking and hand pressing and left copiers weak-wristed, while the all-purpose clerks had to manipulate tall ladders that slid on tracks. The hours were long, the "lounge" facilities minimal. As one worker told *Collier's* magazine: "Your chair is given as your chair and there isn't much point in asking for one that fits beneath the desk or anything else that does not fit."

Of course, to keep up a steady supply of applicants, employers portrayed office girls as superbly competent and attractive, the kind of young professional any girl would want to become. Even department stores started playing similar word games. Their new breed of "lady bookkeeper" was, like her office sister, exceptionally crafty, smart, and unusually honest. As one manager stated: "Lady bookkeepers [are] not so likely to appropriate money that don't belong to them!" Office workers understood that they were supposed to feel lucky—they were, after all, Women of Business—but it was a feeling that one could sustain on most days about as long as it took to reach one's desk.

By 1910, so many women had arrived in offices with so many questions and complaints—Is this "good" job as bad as it seems? Where can I go after this if I have to?—that new advice guides appeared monthly. Among the most popular, and most serious, was an epistolary volume entitled *Letters to a Business Girl: The Personal Letters of a Business Woman to Her Daughter, Replete with Practical Information Regarding the Perplexing Problems . . . By One Who Knows the Inside Facts of Business and the Office Routine and the Relations of Employer to Employee* (1906).

In this book Florence Wenderoth Saunders reveals more about office life and the inherent struggles of office girls than just about any other advice guide, newspaper series, or any realist novel by Sinclair Lewis. Saunders was a middle-aged woman who had worked with great pride in an early office environment, married the boss, then moved with him to the country, where she helped him to run a farm. After his death, she kept at the farm until business plunged—so deeply that she had to send her oldest daughter, just eighteen, off to the city. This was a common enough decision, though still controversial. As Mother writes early on: "I have been severely censured since you left, because I allowed you to leave my protection and care and face the dangers of a business life, particularly in the city."

Readers skimmed Mother's tales of her own heroic stoicism, for example, once walking from Delancey Street up to Thirty-fifth, wearing a cloth coat, in a blizzard, all to save ten cents in trolley fare that she badly needed for something else. Beyond the dire autobiography, young female readers found unusually blunt and specific remarks:

You'll probably hear yourself referred to as a "poor creature" and "the downtrodden working girl" and, even as we used to hear it ourselves, "poor things." Whatever it is there is a lot of "poor" attached to it . . . necessarily the girl who is employed has to give up many things . . . but she gains a far broader knowledge of life than . . . her sisters of leisure. . . . The girl who has once earned her own living knows that if necessary she can earn it again.

And the author had strong views on how that girl, member of an elite female working corps, should conduct herself.

I never saw a businessman's desk that was loaded with the trifles that some of the girls in my office used to have on theirs; photographs, flowers . . . like knickknacks they kept because they were cute. . . . Remember, men have the advantage in business; they have been accustomed to work for generations . . . if [a girl] expects to take her place by [his] side and eventually command the same salary, she must profit from his example . . . keep [your] desk cleared of every article *which is not absolutely essential in the performance of your work.*

The office girl needed a firm, stalwart supporter. Not only was she underpaid and often bored, she also became from time to time a target for paranoid commentators. She had emerged as a new working type just as concern about so-called political and social deviants—suffrage supporters, free-lovers, childless women, Bolsheviks, anarchist bombers—had reached a new high. The unavoidable movement of young women, troops of them, heading off to jobs seemed increasingly suspect. In the minds of certain commentators, a working single woman was by nature uncooperative, potentially radical, and un-American. Why wasn't she at home having babies? Because office girls seemed more serious, more professional, the most hysterical queries were often tossed their way. Was the average typist now spending lunch enmeshed in the works of Hegel, Marx, and Susan B. Anthony? Did she read "lurid fiction"?

Certainly some working girls had read poems by Edna St. Vincent Millay, or at least had heard of her. There were probably some who'd seen a copy of *The Masses* or been taken on an edifying date to some kind of socialist or literary lecture. But the average girl was not trying to reshape the world according to socialist or any other precepts; she was trying, for the time being, to advance in the office and earn more money. And that meant one thing: stenography. Only with this skill might she move her way through the rows of hulking typewriters into the semiprivate outer office of the boss. All she had to do was raise the money for night school. Then she'd add the three hours in classes onto her workday. Then she'd survive it.

Most of what we know about early "business" school—life inside the dry overheated rooms eight flights up—derives from characters like Kitty Foyle, heroine of the eponymous novel by Christopher Morley (1939) and later a film starring Ginger Rogers. Like Tess McGill, the baby-voiced secretary who brilliantly outmaneuvered her corrupt boss in *Working Girl* (1988), Kitty is perceived by the world as all . . . wrong. Wrong address. Wrong accent. Wrong clothes. Wrong man.

In Kitty's case, that's the beautiful son of an old-line WASP family. He sees in Kitty what others are blind to: sharp, sardonic intellect; kindness; and genuine bravery. And not only because she has tolerated the snubs of his family. Despite their involvement, Kitty moves alone to New York City, in order to better support her widowed father. After many visits back and forth, she concludes sadly that she cannot live in his world, nor he in hers, and breaks it off. Soon after, the boy's parents force him into marriage with a suitable girl; Kitty reads about it in the society columns on the same day she has aborted his baby. (Not something that made it into the 1940 Ginger Rogers movie.)

Hoping to move on and to make a better life, Kitty enrolls in night school. "We were pretty serious about it all," she says. "Also pretty damned discouraged by the time we got to diphthongs and disjointed suffixes. That's when you find yourself dreaming shorthand and wake up figuring out the symbol for Indianapolis or San Francisco." The girls in her class form a kind of sorority, pooling resources, going out to movies and occasional dinners and treating themselves to their favorite team drink. ("Every way of life seems to have its own drink," she says; "our shorthand squad specialized on black-and-white sodas.") Together they hunt for jobs, celebrate, and try to assuage their disappointment when shorthand doesn't prove to be the answer to even one or two of life's great difficulties.

Business school works for Kitty Foyle. She "makes her way," gets a better job, and meets a man who, like her employers, finds her personal qualities, not to mention her shorthand skills, truly impressive. For some women, however, business school was not a chance to advance, if slightly, in the world but a means to retreat. It was the place you went when you did not get married. This sad conclusion is best evoked in another novel, *Alice Adams* by Booth Tarkington (1921), the story of an awkward, groping young woman, played in the 1935 film version by a young Katharine Hepburn. Alice is single and poor but nonetheless a determined society aspirant out to "win" a local rich guy played in the film by Fred MacMurray. She attempts this feat by cornering the man on the street, in stores, at parties she wasn't invited to, then maneuvering him out onto a balcony and chattering nervously. In the novel it doesn't work, and with no money and no marital prospects, Alice is last seen climbing the wooden steps of her local business school, up "into the smoky darkness," as if trudging to the guillotine.

As she views her "ominous" prospects: "Pretty girls turn . . . into old maids 'taking dictation'—old maids of a dozen different types, yet all looking a little like herself." (In the movie adaptation Alice triumphs, becoming a wife despite her social gaffes, thus narrowly avoiding slow clerical death.) Florence Wenderoth Saunders would have shaken her head in disgust. As she'd written:

> So many girls look upon their business experiences merely as unpleasant incidents in their lives; to be gotten through, with as little exertion to themselves, and with as great haste as possible. . . . They wed the first man that asks them, for fear that another chance might not come along; whether they love him or not, or whether his salary can be stretched to meet the requirements of

two people, are questions that do not trouble them, all they want is to get away from the office, store or factory and stop working.

For all of Saunders's enthusiasm—her pride in watching her daughter accept a big new job in Washington, D.C.—it's easy to understand how tired and betrayed office workers felt. Far from advancing beyond "shop girl," they had landed in a parallel universe. And one with its own publicity mill. As late as 1935, *Fortune* was still extolling the modern office as a kind of female paradise. As one executive rhapsodized: ". . . the competent woman at the other end of the buzzer . . . the four girls pecking out the boss's initials with pink fingernails on the keyboards of four voluble machines, the half dozen assorted skirts whisking through the filing cases of correspondence, and the elegant miss in the reception room. . . ."

That may have been visual bliss for the men. The "assorted skirts" had their own views. Like the smarter shop girl, the office worker came to understand that "women's" jobs meant those that men had done until they'd moved into a new managerial class. In 1870, less than 1 percent of all clerical workers were women. By 1900, tallying figures received from a thousand or more national employment agencies, the Labor Department estimated that more than 100,000 women worked as stenographers, typists, and secretaries. By 1920, more than 25 percent of all secretaries were women, and by 1965, the figure was 92 percent.* As sociologist C. Wright Mills would later famously state, offices had become "modern nunneries."

Still, like all working single women, the office gal had to make the most of her situation, and enjoy what small amount of time she spent away from her job. Many reported having little energy for rackets and other noisy parties. The time between 10 P.M. and 6 A.M. was on most days devoted to hanging about with roommates or friends from the office and then to sleep. Kitty Foyle, though an invention, provides us with an excellent single-girl scenario:

---

*The most famous ghettoizing process was under way at the phone company. Telephone operator had been a respectable job, meaning a male job, until corporate expansion created several tiers of more challenging positions. By as early as 1902, the Bell Telephone System employed 37,000 female switchboard operators. Their rationale: Women had "more calming" voices and were "more patient."

Molly and Pat and me had so much fun together evenings, going over the day's roughage, we wouldn't even mind we couldn't afford to go out often. Sometimes we had dinner at the wop joint in the yard . . . the one who ate the meatballs slept on the davenport. Then if she wakes at two a.m. . . . she can sit on the edge of the bed and smoke a cigarette without disturbing the others.

In the best cases, an office girl overlooked the obvious, somewhat pathetic obstacles and learned to hustle. Strategize. She looked for the breaks. That meant seeking out a boss she could influence, pushing for overtime pay and promotions, keeping a running tab of better jobs elsewhere, and, of course, considering seriously all marriage proposals.

Kitty Foyle, who'd go on to become a cosmetics-industry executive, agreed that the business girl had to play all the angles. And that strategy was often a more complicated, exhausting business than the business itself. As she says offhandedly, "Lots of career girls have got raises for their ambition that was really Benzedrine sulphate."

LUST FOR A LATCHKEY

All early working girls, regardless of what they did or where they did it, had similar problems. And the greatest of all could be summarized in three words: where to live. The fantasy solution could be summed up in one word: latchkey.

The latchkey, a four- or five-inch-long skeleton key, served for tired, exasperated girls as an amulet, a totem, an admission ticket inside. A key signaled the vanquishing of all boardinghouse breakfasts, the Y, and the landlady, her lieutenants and spies. In 1910 there were an estimated fifteen thousand boarding and furnished rooming houses, where girls were not so much chaperoned but placed on a permanent parole. Wrote one linen saleswoman in *The Independent:* "A [boarding] house like that should be a strictly hotel basis, no Christian stuff, sign this, sign here, be quiet, no guests—oh God, we just want a nice place to live like anybody and not answer questions—where have we been and with who. . . . How is it their business to know?"

Mary Gay Humphreys reported that sixty-eight thousand of the girls who boarded worked as salesladies (their updated term) and hoped to find a place where they might be free of all inquisition. As one male journalist wrote in their defense: "What right has the world to decide that working women must be treated as déclassé until they prove themselves otherwise?"

The working girl understood that like car keys in the 1920s—or car keys now for that matter—the latchkey would guarantee some measure of freedom. But it seemed all apartment keys had been reserved for men. Until the early twentieth century there were no apartments for women. They didn't exist.

There had been interim solutions. The most famous was perhaps the large ocean liner the *Jacob A. Stamler,* owned by businessman John Arbuckle, which had docked for few months, 1907–8, at a Twenty-third Street pier. The offer was to let all rooms on board cheaply and without serious restrictions to "self-respecting girls who'd behave with honor." This lasted a few happy months until the city needed the pier space and the ship moved on; one newspaper printed an etching of tired-looking girls in dark dresses and hats, standing clustered like mourners, watching it go.

No single woman, working or not, had ever been presumed trustworthy, economically solid, or discreet enough to make a desirable tenant. These qualities, if she learned them at all, she would presumably learn from her husband. And she was always suspected of prostitution. But given the statistics, the sheer visual evidence of girls out there, some builders and owners drew up plans for small hotels and apartment houses. Almost every plan, however, was scrapped in the discussion phase; no girl could afford such amenities, and who'd invest?

So it was big news, covered everywhere, when in 1910 the Trowmart Inn, looking for "self-supporting girls tired of the tawdry lodging room and sick of the miserable little rookery," opened its doors. The Trowmart, brainchild of a successful New York merchant, welcomed young women who could prove they held a job earning no more than fifteen dollars per week. They also had to be provably under the age of thirty-five (meaning they were not likely to become indigent spinsters and never leave). A bed inside one of the 228 dormlike rooms cost fifty cents per week. To live with just several others in more private rooms cost $4.50, and for a dollar more per week, a working woman could have a room all to herself. No one had to give references unless she planned to live there permanently. And with no marriage prospects and the age "thirty-five" years away, well, it didn't sound all that bad. The Trowmart served food described as "reasonable" and "pleasant." It was renowned for its "well-appointed" bathrooms. (More expensive rooms had the bathrooms in the room itself!) It had laundry facilities.

The latchkey at last.

Some girls wore their spindly keys on long chains that dangled, while others hid theirs inside a boot or a shoe and stood on it all day to be sure it was safe. It was not an engagement ring, but in its way it symbolized a rite of passage; single female life had at last been deemed a grown-up life. In his 1992 film *Singles*, Cameron Crowe captures the same sort of exultation on the face of Kyra Sedgwick as she holds up her newly acquired garage-door opener. (It's meaningful, really, because it is her own garage, and that garage is just below her own very first ever condo!)

And once the key, one's own private space, had been secured? Then came relief, excitement, and a swiftly spreading sense of disappointment. Girls called the arrangements "better," "more free"—they loved having unsupervised parlor time—but they also used phrases such as "in the overall, small in feeling." One twenty-one-year-old office clerk told *Munsey's Magazine* that the Trowmart and its few imitators had "narrow rooms" with bad lighting and "mincy wardrobes." Many residents took to the parlors, although these filled up rapidly, and so in all kinds of weather packs of girls were out on walks. Out wandering—swiftly wandering so as not to seem vagrant or "loitery"—they often met equally claustrophobic friends, and had marathon teas. A bit later on they escaped to nickelodeons, neighborhood theaters consisting of a small homemade screen and wooden chairs.

There is no document of daily life at the Trowmart Inn. But we can imagine it based on the descriptions of comparable hotels, both the real, for example, the Barbizon—subject of numerous Sunday-magazine features during the 1950s and '60s—and the fictional. There's a great section of

Kitty Foyle in which she describes her life at the fictitious Pocahontas Residence for Women, a dwelling obviously based on the Barbizon. As always, Kitty narrates in a tart but sympathetic manner:

> A neurosis to every room. I can see them yet in the dining room, poor souls with the twice a week chicken croquettes and those rocking little peas, sort of crimped so they wouldn't skid. . . . They called them bachelor girls, but a bachelor is that way on purpose. One evening one of them must have gone haywire [because] she yelled out into the courtyard, "there's a Man in my room! . . . Now, everybody, they had seen the sinister fellow . . . but he was nowhere . . . only . . . a pale phantom of desire."

THE BACHELOR GIRL AND THE BOHEMIAN

By the turn of the twentieth century, so many single girls were visibly out there—working, eating in restaurants, dancing—that it became harder to immediately categorize them. (And arranging single girls into identifiable groupings was a necessity not only among editors, writers, and retail merchandisers. State and U.S. government officials frequently organized mass prostitution raids. An increasingly diverse single population made the task much more difficult. At urban rackets and in the newer Broadway cabarets, government agents became famous for "getting the wrong girl wrong," accusing a shop girl of being a hooker, and "getting whonked for their mistakes," meaning kicked in the ankle.)

One magazine columnist, writing in 1907, put it this way: "In the great cities, thousands of our young women" live in a "swarm of singularity."

But there was an identifiable strain of "new girl" who appeared at the turn of the century, an intense, dramatic type who'd consistently reappear in years to come: the bohemian. Typically our bohemian was a high school or college dropout who had tried but could not *live within the strictures of the bourgeois society she had only narrowly escaped.* She often told reporters, whether she'd been asked or not, that she possessed a "real" self, a poetic artistic self that had been stifled in her previous existence. But now, surrounded by other like souls, in a unique and freeing place, she, or this self, or *something* new and amazing would emerge. Generally speaking, she was hoping for signs of artistic talent or the ability to attract a monied husband who would elicit and encourage her inchoate artistry. One twenty-year-old told the *Saturday Evening Post* in 1905, "It is wonderful to be able to walk along the street, singing. . . . There are men who admire that impulsive daring."

The bohemian had a less deeply poetic, slightly less intense, kind of younger cousin. That was the Bachelor Girl. "The B.G.," as she was known, had come to the city not so much to escape, but to work and send money home. Which she did. But she also developed a taste for rushing after work or whenever possible to Greenwich Village, at that time the city's premiere "artistically inclined place of residence." (I quote from "Why I Am a Bachelor Girl," *The Independent*, 1908.)

By 1910, the Village had settled as an Italian and German enclave, surrounded by the baronial brownstones of Washington Square and Fifth Avenue and pockets of very poor blacks and Irish. For the committed or aspiring bohemian, the setting was perfect—filled with cafés, tearooms, spaghetti parlors, and the unlikeliest and therefore the most interesting people in New York just lounging about. It was still almost a secret. Before 1918, no subway stops connected Greenwich Village to the rest of the city, and one had to practice at navigating its tiny disjointed streets. Many houses, painted pink or blue, had no numbers. Asking directions was useless. Most inhabitants couldn't quite explain it. Didn't know. Didn't feel like it. They spoke, one visitor told the *New York Times*, "in an iambic pentameter, as a bad word play or joke."

Wandering the Village, bohemian and bachelor girls could, to borrow from their own overly dramatic phrasebook, create themselves anew. Margaret Ferguson, of Ruth Suckow's 1934 novel, *The Folks*, makes a wonderful case study of this transformation. We meet her as a girl, the older, misunderstood "dark" daughter of a prosperous Iowa farm family. Not as pretty as her sister, often overlooked, she comes to believe there is "a wonderful shining special fate for her" and that she will find it in New York City. If she didn't take the dare and leave, she would likely wander into a more ordinary female fate, "getting older and older, a spinster daughter like Fannie Allison, who had taught the third grade every year since anyone could remember . . . and lived with her brother and his wife and took care of his children."

Margaret moves to the Village and takes a candlelit cellar apartment that has a green door. At a party a few nights later a strange man sprinkles a few drops of gin on her forehead and she is rechristened Margot.

For real characters, there were many similar declarations of freedom. Taking a walk without interrogation or scrutiny. Entering a restaurant, sitting down, and not feeling the urge to rush out. One might sit for hours in a teahouse, one of those dimly lit and narrow rooms that were always decorated with mismatched furniture and too many dark oil paintings. One might even talk to a man seated nearby and not, for the moment, think: What would Mother say?

Of course, one knew what Mother would say. In the age of the bachelor girls and, worse, bohemians, distraught mothers quickly became as acute a national stereotype, appearing in cartoons and illustrations holding another sibling back from the door, or bent over war-room tables covered with maps of Greenwich Village. This was the start of a war, all right, a protracted generation conflict that would grow more serious and heartbreaking as years passed. In the meantime, there were others more immediately upset by these unnerving young women.

As working gals had inspired absurd terror theories—Will she forgo having children and become a slut?—so these newest strays attracted fresh, outrageous condemnation. Much of this criticism was aimed at upper-class feminist or "womanist" types, but it trickled down to the bachelor girl. In his tirades against "race suicide," Teddy Roosevelt now looked directly at the unmarried white woman, even if she was only eighteen, and called her trouble. There were more immigrants. There were more inexplicably single women—*bohemians*—and so, as he saw it, more than mere laws were in order. (There had already been plenty of legal assistance. Contraception and abortion had been outlawed and between 1889 and 1906, state legislatures passed more than one hundred restrictive divorce laws.) White women of all sorts would have to cooperate!

The true bohemian, like the radical spinster before her, ignored the fuss. The bachelor girl, however, paid attention. There are guilty acknowledgments of this "race suicide" concept throughout my collection of press clippings "re: Bachelor Girl, c. 1908–1914." In stories such as "The Lives and Loves of a Bachelor Miss," "Date with a Bachelor Girl," and "Today's Modern Bachelor Girl—Her Hopes, Dreams, Her Chances in Life," we hear about one's "essential responsibilities," about the "sacred" duties ahead, and more than once about knowing "when the party is over." In the articles "The Bachelor Girl, As Told by One Who Knows," "Bachelor Girls of Today and Yesterday," and "I Am a Bachelor Girl," the phrases "later on in my life, proper," and "when I am settled down," appear three times. Five times in all we hear the phrase "when I am the mother of" followed by the phrase "sweet babes" or "tender babes" or "six or seven babes."

But no matter how often she pledged to defend her future fertility, the bachelor/working/single girl was just as likely to take delight in describing her life as it was at the moment—and especially as the terms "bohemian" (serious, artistic) and "bachelor girl" (worker bee out for fun) began slowly to blur.

We'll call them, along with everyone else, B-girls.

Many wore their hair short, after the girl/boy heroine of *Trilby*, George Du Maurier's 1894 novel. Virginia Woolf called the type "cropheads," the name she'd given Dora Carrington after the young artist chopped off and banged her hair. Some girls went in for a Chinese plait, but the primary fashion influence was Trilby. Trilby had inspired an early rush of icon merchandising (Trilby hats, dresses, waffles), and everyone knew her story: Parisian orphan who boarded with a ragpicker and his wife and lived *la vie bohème* without affectation. She dressed in burlap sacks, and wore sandals on what were, by any standard, huge female feet. (She also had a large, pliable mouth.) For money, she ironed clothing and modeled nude for male artists without a hint of shame. At night she smoked, dressed like a man, and paraded the Quartier Latin, where she was queen of the cancan. (Of course she's taken down—made to feel guilty about her "ways" by the respectable man she deeply loves. He drops her straight into a bog of depression and self-hatred that makes her perfect fodder for the devil, presented here in the form of a music teacher named Svengali.)

Young B-girls expanded on their visions of Trilby. They were reported to wear only "sheaths" or "smocks" and to eat with their hands. In the dark. Often a B-girl had the lights put out as necessary economy, and lived by red candles offset by gauzy veils. There was other folklore about her lifestyle, as one writer put it, "a maze of weird and witching elements." Bathrooms, whether in the hallway or the flat itself, had no doors. Mice were welcome guests and fed at table, which happened to be the floor. Everyone smoked. According to one story in the original *Life*, the B-girls at times "unconsciously interpret[ed] . . . the eating rituals of [one] . . . tribe of Southern Africa . . . this conclusion is further supported by the post-prandial decision to paint their bodies with white and blue stripes and then to dance." (The context of this short piece, wedged between two popular-science stories, makes it hard to say whether the speaker was joking.)

Reporters were out in full on the B-girl beat—the preflapper demimonde that stood to sink our great civilization. One cigarette-holding girl flung open the door (there apparently was a door) and met the press by exclaiming, "Welcome to liberty hall! Here we do exactly as we please!" She told all about her purple robe—no lilac for her but a *purple pure*. She spoke vaguely about a Communist lecture and then asked everyone to please take off their shoes.

"[Their] room[s]," noted one disgusted male correspondent, "[are] a mass of delightful contrivances whereby her gown inhabits the window seat and her frying pan the bookcase. . . . They eat off the ironing board, roaring with laughter about having only cheese to feast upon." More serious stories tried to see past the "nursery antics" and into the inevitable repercussions.

Let's consider the arguments of one Juliet Wilbor Tompkins, who like many writers on the somber subject of race suicide and later, "sexology," used three names in her byline. (It informed the reader that the author was married but independent minded; it further indicated that she had a "career," not a job.) In *Why Women Don't Marry* (1907), she tries to categorize for the reader every possible explanation, outside of sheer perversity, for failing to wed.

Sometimes they are young women of means, who find complete satisfaction in dogs and horses, or in travels and learning or bridge

or nature-study. But more often you will find that they are workers . . . earnest young social workers . . . editors . . . energetic
souls . . . [many] living in an eight-by-ten room, cooking [their]
own chocolate over the gas, and studying avidly . . . full of pity for
the shut-in woman. . . . And they are very happy in the middle
twenties . . . with their battle cry of freedom! To their ignorance,
life offers an enchanting array of possibilities. They see ahead of
them a dozen paths and have but contemptuous pity for the
woman of the past who knew one dull highway.

Others pointed out how many female characters in novels killed themselves rather than admit to failure at bohemian life, that is, the failure of all
that presumed artistic talent or any men whatsoever to emerge. They were
only bachelor girls, after all. Wrote a male reporter in *Munsey's* (1906):

The plain fact is that the bachelor and . . . bohemian girl [are]
merely single women of small means living in the city in order
that [they] may work. . . . As for her chances [with men] she may
become a little harder to suit, but, on the whole, even that is
doubtful. That she stays in her single state is largely due to the fact
that possible men are just as scarce in the domain of the bachelor
girl as in the life of the domestic.

But as bachelor girl Olga Stanley wrote back in 1896: "Probably the
thing which first appeals to us is our absolute freedom, the ability to plan our
time as we will . . . bound by no restrictions, except those imposed upon us
by a due regard for proprieties." As for those who called "her existence 'pathetic,'" what was more pathetic than waiting to find out whether "Tom,
Dick or Harry or whoever he may be turns out to be a good husband?" Of
course she'd take a husband, "forego the delights of female bachelorhood,"
if an excellent opportunity arose. Until then, however, she and her many
unwed sisters would emit "a sigh of thankfulness . . . and draw nearer the
fire, and resting our toes on the fender, lean back in our easy chair and
congratulate ourselves upon our good fortune."

CHAPTER THREE

THIN AND RAGING THINGS: NEW (NEW) WOMEN, GIBSON GODDESSES, FLAPPING AD DARLINGS, AND THE ALL-NEW SPINSTER IN FUR

Am I a boy? Yes I am . . . Not.

> —NELL BRINKLEY, CARTOONIST, BOSTON AMERICAN, 1913

Don't worry girls! Corsets have gone! The American girl is independent! . . . a thinker who will not follow slavishly the ordinances of the past!

> —COLLEEN MOORE, SILENT-FILM STAR, 1920

On the street, you do not recognize old maids and spinsters anymore. You cannot pick them out. But you will be conscious of an increasing number of women who are alert, handsomely dressed, of spirited carriage. That is the picture of today's unmarried woman. You may be very sure she has a fur coat.

> —PROFESSIONAL WOMAN, HARPER'S, 1929

I AM (NEW) WOMAN, WATCH ME SMOKE

It is tricky to reconstruct a group photo of the New Woman. A few visual details float into focus—shirtwaists, suffrage banners, serious-looking girls with their arms around each other—but much of the picture has faded. Over time, the precise meaning of "new woman," like that of the contemporaneous term "free love," has become impossibly blurry.

So let's clarify and state that the new woman, an essential character in the history of single female life, belonged to a group of women considered "individualized" (roughly translated, self-aware and unconventional) that the press began to cover at the start of the twentieth century. At the time, everyone was reporting on single phenomena—the bohemian, the numerous varieties of working girl—and "new woman" sometimes served as an umbrella designation for every newly uncovered independent life-form. ("No one who is not absolutely an old woman," remarked humorist George Ade, "is safe from being considered a new woman.") But the true new woman, a term derived from Henry James and his irreverent moderns Daisy Miller and Isabel Archer, was very much a distinct singular entity. Unlike the average bohemian or bachelor girl, the new woman possessed a leftist intellectual pedigree. Her attitudes and beliefs were descended from the elite early feminists—the singly blessed spinsters of the Civil War era and the later reformers who'd helped found or been among the first to attend the women's colleges.

Our early-twentieth-century new women went to college, and some even managed to argue their way into traditionally all-male graduate schools. Some were suffragists (*ette*, they believed, was a cute, belittling suffix) known for their impromptu speeches and some for their acts of political agitation— hunger strikes, for example, or handcuffing themselves to the fence outside the White House. Some were "womanists," precursors to feminists whose ideology stressed women's social and moral duties as opposed purely to women's rights. Others had unlikely careers—choreographer, economist, journalist, politician, pilot—while still others advocated dress reform, abortion, and contraceptive rights, or simply smoked defiantly in public, a punishable offense after 1908, the year the federal government banned women from smoking. Some new women—Margaret Sanger, writer and economist Charlotte Perkins Gilman, writer Louise Bryant, reporter Ida Tarbell—became living monuments to what many called the "new possibilities."

But the new woman was most famous for her refusal or, rather, polite disinclination, to marry. (And when new women did marry, the unions were almost always unconventional. Margaret Sanger, Charlotte Perkins Gilman, Jane Addams, Edna St. Vincent Millay—all had marriages that involved living apart, sometimes continents apart, "with an understand-ing." There were public and tolerated affairs; in some cases they divorced and husbands took custody of the children.)

The press continued to recycle the prevailing view of matrimony: that no woman was qualified to do anything else but wed. In *The Ladies' Home Journal*, 1900, we learn that "to women, the business world looks to be a great mysterious whirl of which she can understand nothing. . . . To at-tempt . . . comprehension is to strain unnecessarily." In a 1904 survey, *Good Housekeeping* asked five thousand men to list the qualities they required in a potential bride and then those features that "repelled" them. The win-ning prerequisites were an "attractive manner," "Christian tendency," "modesty," and "womanliness," while "career minded-ness," "an argumen-tative nature," "the urge to smoke," and "physical imperfection" doomed an increasingly large percentage of the population to a new old-maidhood.

But I doubt that many in the ranks of new womanhood took subscrip-tions to *Good Housekeeping*. Author Susanne Wilcox, writing in *The Inde-pendent* in 1909, explained, "The desire to participate in what men call the 'game of life' has fastened itself upon many modern women, and their ap-petites are whetted for more abundant and diverting interests than the mere humdrum of household duties."

A male peer writing in the same publication in the same year noted, "The average young American woman, especially if college-bred, now leads a life of mental unfolding and progression abreast with young men . . . many occupations have been thrown open to her. . . . If she does not find a congenial mate, she avails herself of these opportunities and finds much satisfaction."

Here were the true perpetrators of Teddy Roosevelt's alleged "race suicide." Between the years 1880 and 1913, the U.S. marriage rate hit its lowest point in the country's history, and an unprecedented drop in the
birthrate followed. It further seemed that many who'd already married were
determined to get out. In 1870 there had been just 1.5 divorces per 1,000
marriages; by 1890, that figure had doubled, and by 1910, it had risen to
5.5 per 1,000, the majority of petitions filed by women with at least a high
school education.

A researcher studying the 1902 edition of *Who's Who* isolated the
women honorees (977 of a total of 11,000 entries) and investigated details
of their personal lives. He found that 45 percent of these prominent
women had married but that 53.3 percent of them—for the time an enormous number—said they would never marry, viewing it as a "profound dis-
incentive" to serious work. Many new women wrote essays and editorials
in response, pointing out that the majority of white middle-class women
eventually married (which they did—80 percent in 1910). But the notion
of the best and the brightest refusing to marry and reproduce, preferring instead to conduct scientific research, attend conferences, smoke and/or
chain themselves to fences, had taken hold.

According to much-quoted psychologist Stanley G. Hall, "The daughter refuses to do the things her mother did without question . . . higher education is at fault." Charles W. Eliot, writing in the *North American Review*,
agreed. "Girls are being prepared daily, by 'superior education,' to engage,
not in child-bearing and house-work but in clerkships, telegraphy,
newspaper-writing . . . and if they have their 'rights' they will be enabled
to compete with men at the bar, in the pulpit, the Senate, the bench." Because many an average new woman had read Chaucer, spoke French, and
knew chemistry, she had developed, in Hall's phrase, "unreasonable expectations" that led her to "abhor the limitations of married life."

One can almost hear a new woman snort with laughter. Jane Addams
once asked rhetorically: "[Is she] supposed to stay at home, to help her
mother entertain? . . . Take a course in domestic science? . . . How . . . could
any girl stay sane?"

The new women had an altruistic streak. They had come largely from the comfortable middle class—the truly rich upper-class girl did not go to college—and they genuinely hoped to "reclaim" or "uncover" the "individualistic possibilities" in every woman, educated or not. In 1912 Marie Jenny Howe, a nonpracticing Unitarian minister, founded Heterodoxy, the country's first feminist (as opposed to strictly suffragist) group in Greenwich Village. As a nascent consciousness-raising group, it required of each member only that she "not be orthodox in her opinions." It helped if she lived in the Village or at least in the city and could attend the argumentative all-night meetings. But Heterodoxites took their show on the road. They were the first to sponsor popular general-interest meetings about feminism, the first of them, in 1913, called "What Is Feminism?" or, as it was officially titled, "Breaking into the Human Race." These were huge affairs for up to one thousand, and they featured prominent women from around the world addressing every issue imaginable. Here, according to an account, one could "glimpse the women of the future, big spirited, intellectually alert, devoid of the old 'femininity.' "

The language of Heterodoxy briefly entered the national vocabulary, if only as a source of fun. Political cartoonists played for months with phrases such as the "free-willed, self-willed woman" and "the parasitism of the home woman." Marie Jenny Howe's declarations, too, were a source of much joking: "We declare to be ourselves, not just our little female selves, but our whole big human selves" or "we are *feminists!*" Feminism, as a term, did not exactly leap into everyday use. (The *Oxford English Dictionary* would not include it until 1933.) And that was to some extent because it had so quickly, so immediately, been turned into a joke. But it was also true that no one really believed in the prospect of a larger women's movement. No one really believed much would change.

Even Ida Tarbell, the first woman "muckraker," author of *History of the Standard Oil Company* (1904) and defiantly never wed ("it would fetter my freedom"), had her doubts. As she wrote, "In an urban setting, there are now simply more women outside, doing things. There is a sense of freedom, due to numbers of women. . . . But that *doesn't* mean freedom."

In a preview of what would be called "sexological" thinking, psychologist Stanley G. Hall summarized the "new" situation in far more draconian terms. The woman who "abhorred the limitations of domestic life" was not just unconventional, newly or blissfully "devoid of the old femininity." She was "functionally castrated."

SEX O'CLOCK IN AMERICA

To young single women who'd been born just as new womanhood coalesced—say, around 1895—the idea of a "new" woman quickly came to seem kind of old. Even if the woman in question was only thirty, to her younger counterparts she seemed aged due to the impression, even in casual conversation, that she was always giving a speech. Of course there were fights to fight, but as one young woman told *Harper's* magazine, "the New Women don't seem to see how there is . . . life to live!" This dated "new" character with her upstanding shirtwaist and erect posture made one observer think of "a funereal procession of one." New womanhood seemed to be set to a dirge while the young(er) world was starting to move to popular songs.

This generational divide is reminiscent of the gap so painfully in evidence during the late 1980s and '90s. It's fair to say that second-wave feminists were so successful that the entire Western world changed heroically. But if you were a baby while it was changing, if you missed the big battles— and never experienced the old restrictions and unfairnesses—then how could basic freedoms generate a sense of wonder? Of gratitude? How could you be on your guard for hints of sexist regression?

A young woman, twenty-three, an artist's model and aspiring dress designer, told *Life* magazine in 1923 the same thing someone twenty-three might have said eighty years later: "I think many of our women's rights people expect that everyone is going to work for their ideas and causes, even though the battle's already won as much as it will ever be. . . . They get very angry if they sense you have an interest in minor things, in how you *dress*, not in political talk. Or you are not interested in THEM and their struggle to free YOU and your friends. Why aren't we all grateful?"

A symbolic battle had been declared against the tedious new woman—

its rallying cry a slogan borrowed from a *Life* magazine cartoon showing a mother draped in a suffrage banner with a daughter in sporty clothes, holding a tennis racket. The mother is lecturing; the daughter smiles but shrieks to herself: *"Oh, Mother dear, please I do need to leave to go please, please, SHADDUP!"*

A backlash against the educated female had developed from within her own ranks.

In a first-person magazine confessional, "Why I Am an Old Maid" by "A Daughter of New England" (1911), we learn that "men instinctively avoid a woman who can discourse at length on sun spots." More serious statistics seem to bear out this observation—or at least women's belief in it.

Consider some figures from Bryn Mawr College. Between 1889 and 1908, the peak political years of new womanhood, only half of all graduates married. Of those who did, some 62 percent continued on to graduate school and nearly all the married new women continued, according to a university report, "to achieve in their chosen professions." But that changed. Just a few years later an additional 10 percent of all graduates started to marry out of school and the number who continued in their careers simultaneously began to drop. Between the years 1910 and 1918, only 49 percent of married class members continued on to graduate school.

I'll call it the age of the popular as opposed to the reformist new woman, a new woman without the glasses and the prim boater, and in its place a huge yellow hair bow. (And I mean *huge*, as if she were wearing two colorful party balloons joined at the nape of the neck and floating upward. In my grandfather's Springfield, Ohio, high school yearbook, 1911, not one girl in forty-three is minus her gargantuan bow.)

This new girl, known once again as the bachelor girl or "the bachelorette," had grown up, according to the *Saturday Evening Post* (1912) "permeated in the modern world." During the years 1910 to 1913, six states voted in favor of a women's suffrage amendment. Advertisements, popular novels, quick-change fashion trends—all had been present from the start of her conscious life. Our new bachelor girl wore looser-fitting skirts that allowed her to bicycle everywhere. Some had been on aeroplanes, and others boasted that they'd made cross-continental phone calls. With one million plus cars out on the roads, they'd all been out driving, even if they re-tained passenger status (there were no laws against women driving, just, initially at least, a reluctance to let them take control).

Much of the Jazz Age imagery we associate with the 1920s—driving, incessant dancing, loose-fitting clothes—actually took shape around 1913. One *Boston American* columnist described the popular new woman like this: " . . . the 1914 girl: You'll recognize her. Just look for a slim creature who is not on closer inspection a boy in a dress, shaped like a pencil."

One columnist for the *St. Louis Mirror* called the era "sex o'clock in America."

Both these comments were made while writing about the phenome-non known as the thé dansant, or the notorious afternoon tea dance at which gin stood in for the tea. Think of a very small racket—it's crowded and everyone's dancing to a modern gramophone that spins seventy-eight-r.p.m. records. (The tango, imported from Deauville, France, is the dance of the moment, in part because the General Federation of Women's Clubs has banned it as immoral.) It's all very casual. No one has sponsored the dance or sent invitations; like the floating urban clubs of the 1980s, it ap-pears from place to place: in a bachelor's apartment, in someone's parlor—provided the parents are out, of course—or in the back room of a restaurant.

The tea dancers come from all over. There are college girls on break, working girls out on adventure, brides-to-be making their way through long engagements. There are many actressy characters who mix freely with the working girls and, as it's always noted, a contingent of timid girls who look as if they've never been out and aren't exactly sure where they've turned up. All of them play dress-up. Some use sashes to shorten their skirts or change the style altogether, attempting to create straight, narrow frocks that cut just above the knee. Using their ribbons, they tuck up long wavy hair to see how it might look cut bobbed and modern. Long, pointy shoes with buttoned straps radically reveal the ankle. Even-tually, even the little sisters, the timid girls, show up in skinny dresses and Mother Goose shoes. Instead of hair bows, they wear shimmery bands that wrap around the forehead and sprout feathers.

And so tea dancing spreads from city to city, and the late afternoons grow very long. Adults, alone at dinner, slowly take notice.

"DO YOU KNOW WHERE YOUR DAUGHTER IS THIS AFTERNOON?" asked *Harper's* in 1914, anticipating the famed 1970s TV query: "It's ten o'clock. Do you know where your children are?"

One red-faced columnist in the *Boston American* explained precisely where they were: "Tea! Tea! What is this tea!? An excuse, a forum for young girls, many of them obviously of breeding and refinement, dancing cheek by jowl with [female] professionals whose repute is doubtful . . . and learning the insidious habits of the early cocktail."

Belle Moskowitz, an impassioned old-school reformer and later a savvy operative in New York State politics, spoke out on drinking and dancing and the "corrosive" influence of these "other," or lesser, working girls: "[Working] life cries out for rational recreation [but] what? . . . Girls do not of intention select bad places to go to. . . . [But] the girl whose temperament and disposition crave un-natural forms of excitement is nearly beyond the bounds of salvation. . . . she may affect the well being of others."

One of several sudden reports on female criminal tendencies, *The Cause and Cure of Crime* (1914), declared, "Many girls are diseased. Physically and mentally contaminated." The superintendent of one reform school declared, in support, "One bad girl can do more harm than fifty depraved boys . . . many are . . . abnormal or feeble-minded and should be held in custody for a long time or for life."

Slowly, concern that morally corrupt girls were lurking around the thé dansant seemed to fuse with parents' fears about the men who were forever lurking everywhere. And in this age of new womanhood (or "post" or "fun" new womanhood), when there were "simply more women outside doing things," these fears were heightened by the sense that girls faced other, unexpected sources of contamination.

BEWARE THE WHITE SLAVER

For several years during the early teens, the nation was captivated by one villain: the White Slaver. He was that legendary fiend who kidnapped young white girls, drugged them with chloroform-drenched kerchiefs, stuck them with morphine needles, then sold them into prostitution. The slaver, usually a "hit man" for a criminal syndicate, preyed most often on new arrivals to the country, single girls just off the boat, the less English spoken the better. Slavers also worked Upstate New York and Pennsylvania towns, luring girls without prospects by promising—and sometimes actually pretending—to marry them, then at some point drugging them and turning them over to colleagues in New York City.

As one typical headline shrieked in 1913: 50,000 GIRLS DISAPPEAR YEARLY! The subhead: "Before the Chloroform, the plaintive cries: 'Sir, please, I am a decent girl! Who earns her Wages.' "

One girl expanded on this familiar scenario in *The Independent:* "A girl is sitting there at the films. Or on a bench nearby a tree. They creep behind and . . . they force a cloth across your face, there goes the needle in your neck or your ankle or arm, and you go dead black for a time, only to wake up in hell. And no chance of getting back."

As another girl interviewed for the same story put it: "They can take away your own life from you without killing you first."

Quickly this new terror found its way into melodramatic plots. Especially onscreen. By World War I, movies had evolved from primitive hand-cranked "flickers" into longer films shown in makeshift neighborhood theaters. One of the first box-office hits in film history was called *Traffic in Souls* (1913), a white-slaving film that was thought to have no commercial prospects. It was seventy minutes—much too long for nickelodeons, which could handle only one- and two-reelers—and required a legitimate theater (where plays such as *The House of Bondage* and *The Lure* ran briefly before being shut down). More important, as one critic prematurely put it: "Who among us wants to witness a tale of unfortunates abducted, put to sale, forced to the sickening biddings of madam or whoremonger?"

The answer was just about everyone. *Traffic in Souls* grossed $450,000 after showing for a few weeks at twenty-eight theaters in New York City.

It is true that hundreds of young women were kidnapped, drugged, and then sold, usually into out-of-state brothels. And it's true that several state and federal commissions eventually conducted mass investigations. But for a time the white slaver was foremost a mythic devil whose presence seems directly linked to that of the single working woman. Women who had sex outside of marriage, circa 1912, would most definitely have been part of the groupings loosely called "new woman" or "bohemian." The average working woman may have "spooned" ("petted"), but she was likely to have remained a virgin. Despite that technical point, she was still out there, a girl without a husband, alone on the street. In other words, she was a walking sex target. Terms that had been at the edges of the vernacular since Bowery days suddenly began to reappear. A girl was said to be "flaunting it" or "showing what she's got." The white slaver represented, I think, an epic punishment for all those singles who were "flaunting it," asking for it, seeming, whether they were or not, overtly sexual.

(A punishment theme turns up in many of the era's popular-film titles: *The Girl Who Didn't Know*, *The Girl Who Didn't Think*, *The Price She Paid*. In one white-slaving film, *Damaged Goods* (1914), the action came to an abrupt halt about midway through, and a doctor appeared on screen to lecture about syphilis. This seemed an odd non sequitur. But in fact syphilis was a serious sexual threat, a much more common occurrence than white slaving, and there were few ways of discussing it publicly except as a cameo topic in a larger story of female sexual depravity.)

At the same time that white slavery was a vicious cautionary tale, it also served as a secretive sex fantasy. If it was a terrifying act to contemplate, it was also titillating. The language used to describe new women, working women, single women was often so hostile that the male anger behind it is palpable. A destructive or at least demeaning rape narrative was, for some, probably satisfying as a daydream or masturbatory scenario. For single women themselves, guilty or perhaps confused about their sexual impulses, the fantasy of a man rendering them helpless and submissive, with the evil details, the horrid fate left to imagine, well, it could have made the average workday pass a little faster.

That is not to be glib. White slaving was a real and extremely serious crime. The Rockefeller Commission and other smaller committees spent years patrolling docks, brothels, rackets and their upscale counterparts, cabarets, and while few people were ultimately prosecuted, Congress passed the Mann Act, a law prohibiting the transport of underage women across state lines for the purpose of prostitution.

Still, the passage of the Mann Act would not become the lasting legacy of this episode. Nor would the vilification of men who preyed on defenseless young women. The primary message, unspoken but unmistakable, was to condemn women out on their own and also to scare them. The idea that you, as a girl alone, could be lifted from life and that *nobody would notice* became—and would remain—a significant element of single lore.

Perhaps it's not surprising, then, that the first beloved single-girl icon of the twentieth century was not the bachelor girl or the tea dancer or anyone new in between. She was someone who didn't quite exist.

BEHOLD THE GIBSON GODDESS

The Gibson girl, a well-bred upper-class beauty, independent, athletic, and terrifically busy, appeared first as an illustrated character in a 1902 issue of *Collier's*. She was named for her handsome, sociable, much reported-on creator, Charles Dana Gibson, an illustrator who had for years drawn variations of this all-American girl the way someone might doodle the same image over and over at school or work.

The finished product would become the official, polished trademark of new womanhood.

The Gibson girl was classically elegant and feminine—tall and thin, with small hands and feet, china-white skin, and a retroussé nose. But she was also strikingly athletic. Her shoulders were well proportioned. Her hair was piled high, creating the illusion of greater height, and loose strands around the face suggested that she'd just come in from riding or tennis or some other mildly strenuous sport at which she had displayed a calm mastery. She was windswept perfection. A Valkyrie holding a teacup.

At *Collier's*, the girl's home for many years, the staff practiced editorial taxonomy, organizing and subdividing the character's various incarnations into seven distinct types of modern goddess: the Boy-Girl, the Flirt, the Beauty, the Sentimental, the Convinced, the Ambitious, the Well-Balanced or Rounded. Regardless of her precise type, the magazine declared, "she is incarnate, a representation of modernity, individuality, and personality." As a female fan wrote in a letter to the magazine: "We admire most about her the manner in which she keeps her own counsel." When pictured with one of her inevitable suitors, the Gibson girl rarely looked directly at him; rather, she gazed off into the distance, suggesting that she saw on the horizon possibilities beyond that man, or suggesting perhaps to the man that he would never penetrate to the core of her self-containment.

The girl, whether girl-boy athletic, well-balanced friend, flirt, or beauty, became a young single icon in the same way that white slaving became the iconic crime committed against the single girl: through the burgeoning media. The slave scare came alive on film; the Gibson girl was born in print and took on larger life as she was reproduced in a mass-merchandising campaign historic in its scope.

It's true that stage stars and characters such as Trilby had appeared before on wallet cards, postcards, and wall-size posters (many saloons were miniature shrines to certain adored actresses). But the Gibson girl appeared everywhere: on china dishes, drinking glasses, furniture (vanities, dressers, hallway chairs and chests), calendars, flasks, cigarette cases, flatware, paper dolls, dress patterns, hair ribbons, ink blotters, and on down a long list that ends in lockets and thimbles. Her image also inspired look-alike pageants and song and essay contests, and of course she had dances and drinks named for her.

It was as a mass commercial entity that the Gibson girl had her greatest impact on single-womanhood. Nineteenth- and early-twentieth-century advertising concentrated on endorsing and explaining a product's merits, at very great length and often in very tiny print. The emphasis was on solidity and tradition, a confident masculine promise of quality. But as single young women attained some purchasing power, it became clear that the old ways—selling only to wives and mothers—would not hold. Nor would the dull thousand-word odes to the sturdy reliability of a detergent. The Gibson girl provided a form of early branding, a visual shorthand for a product's values that had previously required great amounts of text to describe.

As early as 1915, the Ivory Soap girl, traditionally a symbol of saint-like purity, had become a rouged and healthy-looking Gibson type. These ads contained less text than had previous ads, and the illustration of the girl was larger. In this way, the Gibson prefigured the eventual death of testimonials and the rise of psychological advertising, that is, the use of images to put forth a dream world, a perfect person—things and qualities you might have, that you might actually *be,* if you would only buy the product. Just as early silent films propagated cautionary tales for new women, ads began, just a little bit, to peddle images of freedom and beauty.

Ironically, the Gibson girl also seemed to reassure those who believed that "new woman" was an oxymoron, or should be. Generally speaking, these were confused and troubling times—years of violent strikes and demonstrations, of anarchist bombings. Little more than a decade before, the president, William McKinley, had been assassinated, and the First World War was already under way in Europe. In some drawings the Gibson girl seemed soft and ethereal rather than sharp, and brilliantly new. Sometimes she was just a pretty head that floated high above a soothing landscape, making her less a symbol of modernity and change than an angel.

Ultimately Mr. Gibson grew tired of drawing her, just as his public became slightly bored with her limited exploits. And as it happened, another, far jazzier female icon was already in view.

But first a brief eulogy for the Gibson girl, circa 1916, courtesy of one male columnist in San Francisco: "She is as thrilling as a phone pole."

COME FLAP WITH ME

In 1920, the year the suffrage amendment became law, the Flapper—not the suffragist or anyone remotely like her—emerged as the supreme incarnation of the early-century single woman.

She burst to life in all forms of popular media as a much more precise and confident variation of the "1914 girl," the bachelor girl who'd snuck out to the tea dance, her hair tied up in imitation of a bob. Now all hair was short, waved, and often covered by a cloche modeled on a World War I GI helmet; dresses, tubular sheaths set off by long strands of beads, hung from the shoulders. The eyes were kohl-lined and the lipstick so dark it almost looked purple. (Ann Douglas in her remarkable study of New York in the 1920s, *Terrible Honesty*, reports that one popular lipstick brand was called "Eternal Wound.") Above the regiment of pointed shoes, the flapper wore sheer hose that she often rolled down several inches along the thigh, suggesting socks and schoolgirls while at the same time alluding to a stripper. According to flapper legend, as created largely by enamored advertisers, corsets had been banished and beneath her boyish yet exotic finery she wore lingerie. My favorite brand name of the era: "Silk and Nothingness."

The Bowery girls, like the shoppies, had formed a premodern female youth group based on work and class. The new women were an educated contingent of serious and brave politicos, the bohemians a diverse band of self-declared eccentrics. The flappers were singular democrats. Anyone could join. Whether she worked, studied, taught, performed, or played around, all a woman needed "to flap" was a youthful appearance and attitude—a sassy vocabulary, a cool way with men, a bit of daring, humor, and some professional smarts. Lacking these latter qualities, one could easily just dress the part. (A sheath was much simpler, and cheaper, to sew than a shirtwaist.) One talent-agency secretary, interviewed in *Look* during the 1960s about her flapping years, explained:

> I was a shy girl, not a girl who danced on tables at roadhouses, or not even on the dancefloor . . . [but] I liked the clothes, how modern and how comfortable they felt. . . . You dressed in your flapper's clothes, you drove around—everybody drove around—you seemed to belong to a club . . . you seemed more confident. You . . . were looked at as one of the "popular kids" [and] . . . you could start to feel that way. Big deal that you had two left feet, couldn't drive either. . . . You were the most up-to-date Modern there was. That's what everyone saw.

It was during the postwar, postvote flapper era that modern life as we'd recognize it began to take shape. In 1920 the country was officially declared an urban rather than an agrarian nation—a cityscape wired for communication via telephones, telegraphs, movies, and radios. Speed had insinuated itself into every area of modern life, and nowhere was this acceleration more heightened and intriguing than in Manhattan. It wasn't only all the cars, or the young women in the cars (called "rolling hotels") riding with men they had previously courted at home in sight of parents. Neither was it jazz nor the complex new dances that made the spiel look crude and dated. A slightly manic style was spreading in all sectors of the New York population: Housewives, using "revolutionary home technologies," finished their work in several hours, then rushed around trying to fill in their afternoons. Shop girls and businessmen alike "wolfed down" lunch while standing at counters. Society parties vied with secretive, strange, but no less ambitious costume balls in Greenwich Village; single girls threw parties; coeds threw parties. Everyone went out, drove somewhere, walked briskly; people started running for sport.

The flapper was the female embodiment of this tempo shift.

She was the first single woman ever to wear a wristwatch. To drive and possibly own a car and to have her own "revolutionary home technologies" in the form of unusual new products. The most important among these were tampons (developed by nurses during the war and later patented by a male doctor), depilatories, and tanning lotions, this last essential ever since Coco Chanel had decreed that to be modern was to have been running around, exercising, in the sun.

If flappers were the embodiment, the "supreme incarnation" of all this newness, that's because they were the first singles to be viewed as a peer group *and* as a peer demographic—a distinct subset of the population interesting from a sociological as well as an economic perspective. Like that late-1940s creation, the teenager, flappers were identified as unique consumers to be studied and pampered as if they had the buying power of wives. Or something close to it. In 1900 there were 5,237 female college graduates in the United States; by 1910 there were 8,437; and in 1921, more than ten thousand young women had graduated either from college

or graduate school. Combined with all those already out there in the workplace, these young women formed the rearguard forces of a significant social movement: more women living for longer periods of time on their own
before marriage. If they weren't likely to rush out and buy major appliances, they would buy much more expensive merchandise, and more of it,
than ever before. Advertisers, primitive marketers, set out to "speak" to
them, as if through a national megaphone.

For years, most female ads featured women's faces or women posed behind counters, most often kitchen counters that cut them off at the waist.
And that included the all-modern Gibson girl Ivory Soap ad; she had appeared as a blushing face inside a circle. The Gibson may have advanced
the concept of single-girl "branding," of targeting and specifically addressing an identifiable single woman, but flappers took it further. Flappers appeared whole—walking dogs, stretched out across cars, crouched and set to
dive wearing shiny Jantzen bathing suits. The point, lost on very few young
women, was that for a time they could seem wholly formed without marriage, or while ostensibly in search of marriage. The point was further made
to women no longer considered young at all.

In 1915 *Cosmopolitan* had pronounced that women of "all, all ages,
every one" could and should be "beautiful, fascinating, attractive." Ten
years later a male correspondent for the *Saturday Evening Post* marveled
that beneath "the aegis of flapperdom" women pushing thirty, even thirty-
five, were now saved from the taint of spinsterism.

> It was that war, cracked open the world! . . . Now these benefici-
> aries of war work . . . [have] evolved into the business-like art-
> loving fashion-setting spinsters of today . . . burst free from her
> thin-necked anxious service-without-pay chrysalis, [she] spreads
> her purple and gold wings . . . sail[ing] gracefully into the horizon
> blue of a new existence.

The term "flapper" actually dates from the First World War, although
there are still disagreements about its origins. Critic Edmund Wilson wrote
that it was derived from the flapping sound of a baby duck's wings as it

struggled to fly. Others have pointed out that "flapper" is an old term for a young prostitute, while still others have nominated the clacking sound of those long beads as a girl ran out of the house or as she danced. But the preferred theory of origin lies with the "beneficiaries" of wartime jobs.* In bad weather, many factory workers put on enormous boots they did not bother to buckle as they left work. Perhaps they were too exhausted. Perhaps they liked the sound of buckles jangling as six girls wandered the street. Six girls across, six pairs of flopping boots, and a lot of giggling: That was the original sound of flapping.

The finalized flapper icon was likewise a product of the war years. By 1918, there were more than three hundred films circulating the country at any given time, many of them featuring well-defined flapper characters. The movie bibles *Photoplay* and *Modern Picture World* (b. 1911) referred to the actresses who played them as "America's Pals," girls just like the reader, with one enormous exception. The pals all had "It." As defined by scenarist and director Elinor Glyn, It—the quintessential flapper trait—was a form of perceptual physics. In the heat of a media frenzy, the celebration of something "new," all of a culture's most desirable traits attached themselves to one young icon everyone else then imitated. But It, the sum total of many tiny acts of adorability, was hard to mimic. It just came to you: a shoe positioned at a clever angle. Well-timed winking. Clever tap-dancing moves away from lecherous men. A fashion columnist summarized in *Vogue*, "One has IT or one does not."

But most every silent screen star, and many of the women who watched and read about them tried hard to evolve their own unique sense of It.

Gloria Swanson and Joan Crawford began their careers playing richgirl flappers, roadhouse dollies, and office workers who expressed their sense of It by suggestively blowing cigarette smoke into the faces of their leading men. Colleen Moore and Louise Brooks introduced the slick

---

*Historian Eleanor Flexner notes that it took four pages of small type to list all the male occupations women took over during the war. Without the influence of World War II–style propaganda, women of all ages had trained to build armaments, to repair furnaces, while a very large corps of nurses traveled, often driving ambulances, between battle sites. Many continued their work, putting themselves at enormous risk throughout the flu pandemic of 1918.

black helmet haircut and a speedy double-talking sense of It that was deceptively fun and eccentric. If asked to be fully candid, their characters might have confessed: "I am so cute and charming, you will inevitably fail to understand that I am also crazy, irresponsible, and destructive!" Even D. W. Griffith, master of the epochal silent film, took on a flapper who, in attaining It, seemed to have injected amphetamines. Carole Dempster, a wild-eyed, frizzy-haired actress, swam marathons, rode bikes or horses, played tennis, tossed hatchets, and, whenever possible, did the jitterbug, which had been called "a dance of anxiety and bitterness." All within the course of one movie.

But the star with the essence of It was Clara Bow, a redhead with a strategically placed beauty mark and a Brooklyn squawk that would ruin her career in the sound era. She played all variety of flapperish working girls—a manicurist in *Red Hair* (1928), a swimming instructor in *Kid Boots* (1926), and, among many others, a lingerie shop girl in *It* (1927), a film that grossed an astonishing one million dollars. The Bow characters were distinguished by their effervescent refusal to accept class distinctions. In many of her films, her characters "land" a better kind of guy by easing in and out of social milieus (the Ritz *and* Coney Island all in a weekend!) relying only on their high-spirited personalities to erase any awkwardness.

But having It, running around, trying hard to seem fresh and daring, could be interpreted in other ways. To many Americans, the flapper, as depicted on-screen and in the three thousand magazines published monthly circa 1923, was little more than a potential slut.

Sex and danger were big selling points in flapper films, as reflected in their titles: *Strictly Unconventional, Speed Crazed, Wickedness Preferred, In Search of Sinners, Dangerous Business*. And the flappers, the *It* girls, were portrayed, at best, as lightly naughty. For example, they shoplifted. They stole boyfriends. Drank. Or, in many cases, they were chorus girls, a job title that encompassed all the above tendencies. The American Film Institute has cataloged 101 flapper films that featured "chorines," among them, *Sally of the Scandals* and *An Affair of the Follies*. The naughty fictional flapper was also sometimes a schoolgirl. In two-reelers typically entitled *Honey* and *Sweetie*, student flappers lounged around their rooms

smoking and—this was often depicted as an activity—"wearing lingerie." After a while the coeds put on clothes and attended their classes.
For the rest of the film they flirted with handsome professors, who
seemed frightened.

Naturally these films were accused of encouraging the worst aspects of
It: sexy, louche behavior that could ruin lives. In fact, they seem most to
have encouraged female viewers, potential *It* girls, to become actors. Many
1920s movie stars, all those friendly "pals," seemed less talented thespians
than they did cute, clever girls. How hard could it be? As early as 1920, the
Department of Labor estimated that 14,354 young women listed their occupation as "actress." And so "actress" entered the flapper pantheon, along
with "showgirl" and "lingerie saleslady," as something tawdry.

The first Miss America pageant, held in 1921, barred both divorcées
and actresses from the competition and looked very closely at those girls
dressed as flappers. Local censorship boards drew up laundry lists of things
actresses, playing flappers, could not do or have done to them. In Port
Arthur, Texas, one could not "make goo-goo eyes at the flappers." In Pennsylvania, "views of women smoking will not be disproved as such, but when
actresses are shown in suggestive positions or their smoking is . . . degrad-
ing, such scenes will be disproved." In Kansas, no kiss could last longer
than thirty feet of film, and in Connecticut and several other states directors could not stage activity in a bedroom or a kitchen. How else to keep
flappers, actresses—all these swarming sexual girls—in proper check?
Their insidious influence was felt everywhere.

The backs of magazines were repositories of tiny ads promoting
"French cures," euphemisms for abortions, as well as paid testimonials to
the miraculous "harnessing of vulcanized rubber," a miracle product like
Flubber. It could make a tire! Or a bouncing ball! More to the point, it
could and would make a condom. By 1926, this latter item could be purchased in almost any drugstore or gas station in the United States, and it
was widely known to be advertised in the Sears catalogue.

But the flapper—student, actress, or career girl—was not in most cases
a sexual vixen. She was trying on a part and playing a tease. And she always learned her lesson. One of many films to teach it to her was called

Wine of Youth (1924). We start with Grandma and the man who would be Grandpa, on the couch, happily holding hands. The screen fades and it's the same couch, only on it now we see Mother and her fiancé, soon to be Father. Fade to the present, where Mary, the modern daughter and her modern friend Trish announce that they each plan to take what they call a "trial honeymoon." No sedentary courtship for them. Together, with their fiancés, they plan a camping trip. Mary explains the point: "to know . . . how a man is in everyday life before you give your all." But as it turns out there are things about the prospective grooms—how they look in the morning, for example—that a girl doesn't need to know right away. She needs time to adjust. In the end, we see the same couch again. On it the modern couple, Mary and her man, is shown chastely holding hands.

"In the end, she was a good girl," Colleen Moore told the *New York Times* in 1971 about the flapper. "All she did was have a cocktail and smoke a cigarette." Others pointed out that while she drove and danced and all the rest, she also went to school in greater numbers than any women before her. The flapper, in short, was more than a silly screen icon or someone's shorthand for "troubling young woman." She was a real young woman with complex views and expectations, and she left us a useful pile of press clippings to explain them.

Many of these "New Girl Sounds Off" stories established journalistic formats still in use, for example, point-counterpoint or He says/She says; going undercover as a kid; the luncheon interview in which the reporter watches the girl eat as she gives a four-hour account of her life. There were always two recurrent topics. One was men. And there was Mother.

I've excavated two variations on the problematic mother.

The first was the educated and slightly bored Lady of the House. To many girls, Mother, other people's mothers—the idea of mothers, generally—suggested a nation of cultural gatekeepers, fierce defenders of cleanliness and manners and the so-called finer things. The slightly bored lady of the house is often pictured as pearled and buxom, like the club-lady matrons in the Laurel and Hardy shorts. The fat-and-skinny twosome are always moving her piano or painting her parlor and, as they go about it, creating a horrible mess. Gradually, they destroy the matron's precious aesthetic order, ruining paintings, smashing curios, obliterating the palace. (It was as a wrecking team of big, fat female life that Laurel and Hardy attained their greatest popularity.)

Mother Number Two was a new woman, a onetime progressive reformer, desperate because her own daughter had no political views and had never even heard of the National Women's Party, the ERA-devoted Congressional Union, the Women's Trade Union League, nor even the National American Woman Suffrage Association. What views the girl held seemed to concern her right to act as she chose and to denounce her mother. Consider some of the contemporary first-person story titles: "The Harm My Education Did Me," "Confessions of an Ex-Feminist," or, more to the point, "The Injurious Strain of My Mother's Devotion." As far as one girl was concerned, such impossible new women had "crammed their bookshelves with pamphlets on venereal diseases [and] suspected all . . . male acquaintances of harbouring a venereal taint."

As if writing for the girl groups of the early sixties, another annoyed daughter wrote: "I'm out of here, mama, and don't you try to come my way, too."

Still, it was sometimes mothers who provided the most insightful information about their daughters. An excellent example is "A Tale of Not So Flaming Youth," by Mrs. Virginia Kirk, published in *McCall's* in 1929 and deemed so compelling it was reprinted in the *Literary Digest* in May 1930.

Mrs. Kirk was concerned. Her "own daughter was nearly ready for that stage in her education [high school]; and she wanted to know what the girl had to face." Although she was "ten years out of university" Mrs. Kirk appeared so youthful "that she could pass for seventeen." And so, posing as a student, she infiltrated the high school scene.

She got it firsthand. The number of girls who smoked was on the rise. Nearly 95 percent of all students did not attend church, although most seemed to have notions of a "secret personal religion." Moving on to the primary topic, she reported that sexual behavior remained the same as in her day. Boys craved physical contact. So did girls, though they were "afraid of the social and biological consequence, not to mention the religious aspects and reasons." But, she emphasized, sex had lost some mystery due to "semi-realistic and suggestive" film content. Any mother who ignored the subject or "berated" her daughter was pushing the girl "closer" to an unmarried sexual encounter.

Mothers also needed to know that "treating," the ancient dating ritual, had become a standardized business transaction. Boys understood that they were to fund goods and activities—a corsage, car, food, movies, plays—and girls were expected to allow an increasing degree of sexual progress as dates and sums accumulated. But of course many girls were reluctant. And of course boys resented this fact and punished the recalcitrant girl by calling her a "gold digger," a bitch out for only one thing: boys who could produce a paycheck from a part-time job or generous parental grants. Girls denied the charges. But how to explain? Although they were flappers, flirtatious and bold, they still were nervous. And because they were flappers, because they were flirtatious and bold, they had their doubts about men and the romantic scheme in general.

Wrote Mrs. Kirk: "Marriage can no longer be represented to them as an infallibly ideal state, since they only need to look around to see scores of their elders making a failure of it."

To a reporter, at lunch or over drinks, some young women tried to explain their conflicted feelings, their "inability to live life according to the rules" or their "unwillingness to conform." Most hoped to explain how "in due course [they would] do something quite grand."

The interviewer was always intrigued by his subject and at the same time scornful. In my favorite, "An Interview with a Young Lady" (1927), the subject, an "aspiring writer" who has taken "a man's point of view as her mother never could," explains herself well, then gaily leaves the interview that's posed as lunch. Having observed her manner, her "tendencies" (the blotting of lipstick on linen napkins, uncrossed legs, and a hat that never left her head), the interrogator watches her swish out to the street, "confident, with a new kind of walk." But, like all others of her kind, she was unknowingly "dogged by a slinking gray figure with horrible designs upon the security of her later years." In fact, the interviewer had throughout the lunch glimpsed the "gray figure," the phantom spinster right there in the restaurant, "huddled in the corner." As "the beautiful young lady" passed through the door, the "repulsive gray figure . . . winked slyly . . . pointed after her," and followed.

After several years of such stories, the girls' "divergence from the normative," the "contrarian stands" and "elaborate risk-taking," as it was said, became annoying. Enough was enough.

"These little jabs at our customs and traditions can not continue indefinitely . . ." wrote one columnist. "Human beings are born to marry, as they are born to die. Nature has overloaded men and women with the instinct that leads to marriage, that the race may be perpetuated; and at the proper age the young man turns to the young woman, as she also turns to him. . . . Such is the nature of human creatures."

Doctors began to warn against "foolish flapper fads," especially a "wearing down" of the internal organs due to late nights and too much alcohol. In 1926 Dr. Charles Pabst, writing in the *Literary Digest* (below a photo of himself holding a test tube), reported, "The girl of today confronts severe internal derangement and general ill-health." She also risked ruined skin and lung trouble, due to "roofless cars," cigarettes, and "funny" diets. (The most popular, said to have worked wonders for several screen stars, consisted of tomatoes, spinach, and orange juice). Most terrifying, said Dr. Pabst, was the undocumented "fact" that the flapper increased her chance of contracting TB by 100 percent. At around the same time, another doctor, writing in the *Journal American*, discussed the possibility of flapper sanitariums that would be designed in "modish surroundings" to "pacify" the girl so she would not die, running off in the woods, to escape.

In the meantime, with few, if any, actual TB cases linked to flapperism, Dr. Pabst addressed more mundane health issues such as boils, advanced dermatitis, and haircut risks, for instance, "folliculitis," commonly known as "pimply mange," a severe rash that resulted from shaving the back of one's neck. Hair dye, too, seemed problematic. Many thousands of flappers had dyed their hair blond using peroxide and other crude chemicals that left them with scalp burns, lacerations, severe skin peeling, and hair loss.

There was also an inevitable "moral derangement," a slackening of values in flappers themselves and in younger women who'd missed the first wave but had nonetheless been sadly influenced. In a series of studies, 1928–1931, designed to measure movies' influence on young women, several academic researchers determined that 17.5 million kids, mostly girls between the ages of fourteen and twenty-one, regularly attended movies. Their favorite star: Joan Crawford, then a brassy flapper who seemed to spend entire films dressed in lingerie and often, for fun, jumped off of yachts. As one girl told an interviewer: "When I go to see a modern picture, like *Our Dancing Daughters*, I am thrilled. These modern pictures give me a feeling to imitate their ways. I believe that nothing will happen to the carefree girl like Joan Crawford, but it is the quiet girl who is always getting into trouble."

Soon after, the *New York Times* ran a story entitled "How the Flapper Aids Church." It seemed that this overly energetic female was driving men into the ministry in unprecedented numbers. The president of the Christian Missionary Alliance stated with great conviction, "Better a hungry heathen with a club than a thirsty flapper with a lipstick."

By 1927, some relief seemed in sight. The first generation of "jazz babies" had grown up and retired from the scene. A surprisingly large number seemed to have transformed themselves into something else entirely: flapper graduates. As alumnae of this movement, they went out into the world with confidence, insouciance, and a wardrobe and vocabulary to match.

Commentators, editorialists, and well-dressed ladies worried that second-stage flapperism might become a way of life. Imagine it: Each year more girls went to college, fooled around yet somehow still graduated, then, well-dressed and outspoken, became career women. As it turned out, more women during this time married and had babies than any peer group in thirty years. But the impression of a dangerous "flaming youth" refused to die a natural death.

There was no choice but to kill her.

At the close of 1928, the *New York Times* ran a front-page obituary for the Flapper. To replace her, editors endorsed a diaphanous, vaguely European creature called the Siren. She was an imaginary woman of great style and mystery who possessed an "air of knowing much and saying little . . . a mysterious allure." These truly feminine qualities, especially the part about saying little, "spelled death" for the flapper, that "fashion-killing" young woman who through sheer "force of violence established the feminine right to equal rights in such formerly masculine fields as smoking and drinking, sweating, petting, and disturbing the peace."

The siren quickly would be revealed as the brainchild of French couturiers concerned about the straight, unremarkable silhouette of flapper dress styles. And the attempt to delete flappers from the cultural record would ultimately fail—but not because the siren proved so blatantly artificial. Those much-feared "second stage" flappers, the ones said to have transposed young flapper moxie into grown-up careers and single lives, simply refused to give it up. They had moved on in life, but their "true selves," as one put it, lay hidden behind a "jazz mask."

Writing in *The New York Times Book Review*, an "unrepentant flapper" recalled:

> dancing brown-skinned in a hula-hula skirt . . . learning how to smoke and swear and stand up for myself . . . proud of my nerve . . . shameless, selfish and honest, but at the same time consider[ing] these attributes virtues . . . with the sharp points (worn) down . . . the [flapper's] smoothly polished surface [will] provide interesting, articulate, unstuffy companionship to men in years to come. . . . Be thankful that we could be the mothers of the next generation.

Many feared that women who cherished their memories of younger years (even if that meant life three years before), would not, en masse, become the next mothers. They would never wear down peacefully into housewives who bought large appliances. They would not even make proper spinsters.

THE ALL-NEW IMPROVED SPINSTER

So we come to the last of the Jazz Age single icons: the New Spinster, the single icon most likely to be crowned ancestral career woman. She had a surprisingly good job. A nicely decorated place of her own, in which she was often pictured seated in an art moderne chair beside her telephoning table. She was well dressed, she had her own car, and her days were so busy she required a diary, an antique sort of Filofax made of red leather, monogrammed and chrome-bound, with a lipstick case to match. As she perceived it, the mechanics, "the orientation," of her own life "allowed her to glide along smoothly." All she had to do was to slip into a casual dress or blouse with skirt, toss on a jacket and a pair of pumps, and rush to her car, without asking anyone's permission. One reporter described her like this:

> Today's spinster is fashionable to a fault. She . . . knows how to buy and because she is spending money she has earned, she has both assurance and discretion . . . And because she had avoided the extra duty and unexpected worry which are so often part of married life [she's] kept her looks . . . at 35 or 40 the unmarried woman looks fresher and younger than many a married woman of the same age!

And she was patient in a way only a mature, confident person could be. When barraged with public queries—"How could she *bear* missing the truly grand things in life? Husbands? Tender babes?"—she calmly explained that nothing had been ruled out and that her life was full. She further ignored all melancholy longings for the spinster of yore, that sad, faded dame missing her teeth. (The same annoyed question—Who would perform the vital free labor spinsters once provided?—had been raised in 1860 and would arise again in the early 1960s.) As she saw it, the advantage was hers. She had not gone soft in the middle (or, some added, the brain) as had her married sisters and friends. And she knew men "in a way no wives would ever" because she worked so closely with them.

Occasionally new spinsters wrote about life and inserted the slightly regretful "I look at my beatific sister with seven beautiful children . . ." sentence. But the majority of them wrote about their lives the way this thirty-year-old woman did in *The New York Times Book Review*, 1928: "The average spinster of today is . . . as a rule self-supporting, independent, very busy and surprisingly contented. If she is missing the best things in life, she does not seem to realize it!"

Of course this newest spinster confronted some of the same problems as had her predecessors. As Charlotte Perkins Gilman wrote at the time: "There has occurred a rush of activity such as no one could have predicted even a decade ago . . . still values have not fundamentally changed."

In other words, no matter how fashionable she appeared, she could not always peel off the scarifying old spinster markings. For example, many wives maintained a "considerate" refusal to discuss sex in the spinster's presence, so that she would not "too acutely feel her loss."

More significant, an unwed woman was still considered on permanent call to her family. Just as immigrant girls had been required to hand over their paychecks, so new spinsters were expected to keep an open-wallet policy. In the early sound film *Mannequin*, proud factory worker Joan Crawford explodes at her poor potato-peeling mother who has given her b'hoy of a brother (played, appropriately, by Bowery-boy star Leo Gorcey) her own week's pay. Whipping a tea towel on a chopping block, she shouts: "I coulda bought a pair of stockings with two dollars, and I needed them. . . . he doesn't want to find a job, and why should he? When he can get enough quarters and dimes outta my salary to throw around the pool hall. I'm sick of it!"

Among more firmly middle-class families, the situation was even worse. Mothers loved to throw lavish Sunday dinners. "Enormous chunks of meat for all!" read the caption of a cartoon defending the single girl who'd been asked to "bring in a few things." There's a horde of people in the background, watching her, waiting for her to leave and get the ham, the roast beef, bread, vegetables, puddings, cakes, and anything else that will be needed. The point seemed to be that because she supported no one but herself, she could contribute lavishly to the family fund. Brothers seemed to have felt this entitlement most acutely. Even if these men had jobs, the jobs never brought in enough cash. They had children, demanding wives, and other personal interests to support. And so, as it was reported again and again, brothers hit up their single sisters for cash, knowing that loyal single sisters would keep it secret. Many sisters came through. Thus, in the story, her moral superiority to the family is revealed not by hard work and generosity but by loyalty and discretion.

Of course some sisters saw it differently, and they wrote about it, one calling the condition "the New Dependency." For years after, novels and short stories took on the issue. In Josephine Lawrence's novel *But You Are Young* (1940), heroine Kelsie Wright, a savvy manicurist, is furious at her vampirish family, who wait each week, in a row, for the communal envelope. Kelsie rushes into a difficult marriage as if she were an immigrant panicked to get a green card.*

The new dependency became a subject not only for married-women/single-girl debates (by then as common as ads for talcum powder). Editorialists and college presidents joined in the discussion. Unanimously they sympathized with the sponger and somehow blamed the giving sister. One much-circulated and reprinted pamphlet explained this point of view: "How can this young man ever hope to get back on his feet when he is demoralized into taking such 'gifts' from an unwed sister? It saps the moral strength, turns our bright young men soft, unenterprising . . . ruined for all chances of manhood by the humiliation of taking handouts from a sister."

And there was worse in store for the new spinster.

SEXOLOGY AND THE SINGLE GIRL

The response, or backlash, came in the form of sexology, a pre-Freudian system designed to scientifically classify types of sexual behaviors. Sexology was often confused with "free love," the thrilling, somewhat baroque concept popularized in the novels of D. H. Lawrence and Henry Miller. In fact, sexology, a conservative response to new women workers, concerned just the

---

*The saddest new-dependency story belongs to blond thirties screen idol Jean Harlow, who was shoved into the film business by an insensitive, piggy mother and a lecherous stepfather. Never satisfied she'd done enough for them, they pushed her harder, and spent a great deal of her money. Eventually she broke free of them but had only a few years on her own. She died at twenty-six of a botched abortion.

opposite. It reworked elements of phrenology (the categorizing of persons according to skull differentiations) and eugenics, the study of superior human breeding, to codify acceptable sexual practices, and then to regulate it.

An antivalentine to the single women of America, sexology propounded that sex was good, wondrous, life-affirming—*if* it was the right kind of sex. That meant married sex, as performed in the missionary position, either for the purpose of procreation—that most erotic aspect of female sexuality—or to make marriage stronger, more "companionate." Women who were awkward, embarrassed, or for whatever reason uninterested, were diagnosed as cold or, a new and frightening word, frigid. Single women, who were presumed to miss out on intercourse entirely, were thus automatically considered frigid.

As far back as 1910, when "race suicide" was a familiar and threatening term, bookstores had been stocked with antisingular tracts condemning the "social worker" or "New Woman." They had titles like *Antipathy and Coldness in Women* and *The Poison of Prudery*. Now sexology made the point specific to the flapper and the new spinster and any other variation of single working women. *What Should We Do with Our Daughters?*, a 1921 compendium of expert commentary, featured many viewpoints, although most may be summarized by one Dr. Ely Van de Warker, who declared, "The effort of women to invade all the higher forms of labor is a force battling with the established order of sexual relations."

From another doctor: "Discovering . . . her innate feminine charm in the selling of dry goods [treating it] as a more alluring expression of her female self than that of the homely status of wife and mother, the girl exposes the grave crisis of the modern age. . . . This bounding into the world represents a futile struggle against nature . . . it touches on disease."

The experts were very precise about the origins, symptoms, and lasting effects of this disease. There were several different strains among unmarried women.

First, there was the "war working woman," the woman who'd bravely pitched in during the Great War and was thus also referred to as "a warrior maid." More commonly she was called an intersexual, a single woman who because of her odd experience somehow had fused with a male inner soul and who, though she appeared female, acted like a man. Charlotte Haldane, writer and antifeminist, viewed this "specimen" as a "significant enemy of motherhood." As she explained, "The development through the experience of war work [led to] the phenomenon of the war working woman," also the "more or less unsexed or undersexed specimen."

Next came the so-called "mannish lesbian" or "mannish woman" who took things further by dressing the part. (The definition of "lesbian" as we know it still had not settled and the term was often used to describe a woman who dressed like a man.) In medical journals and many popular articles—the word *warning* often appeared in the headline—these women were referred to as subnormal or inverts. Inversion, as described by Havelock Ellis, the father of sexology, matched precisely the traits ascribed to the new woman/flapper/new spinster:

> Not only is there frequently a pronounced taste for smoking cigarettes . . . but a . . . toleration for cigars. There is also a dislike of needlework, and domestic occupations while there is some capacity for athletics . . . brusque energetic movements . . . direct speech . . . [and] an attitude towards men, free from any suggestion of shyness . . . these will often suggest the underlying psychic abnormality to a keen observer.

Ultimately in the late 1920s, lesbianism began to take on its modern denotation: two women in a romantic and sexual pairing. No longer was the word used as a universal term gathering together schoolgirl smashes, the living situations of women in settlement houses, and heterosexual women who suffered subnormality and inversion. Lesbianism was, in sexological terms, about as bad as it got. As early as 1902, the *Pacific Medical Journal* had declared that "female boarding schools and colleges are great breeding grounds of artificial [acquired] homosexuality. . . . If carried into life, such learned perversities would lead to permanently skewed relations with men." By 1925, the situation was much worse. Commented a woman sexologist that year: "Such a fate is so contrary to the fullness of female human development little can be said to express its horror."

Statistics on lesbians, as so defined, are difficult to find, but one can find a bizarre number of estimates concerning frigidity. In 1925 leading sexologists estimated that 40 to 50 percent of all women were frigid, the highest numbers to be found among the more educated classes. According to experienced sexologist Weith Knudson, there were five categories of frigidity. Twenty percent of all women had turned out to be "cold," 25 percent could be called "indifferent," 30 percent "compliant," 15 percent "warm," and just 10 percent "passionate."

From a sexological point of view, women living alone, especially those who made no effort to find a husband, were to blame. Knudson wrote angrily, "I have emphasized repeatedly that dysparunia"—the technical label for frigidity—"signals an inner negation. . . . obstinacy cancels the will to submission. . . . There are women who refuse to be made happy; they resent the thought that the man has saved them, that they owe him everything."

But readers were assured that such an ungrateful unwed female would suffer for her obstinacy.

Walter Heape, an active commentator on sexological matters, called spinsters—all varieties—the "waste products of our female population . . . vicious and destructive creatures." He suggested that like wounded dogs, they might, with the slightest provocation, snap entirely. "A thwarted instinct does not meekly subside," he declared. "It seeks compensation and damages for its rebuff. . . . As the number of these women increases every year and, in systematic depreciation of the value of life, they are joined and supported by thousands of disillusioned married women who also scoff at marriage and motherhood as the only satisfactory calling for women."

In other words, the single idea was contagious, and as it spread these women became increasingly scary. By 1929, the vicious psycho-spinster, a frustrated, vindictive harridan, had debuted as an American character. Walter Heape was one of many who characterized the evolving nightmare. Here is a part of his 1928 study of "inherently frustrated women who have failed to marry by the 25th year": "She is . . . the guardian . . . [seated] in every auditorium of every theatre . . . haunt[ing] every library . . . in our schools, she takes little children and day by day they breathe in the atmosphere of her violated spirit."

Sexology promoted itself as a salvation, a means for innately shy, prudish young girls—or girls who'd been wrongly swayed while at school—to marry and to enjoy a natural womanly sex life that led to many wonderful babies. There was the promise of great joy, if only a woman cooperated and did it right. Even the frigid might be brought back to life. But it was also true that some new spinsters were so deeply frigid, so mentally scarred, that there was no hope for their recovery or return to life.

This sad old girl was shown, as always, to be socially pathetic ("The normal woman must have something to live for, if it be only a cat," wrote Mrs. Juliet Wilbor Tompkins in 1927.) But now she was also potentially sick. According to Tompkins in "Why Women Don't Marry," *Cosmopolitan,* for some new spinster misfits the "ways of sex will always remain a sealed—and rather horrid—book she reads at her peril." Others of these "nuns by blood" would evolve a "repose, a gentle power of indifference" that sometimes made them "bewilderingly" interesting to men "who wonder if they may not be awakened." The sad truth, however, was they would always be dormant. Even if they wed, their strange stillness would render any union abnormal. "Such women may marry and have ten children without seeming to come into any close relations with life: to the end they are stray angels, cool and aloof. The man who marries one of them will have no tempests to encounter, yet his way will not be . . . easy . . . for he can never fall back on his sex with her."

The language of sexology, its strict hierarchies of frigidity and lesbianism, suggested that there was serious scientific proof for such claims. If anything, sexology gives us proof that female freedom was so terrifying, so unthinkable, that it had to be killed off—and not just by inventing replacement icons. Finally, all female abnormality would be smothered beneath a pile of specious scientific findings.

HOW THE NEW SPINSTER MADE OUT

In spite of these warnings, most young women still felt "a Ferris-wheel-at-the-top thrill," as one of my own subjects put it, about trying on a single life. Even if the top jobs were closed to women,* there were still so many dizzying possibilities they seemed to pass by as if in a movie montage. My favorite character in search of career is the fictional Carol Kennicott, the determined, unintentionally hilarious heroine of Sinclair Lewis's *Main Street* (1920). In one early packed paragraph, we learn that Carol had "hoped to discover that she had an unusual voice, a talent for the piano, the ability to act, to write, to manage organizations," and that with each disappointment, she "evanesced anew—becoming a missionary, painting scenery, soliciting advertisements," and on and on until she's talked into marriage by a doctor from the Midwest with the promise of his rising hometown for her to conquer. Stuck in dreary little Gopher Prairie, Minnesota, she takes up urban planning, working to change street directions and move buildings, not that anyone has asked her to. She runs away once, to Washington, but comes back, because she's waited too long. She has a child. She is not a career girl at this point but a middle-aged woman from, and even she has to admit it, Gopher Prairie.

Had it worked out for her in the big city, Carol might have discovered what many real young women had discovered: Jobs were not, as the *Atlantic Monthly* had concluded, "open-sesame's to life." They were, as any man could have testified, only jobs. Una Golden, hero of an earlier Lewis novel, *The Job* (1917), skips out on small-town life and rushes to the city where she finds work in an office, a new world that sustains her for about half the book. That is, until the day Una understands that it will never change. She asks herself, "[what are] days . . . beyond a dull consistency of . . . machines and shift keys and sore wrists?" Not much, and at the end Una establishes herself and her fiancé in a successful real estate brokerage.†

She was one lucky character. In the late 1920s, the lawyer, writer, lecturer, and feminist Crystal Eastman prophetically stated, "Women who are

---

*Most American medical schools placed a 5 percent quota on female admissions, 1915–1945; Columbia and Harvard law schools still excluded women applicants until 1937, as did the New York City Bar Association.

†It's interesting that Sinclair Lewis, the man, seems to have had a personal change of heart about career women when his own wife, former journalist Dorothy Thompson, became exasperated with marriage and his drinking and went off to cover World War II. He left her in 1937, claiming that her work had destroyed their relationship. "American women are like that," he concluded, "killers of talent."

creative . . . with administrative gifts or business ability and who are ambitious to achieve and fulfill themselves along these lines, if they also have the normal desire to be mothers, must make up their minds to be sort of superman."

Margaret Culkin Banning, who wrote sensible new-spinster stories for the *Saturday Evening Post*, continued well into the 1920s to praise the new spinster as that sleek figure in a modish cap, freed of the troubles of her married friends. But she understood the point Crystal Eastman had to make. It would increasingly be difficult. With some resignation, she wrote in 1929,

> The normal social unit is made up of a man and a woman in love, courting or married. The unmarried woman who has made a job the other half of her social unit . . . is bound to be somewhat extraneous . . . out of the social picture. . . . The masses . . . administer printed condolences and sedative terms—"new woman," "bachelor girl,"—but the world in general has not approved the sight of a lady jogging through life alone.

All of this discussion came to an instantaneous halt with the 1929 stock-market crash. Within weeks, it seemed, the troubling unwed American female—whether professional, fun, academic, political—slipped from beneath the cultural microscope. The U.S. Women's Bureau estimated that just six months after the crash, two million women, many single, had lost their jobs. It was made very clear, however, that men had suffered more. They'd lost more than just jobs; they'd lost their essential core of masculinity. Amidst a collapse so hulking and vast, there was little energy left to think about the single woman. But there would always be something to say.

CHAPTER FOUR

THE SUSPICIOUS SINGLE: JOB STEALERS, THE RIVETING ROSIE, AND THE NEUROTIC HUSBAND HUNTER

—*"But aren't ya ever going to fall in love?"*
—*"A career itself is a romance. I haven't the time . . ."*
—*"Aren't ya ever going to marry?"*
—*"My de-aah, when you spend 14 hours a day with your dearest illusion, it loses something."*
—RUTH CHATTERTON EXPLAINS LIFE IN *FEMALE*, 1933

Now, listen . . . forget about yourself . . . You know what it means to the girls in this show? Those poor kids gave up jobs and will never be able to find other ones! . . . If you let them down . . . they'll have to do things I wouldn't want on my conscience and it'll be on yours!
—ALINE MACMAHON, THE SMART CHORINE, GIVING HELL TO HER DELINQUENT PRODUCER, *GOLD DIGGERS OF 1933*

Let him know you are tired of living alone. . . . You want him to take charge. You want now to have your nails done.
—U.S. GOVERNMENT "READJUSTMENT" GUIDE, 1945

SINGLE GIRLS ONLY NEED APPLY

If attention turned to the single woman—and occasionally, of course, it did—there was just one question for her: Did she work?

If the answer was yes, the response was almost always angry. Women, during the Depression, were not under any conditions supposed to hold jobs. Jobs were for men—all those guys thrown out on their asses and depicted sitting home, too depressed to lift their feet for the carpet sweeper. Women seen dressed for work, entering an elevator in an office building, made this horrific situation, this stigma of compromised manhood, that much worse. Even if she was en route to a job no man would take, the stares, the muffled traitor talk, reminded her of life's primary motto: "DON'T STEAL A JOB FROM A MAN!"

This made life tense and difficult for single women, because single women were just about the only women out there working—and sometimes there were more of them working than men. By 1932, legislation in twenty-six states prohibited married women from holding any jobs whatsoever, and that included teaching and positions in the Civil Service should a relative already hold one. In states where getting married didn't require retirement, an employed woman who married was nonetheless expected to make a "full disclosure" or risk losing that job or incurring fines for "misleading statements." And that applied even to women in those female jobs no man would take—typing, filing, cleaning.

My father, a schoolboy during these years, recalls: "If we found out a woman who worked in our school was married, we were shocked. I think at one point there was talk that the librarian had a husband and we wondered, why does she have a job? Why is she working? If her husband is a dentist or a lawyer or a truck driver, what does *she* have a job for?"

There was much discussion of job-hogging acts of afemininity. However, little was said about the myriad problems, anxiety, and sacrifices of single women, many of whom were also supporting their families, parents, siblings, grandparents—the new dependency in crisis mode. Millions of unemployed single men would ultimately regain jobs and misplaced respect. So would some single women. But more than a quarter of all women who'd been between twenty and thirty during the Depression years would never have careers. They also stood to lose much more.

"A quarter of all women" is a much repeated estimate that's hard to break down. But it's known that thousands would not, as planned, attend college or at least finish up their degrees. Hundreds of thousands who would have married never wed, never had children, and by 1932 the U.S. marriage rate had hit a historic low, while the birthrate had dropped to its lowest point since 1900. And many of those who married simply did not consider themselves financially stable enough to have children. Despite the danger and illegality, abortion was commonplace, and according to a 1933 Gallup Poll, 63 percent of the population favored "some form of birth control." In 1933 the condom industry, a $350 million enterprise, produced something like one million units a day. Wives could obtain an early form of diaphragm known as a pessary, and so could single women, as long as they posed as wives and appeared in doctors' offices wearing wedding rings.

Mary McCarthy* describes the complex procurement process in her novel *The Group*, set in the thirties and written in 1966. For weeks one character schemes and plans to get the item, telling her prospective lover that she will call him as soon as she has it in her hands. After an embarrassing doctor's "fitting"—what is perhaps the first flying-diaphragm scene in all literature—she leaves with her secretive bag and calls him to find he's not in. She walks around, calls again, then again, and finally tells his landlady that she is waiting in Washington Square Park. Seated on a bench, the precious treasure on her lap, she starts to reconsider. Hours have passed and obviously he's not coming. Ultimately she leaves the bag beneath the bench and walks off feeling terribly alone and embarrassed.

*Some of the best recorded sex in all thirties literature can be found not in the sexologized males of the period but in Mary McCarthy, particularly in the interwoven short stories *The Company She Keeps*. On a long train ride after leaving her husband, a sophisticated, educated young woman, a self-styled radical and intellectual, finds herself with no one to talk to and so chats morosely with a red-cheeked Midwestern type, probably a salesman. They get violently drunk, then for hours on end perform every imaginable sex act in his berth. In the aftermath, he declares that he will leave his wife or take her for his permanent mistress. She claims to have been blacked out through most of it and, recalling the rest, would like to jump from the train. In the end, ignoring his entreaties, she decides to collect it as an experience, knowing the purple love bites and hand marks still visible on her buttocks will go soon enough, and she will be once more her sophisticated self.

Many real single women spent the Depression years feeling terribly alone and desperate. Work was hard to find and no matter how irrational it came to seem, there was still a stigma attached to the job hunt. The compromised "forgotten" man—he was the one who needed work. But there were also needy women, and some of them literally began to starve. Fainting, in fact, became a common melodramatic plot point in the numerous backstage musicals of the time. The starving girls were almost always revived by Broadway stars who just happened to be passing by and who went on to make the emaciated girls tap-dancing miracles. Back on earth, of course, fainting was not a career option. Most women who could, as well as those who couldn't, typed. Even college graduates typed. Barnard College reported that only one third of the class of 1932 who sought jobs found them, and that most of the class at some point took up typing.

"Most of the girls I knew in those years were typists or bookkeepers who had their jobs because they were the only ones who knew how some cigar-reeker of a slob kept his files," recalled Bess, now seventy-nine and herself a bookkeeper who worked until 1997. "Women weren't taking over men's places. What man do you know who wants to cross his legs and take dictation?"

This was still an age of classifieds listing "Jobs—male" and "Jobs—female." (In fact, this age would last until the late 1960s, when protests and sit-ins inspired newspapers to blend the job offerings.) And it was "Jobs—male," the jobs in heavy industry, that took the biggest hits during the thirties. Clerical jobs, like all others, thinned out but never to the point where there was nothing. Women who held these jobs both hated and cherished them. There was little else out there and, for the city emigrants, nothing at all to return to.

But there were a few positions beyond typist, telephone operator, unwed teacher, and a handful of actress jobs. The biggest professional openings were in journalism, specifically, in the women's sections, what were known well into the 1970s as "4F" for "food, furnishings, fashion, and family." From the 1935 handbook "So You Want to Be a Reporter: A Hard-Boiled Look at the Profession for Eager Cubs," we learn just how difficult a challenge it will be. A wizened Chicago newspaperman, or someone imitating one, says:

Most of you perusing this little pamphlet have in all probability given many of your youthful Saturdays to the movies. In the films you have seen, there have been women who find work as reporters and go on to break the big story. Fairy dust, ladies, fairy dust. Let's set the record straight up top. . . . The majority of reporters are men, many with military records and other distinguished accomplishments to back them up. . . . But there is a place for the modern woman, if she is well educated, properly bred . . . but if you imagine in your dreams that'll be you covering the presidential press conference, take a good deep breath and remember that you are a Susie. "Susie?" Didn't I mention Susie? All the gang call the new female recruits "Susie" until they do something outstanding and earn themselves another nickname.

It goes on to describe a life so grueling one might be reading a publication of the U.S. military. Yet by 1934, the Labor Department estimated that there were 15,000 "girl reporters" (compared with a total of only 7,105 in 1920), including several hundred editors across the country. Although most of these young women found themselves on the casserole-and-sweater beats, they kept at it, and by 1950, there were 28,595 female journalists.

Within a few years, the existence of so many reporters would inspire a rush of "girl-reporter" movies as well as the birth of comic-strip perennial Brenda Starr. But at the time, books and movie serials featured reporterlike snoops, detectives with blond hair, nice manners, and remarkable powers of deduction. Nancy Drew, who debuted in 1930, drove a blue coupe and with her two girl pals, Bess and George, solved community mysteries. Detective Judy Bolton went to work in 1932, and that same year Joan Blondell, best known for playing sardonic chorines with a past, became Miss Pinkerton, a nurse who investigates a murder on the large estate where she lives and works.

These fantasies tried to pull struggling women into small mysteries and story lines more captivating than those of their own lives. But plenty of women were out there having real-life wild adventures of their own.

ON THE ROAD, FEMALE EDITION

There were always a few women reporters who published more than their recipes. Many of these writers had been encouraged by Eleanor Roosevelt, who held a weekly woman-only press conference, inviting prominent journalists including Lorena Hickok of the Associated Press; Genevieve Forbes Herrick of the *Chicago Tribune*; Marjorie C. Driscoll from the *Los Angeles Examiner*; Grace Robinson, the New York *Daily News*; Elenore Kellogg, the *New York World*; Ruth Finney of Scripps-Howard, and Emma Bugbee from the *New York Herald Tribune*. Over time, the First Lady had come to view women as a class apart, a group having its own distinct, neglected problems, and she believed reporters might best bring these postsuffrage issues into public debate. Even those not within the inner circle got the message. Freelance writer Grace Hutchins makes the perfect example.

During the mid-thirties, Hutchins spent two years traveling the country in search of the Forgotten Woman. She found a great one: Miss Bertha Thompson, aka Boxcar Bertha, the famed lifelong female hobo. At age thirty or thirty-two—she wasn't quite sure—Bertha told Hutchins her life story. How her family had hit the road in desperation years earlier. How she'd learned to read and spell by sounding out the words painted on the sides of passing freight cars. Her mother taught her the rest of what she needed to know, a body of knowledge that might be entitled "Don't Count on Men."

At the time Hutchins met her, Bertha had established a chain of female "transient bureaus" that functioned as M.A.S.H. units and impromptu wilderness kaffeeklatsches. She described her fellow travelers as a "great army of women, all motivated by the same things . . . no work, family barely on relief . . . no prospect of marriage, the need for a lark, for sex, freedom, living and the great urge to know what other women were doing."

Bertha couldn't possibly have kept up with the traffic. According to Hutchins, there were between 100,000 and 150,000 homeless women wandering around, many of them teenaged runaways who slept outside. The YWCA estimated in its 1933 Christmas message that there were 145,000 women who "very well could be" described as "home-less and footloose . . . at dangerous odds." In 1935 the Salvation Army reported that in eight hundred cities across America there were 10,000 women a night asking for shelter. Another source of information about transient women was social scientist Thomas Menehin, who wrote of his travels "hoboing" his way around the country in 1936. His estimates: One out of every twenty tramps was a "girl," although many, like Veronica Lake in *Sullivan's Travels* (1942), dressed as a man for protection. Life on the road was extremely tough; women were in constant danger of rape, especially in the public shelters.

Or so it was assumed. Menehin, like others, did not have any hard data on what homeless women did at night or, for that matter, by day. Did they band together, or was it a rule of the road to trust no one? Where did they sleep? "The Forgotten Man" became a vivid national icon in part because he turned up in newsreels. With the colorful exception of Boxcar Bertha, Forgotten Women were invisible. Writer Meridel LeSueur asked, point-blank, in a 1932 issue of *The Masses*:

> Where do they go when they are out of work and hungry? . . . they are not on the breadlines. There are no flophouses for women . . . you don't see women lying on the floor of the mission in the free flops . . . or under newspapers in the park and trying to get into the Y without any money or looking down at the heel. Charities take . . . only those called "deserving." The lone girl is under sus-picion by the virgin women who dispense charity. . . . Where do these women go?

One read about these women on very slow news days, in stories that often seemed more like public-service announcements. Women who made the news were valorous like Eleanor Roosevelt, brave and spunky like Anne Morrow Lindbergh, glamorous—the duchess of Windsor, Marlene Dietrich—or extraordinary, like Babe Didrikson Zaharias, the mega-sportswoman. (At a time when there were no organized women's sports, Zaharias served as a one-woman Olympic team. Asked once if there was anything she didn't play, she answered, "Dolls.") But the average single woman wasn't asked very often what she thought or did. And when some-one—a man, an official—happened to ask, certain assumptions about her character seemed always to creep their way into the questions.

THE CASE OF THE MISSING HEART

One of the key single-female motifs in Depression-era America was the heartless woman. She stole jobs from men. She stole herself away from men who needed her. She even stole cosmetics from stores. She could not help herself. Either she'd been born hard or, to paraphrase from numerous mag-azines and dime novels, something human had been ground out of her in hard times. She was missing a vital piece. The word *malevolent* began to ap-pear before the words *woman* or *female*.

The mannish sexological ice block seemed healthy and whole in com-parison. Here was a woman missing more than sexual warmth or desire. She was missing her heart. And this freak condition was best open to ex-ploratory surgery on film. As early as the mid-twenties movies had featured intense, almost rabid female bosses who spit out orders. They hired! They fired! They lived in art moderne palaces around servants they hired and fired! Most important, they dismissed romantic love as a plebeian distrac-tion. At least for the first forty-five minutes of the movie. A classic exam-ple in this brittle-bitch genre is *Smouldering Fires* (1925), starring Pauline Frederick as a corporate executive named Jane Vale (that's for "vale of tears" as opposed to "wedding veil"). Miss Vale shrieks her way through staff meetings. She yells at ninny secretaries who seriously discuss makeup and men. She has a signature motto: "Be necessary to others and let no man be necessary to you."

Then, unexpectedly, Miss Vale falls in love with a younger man and seems to change, but not in the way we anticipate. Instead of becoming a "real" woman—warm and sexually receptive to her husband—she becomes a female martyr. Reworking a classic spinster story line, Miss Vale relin-quishes her man to the one person on earth she feels for at all, her younger sister. The girl is nineteen or so, an eager, sweet college kid; the hero is thirty-seven. At one point, watching her fiancé and sister dance, remarking on how "young" they seem, she realizes that she has missed the boat or, more appropriately, gotten on the wrong elevator. She lets them go. During the Depression years, she might not have been quite so giving.

In *Baby Face* (1933), a heartless-woman masterpiece, Barbara Stanwyck, a speakeasy bartender, puts on a decent dress and works her way up within a corporation, starting on the first floor as a filing clerk. We know immediately that she's an operator. She casually asks a colleague how she got *such* a great perm. She asks another one where she got the *fabulous* shoes. She shows up with the perm and identical shoes the next day. Soon she's headed up the corporate skyscraper. On each new floor (accounting, mortgages, et cetera) she's transformed: better clothes and hairstyles, an entirely new professional manner. At each stop she lures then abruptly drops at least one ardent lover, although one man she keeps around—a strategist and booster, who's advised her and helped finance her climb. Finally we see her at the top, draped in one of those sparkly floor-length gowns so many thirties heroines wear just to swish around the house. In this key scene, the lover and friend charges into her office. He needs cash. He's desperate. And he asks her point-blank for some jewels he once helped her buy. She stares at him. Thinks. And then she delivers a heartless-woman manifesto: "I have to think of myself. I've gone through a lot to get those things. My life has been bitter and hard. I'm not like other women. All the gentleness and kindness in me has been killed. All I've got is those things. Without them, I'd be nothing . . . I'd have to go back to what I was! No! I won't do it, I tell you, I won't."

And she doesn't.

In *Dangerous* (1935), Bette Davis plays an actress who when refused a divorce, tries to kill her husband by smashing the passenger side of their car, his side, into a tree. (The staged accident was a common heartless-woman maneuver that would be adopted by the overly anxious, neurotic single bitch of the late forties.) To her dismay, the husband lives as a cripple. As a heartless bitch, naturally, she has to leave him, and ruin her own life—retiring from the stage and wandering the city drunk. One evening, a fan spies her out having her liquid supper. He comes over and compliments her, though she alternately ignores him and denies who she is. After much back-and-forth and many drinks, she admits her identity. A romance grows slowly. When he gets too romantic, however, she barks, "Oh, don't be so *intense!*" He asks her to marry him. Her response: "Oh, it makes such an *issue* of everything!" And, as it happens, she's still married to the man she disfigured. After more drinks and many fights, plus a failed rehab sequence, she goes back to the husband, begrudgingly attempting to act the wife. Let's put it this way: If the guy could have moved, he would have killed her.

The greatest entry in the heartless-woman genre is *Three on a Match* (1932). In this bizarre tale, three old school friends meet by chance, each having turned out just as a childhood prologue had predicted. Joan Blondell, recently out of prison for theft, works as a chorus girl. Bette Davis, very young, skinny, and timid, is a stenographer. Elegant Ann Dvorak is married, wealthy, and has an adorable child.

They meet for lunch. Ann, at one point, turns to Joan, the ex-con, and says, "It's *you* I really envy—your independence and your courage . . . I accepted the first man who wanted to marry me—I thought it meant comfort and security." The two friends stare at Ann in disbelief. She goes on: "Oh, I suppose I should be the happiest woman in the world—a beautiful home, successful husband, and nice youngster. But somehow the things that make other people happy leave me cold. I guess something must have been left out of my makeup."

As if on cue, they light their Chesterfields—three to one match. According to superstition, one says, the last to get her cigarette in there and lit will suffer a horrible fate. In this case, no big surprise, that's Ann Dvorak. Whatever it was "left out of [her] makeup" kicks in like a drug.

She flees her home, taking the child with her onto a cruise. Then, leaving him alone in her stateroom, she wanders the ballrooms looking for men. She picks out a scary sort, a gangster with a round face and tight striped suit, and off they go at port, leaving the boy on the ship. (The father eventually rescues him.) Inexplicably, then, she cuts off all contact with her family and begins a life of petty crime. One day months later the husband runs into the girlfriends, Bette and Joan, and decides to make a new life with them—that they will be the "three." He marries Joan and hires steno girl Bette as the little boy's governess.

Another day months later Ann shows up outside the house, her thuggish boyfriend looming behind. Annoyed, he pushes the ragged-looking Ann toward a smart-looking woman approaching in furs. Ann looks up to see Joan, her replacement, home from shopping. She asks after the boy, then gets to the point. She needs money. Joan gives her a little, and Ann is gone, back to her gangster. She gives him the money; he shoves her. "Hey!" he shouts, "ain't that dame married to your husband?"

Throughout these years, single women were objects of suspicion. Perhaps they worked when men did not. Perhaps broke and alone, they hitchhiked from place to place—as unwomanly a thing as a knife fight. In mass-movie fantasy, some grew into self-contained man-eating monsters.

But most real women, like most men, were just frustrated. They had been forced to take an unexpected detour from what they once would have called "the normal things." And this tangent had lasted so long that the once-upon-a-time state known as Normal now seemed exotic. Especially for the young among them—all those who had grown up without dance crazes and arguments about flappers and smoking. Asked what she remembered about these years of "massive economic dislocation" (as common a phrase as "Jazz Age"), Bess the bookkeeper said, "I wanted panty hose. I wanted a room that had fewer than four sisters and a cousin in it. I wanted to get married—well, forget that. Forget the room while we're at it. Panty hose."

THE SWING OF THINGS

The original new women, now in their fifties, had organized their networks and pushed hard for their causes—aid to indigent families with children, civil rights, minimum-wage laws, nationally sponsored health care—and they had a stalwart ally in Eleanor Roosevelt. Several of the circle headed New Deal agencies, and as a unified block they spoke out about the unspoken everything, from the harassment of unwed mothers to the instant need for antilynching legislation. Now they looked toward Europe.

Genevieve Parkhurst asked in a 1935 issue of *Harper's*: "Are the women of America going to realize the destiny marked out for them when they began their long march toward emancipation? Or are they, like the women of Germany, to stand accused of having betrayed themselves?"

The American Women's Association called upon all American women to fight fascism, which dictated that women stay in their homes and reproduce for the glory of the Fatherland.

I imagine average American women hearing this and blinking up into the light, confused, exhausted, and mumbling something like "panty hose." As historian Lois Scharf wrote in *Holding Their Own* (1982): "The massive economic dislocation . . . riveted the attention of Americans along the entire ideological spectrum . . . events overseas . . . [were] completely subsumed by anxiety . . . demoralized . . . disintegrating families," and within a few years, she might have added, the complete indifference of many young women.

In 1935, shortly before her death, Charlotte Perkins Gilman lamented that the original new women had failed to train successors. Others admitted that they had, in fact, alienated many young women by publicly insulting the popular culture of the 1920s. All that was true. But if many young women were apolitical, it was not because they felt excluded by older feminists. With the exception of the very wealthy and the very lucky, most young women had missed out on the basic things they'd been raised to expect, as one young woman told the *New York Times*: "dating, driving, horseback riding. . . . I never went ice skating or out dancing. . . . One year our school play was canceled because the stage was considered unsafe and there was no money to replace it. Also we had no sets and costumes."

As the Depression finally eased, this young woman, like thousands of others, would officially attempt to have fun. As early teenagers, these "kids" threw parties, listened to music—big-band, swing—that offended their parents, evolved an inside slang ("ugly duck" and "scrag" versus the "fly" or "nifty" girl), and traveled in high school packs, kid constituencies that, as in the 1920s, formed a discernible if less extravagant youth group.

As one salesman put it, there was scattered throughout the country a whole generation, sixteen to twenty, "none of whom have owned a second pair of shoes. Can they know what it is to have a closet full of shirts? Wearing the same clothes every day for weeks, months on end. . . . How many recordings does the average youngster own? No need to start counting. . . . Imagine having your own radio!"

This atmosphere was captured by one of my oldest subjects, who declines to give her age but says, "My name is Ida-Mae, that's how old I am":

> There was a longing to run around with your friends, and talk fast about . . . pure nothing. . . . I remember our mothers couldn't understand why we wanted to have many boyfriends, instead of just one. And music, oh yes! My mother, I remember this, called it "Jewish sex music"! Maybe the clarinet was too phallic for her. Benny Goodman was prominent. . . . We were always dancing, in basements or someone's living room. Sometimes it got a little lewd. But, believe me, in the average crowd, nobody had sex. We ran around with boys. . . . After the Depression years, going out for a soda—that was fun. Oh boy! And if you happened to go with fifteen other kids who all wanted to sit in the same booth—even better! . . . Nobody knew what was coming. I remember thinking about two things. I was going to find a husband. And I was going to college. Not in that order.

But, like others, she encountered resistance to what she called "the college end of the bargain." With the wane of the crisis came a renewal of public arguments about the purpose of higher education for women. Why, and especially after this enormous social mess, would the average girl want more than a home? And if that was to be her destination, was it fair to men, who had suffered, that she take up needed space in classrooms? The *Atlantic Monthly*, 1937, solemnly noted: "When the point is reached where, in order to secure a higher salary, she must study for a master's degree, she may realize with a sudden anguish that her chance of marriage [is] growing more remote and that the pattern of her life is more and more following the lines of spinsterhood."

During the late 1930s universities were referred to as "spinster facto-

ries." And as in the Victorian period, prescribed remedies to this factory
life turned up in the media. A typical *Life* feature demonstrated how a
mother might work on a girl when she was young so that when it came
time for college that girl would already be married. One 1937 story consisted of several panels in which the chosen girl, Susan, eleven, was pictured deep in training to be "a winning female!"

In one panel, Susan makes beds. In another, she studies the way her
mother fixes her potentially "beguiling" nails. In still another photo, Susan
sets the table. "Homemaking doesn't come instinctively to a teenaged girl,"
Life explained. "It's easier to teach a little girl than to nag at an older
one. . . . Now the child can do simple meal planning and cooking, cred-
itable bed making and charming table setting."

It was a familiar process. Evidence is dragged forth to prove that what
society wants for single girls is what these girls want for themselves. Back
in the nineteenth century, no intelligent young woman wished for bedrest,
the prescribed "cure" for hysterical antifeminine behavior. Yet after all
she'd been through—the shrieking fights with mother! Her insane demands not to wed!—wasn't bedrest what she secretly craved? Likewise,
after the Depression, after all she'd been through, did she really want to
do tough academic work? Ignore for a moment the actual facts, for example, that 15 percent more women were enrolled in college in 1938
than in 1933. Instead consider some of the expert arguments.

To begin with, the number of female professionals had increased by a
mere 8.5 percent during the 1920s. If single women were serious about careers, as opposed to mere jobs, wouldn't that figure be higher? It was further
noted that professional women earned less than their male counterparts, so
much less that they could not possibly be serious about sustained and important careers. And even in "female" professions, men outearned them. In
1939 male teachers averaged $1,953 a year, women just $1,394; male social
workers received $1,718 compared with women's $1,442.

Young women continued to draw up their own personal blueprints,
and to present their own plans. And they were continually besieged with
these retorts. In one 1938 *Coronet* piece, a twenty-year-old relates a conversation she had with her mother. The daughter said she wanted to see

France; her mother replied, "So did Amelia Earhart," the aviator who'd recently gone missing. "See to getting yourself settled! Figure that and someday you can take a trip."

Those who took the solo trips—college, careers without husbands,
forays to Greenwich Village—found it no more difficult, than those
who'd gone before. But they were viewed differently in the post-
Depression world. Why now would anyone risk their security? In novels
and stories, we find images of women missing more than their hearts;
they are falling apart.

Let's look at two popular novels. *Ann Vickers* (1933), by Sinclair
Lewis, concerns an ambitious social worker who becomes a prison warden and reform advocate, somewhat like Clara Barton. In coordinating
such a difficult career, Ann Vickers has sacrificed anything resembling a
coherent personal life. She has an illegal abortion. When she does finally marry, it ends in divorce, and she takes up with a gangster. Although successful (and popular!) as a prison warden, she suffers a
nervous breakdown.

In *The Folks*, Ruth Suckow's novel about the Iowa farm family, we pick
up the story of Margaret Ferguson, the dark and arty girl who ran off to
Greenwich Village and rechristened herself Margot. Finally, after several
years spent living in New Mexico with her married lover, she returns to
New York City. Margot's life has been, to choose one word, controversial.
Her family doesn't understand; in fact, only one small-town neighbor has
ever understood at all. "Margaret's generation of girls is wonderful!" she
had said to herself during one of Margot's rare visits home. "They went out
and grabbed at life." Margot's thoughts precisely. Yet that was years ago,
and now, at almost thirty, she finds the city of dreams and adventure
changed and cold. "She felt a bitter hatred of the noise and the hugeness
around [Grand Central] station, making her think of how she was now to
earn a living. Everywhere [she] seemed to see these smooth metallic girls
whom she hated. They were like the modern buildings, not individualized
but stylized . . . groomed into urban smoothness."

Later, wandering her old neighborhood, Margot is stopped by a sight
even worse: a "hag" selling pencils on a street corner near the apartment

where she once had burned candles and danced with scarves. It's an archetypal moment in the single narrative: The younger woman sees her future in the older one, in the lonely and forgotten hag selling "pencils she knew no one wanted to buy." During the mid- and late thirties, protagonists like Margaret-Margot were held up as icons of female disaster. If college and career could make you crazy, the unconventional life was like a suicide. Usually writers posed it as a question: What became of runaway girls, not just the down-and-out but the bohemians, the superannuated flappers, the Margots, who'd set out to see the world without a guidebook? The answer: Either they'd wise up and marry or they'd eventually take a place on the street corner.

Jean Rhys, in her melancholy novels, was a premiere chronicler of the aging adventurer now about to fall apart. The best of her slender oeuvre is *After Leaving Mr. Mackenzie* (1930). Here we have the problem called Julia, a Londoner long ago self-exiled to Paris, where she's had her share of exotic experiences. Now she is older and broke. One former lover, noting her shabby clothes, observes, "It was obvious that she had been principally living on the money given to her by various men. Going from one to another had become a habit . . . she had not saved a penny." All true. As Julia explains to one of them, "You see, a time comes in your life when, if you have money, you can go one way. . . . If you have nothing at all . . . you go another." And sometimes rather than fight, you take up residence in a fantasy world. "Every day is a new day," Julia dreamily tells herself. "Every day you are a new person."

There were millions of single women in 1940—office drones, struggling reporters and nurses, end-of-the-road new women, the homeless, and all those still waving a tattered bohemian flag. But what became of any of them was once again a question put indefinitely on hold.

HOW I WON THE WAR

So much has been written about the experiences of women during World War II that I will not describe in the usual minute detail how they "answered the call to duty," as invoked by the deep, paternalistic urgings of midcentury newsmen—Walter Cronkite, Eric Sevareid, Edward R. Murrow, and Lowell Thomas.

Let's instead look at it this way: The entire female population was for an odd slip of time effectively single. No one knew if their fiancés, boyfriends, lovers would ever return. As one California woman wrote in her diary in 1942, "All plans changed last week or fell away." Single meant "available," but not as prospective brides to men. The War Manpower Commission, supported by the Office of War Information, produced voluminous amounts of working-girl propaganda to fill the void.

Millions of suddenly essential female workers took over male positions such as cabdriver, elevator operator, bus driver, and security guard. In one year, the number of female defense-factory workers increased by 460 percent, a figure that translated into 2.5 million women assigned to the unlikeliest tasks. Instead of making carbon copies or assigning homework, many women now manufactured tank parts, plane frames, engine propellers, parachutes, ships, gas masks, life rafts, ammunition, and artillery. Another two million women continued in or picked up clerical work; the number of newly indoctrinated typists would double before the end of the war. And for the more serious, educated woman, the absence of men presented a guilty holiday. For the first time, many women found positions in symphonies, as chemists, and in some states, as lawyers. Harvard University accepted its first small number of female medical students in 1944.

Suddenly it was glorious and patriotic to be single. Newsreels with titles such as "Glamour Girls of 1943" reported that with "industrial advances" a girl might do "practically anything!" There were no limits to "the types of jobs a woman could do. . . . whether she has a husband or not." Any single gal who didn't step up, sign on, *cooperate*, was considered as much a disappointment and failure as those who had favored a career over marriage in decades past.

One female worker recruitment film, entitled *To the Ladies*, and shown as part of newsreels throughout 1942 and '43, opens with an establishing shot of fictional Middletown, USA. The camera pans the sidewalks, town squares, store windows and finds only women. They're young, hair down, in flowered dresses, or they're older, more professional-looking, hair piled up, shoulder pads piled up nearly as high. We intercut between life scenes: girls at a drugstore counter giggling over sodas and twirling in their seats . . . women buying nail polish . . . women having lunch . . . women going to the movies in the afternoon. The Voice of Authority asks us to compare this lackadaisical portrait with others from around the world.

Why, look at the women of England! Forced to send their kids off to the country or into tube stations. And the French! Here we cut briefly to fashionable women tearing up their last good clothing to use as tourniquets for bleeding soldiers. We also watch a Russian grandmother building some-thing in her kitchen that looks like a bomb. Meanwhile, back in innocuous Middletown, idle females carried out the "meaningless household chores" that had previously been declared their purpose in life. As the camera moves back and away from the street set, the women look like little kids rushing around as they play.

As if the point hadn't been made, a companion film, *Women of Steel*, introduced a shop-girl welder and her Hungarian great-grandmother who, using her blowtorch, lit a male coworker's cigarette.

There she was, the one singular female icon to arise from this antisingu-lar period: Rosie the Riveter, industrial pinup, her hair back in a snood or ker-chief, her body swimming inside overalls, one hand holding the signature blowtorch. What's rarely mentioned is how few ever made it to welder status and the coveted role of human cigarette lighter. And of the few who did, 99 percent were white. At the time, many didn't take note or find such discrim-ination unusual; the society was segregated, and most whites had never before worked with those then referred to as Negroes. (If white women worked in of-fices, black women were lucky to clean them at ten P.M.)

It's one of the first things we learn during the average "Rosie" docu-mentary, most made during the late 1960s and early 1970s. The Jewish, Italian, and Irish workers recall the exhaustion and exhilaration. They all talk about loneliness. When we come at last to a black worker it's clear that wartime single life was often lonelier than any white women might have imagined. One former black welder spoke in a 1972 documentary.

I had done all the requirements, the hours, but it was just the case they'd never put anybody in the more interesting welder jobs unless she was white. . . . three years of me watching—it seemed like hundreds of girls get in there before me . . . yeah, I finally got in. And they think I don't know they paid me less than half [the salary] of the whites? . . . when it was leaving time, they always made me and the others wait until the white ones had left first. So we never talked. . . . I remember thinking one day, oh God, is this stupidity? . . . Here we were all alone pretty much. None of us, just from the faces you could see, was going home to very much. . . . It was a strange time, very tough, and I couldn't get over that we couldn't break it down a little, stick it out together.

They had at least this in common: Despite reports indicating that as many as 75 percent of *all* working women wished to keep their jobs after the war—black women, for example, had increased their presence in the clerical sector by five thousand jobs—Rosie and all her sisters were to become the century's most exotic, briefly celebrated temps. At the time, they would never have believed it.

In May 1942 *Business Week* reported that airplane plants considered women 50 to 100 percent more efficient in wiring instrument panels than men, due to general carefulness and a greater attention to detail. The authors of this survey felt confident in stating that women could perform 80 percent of all war-industry jobs and all but 80 out of 937 jobs in civilian industry. Boeing Aircraft in Seattle utilized squads of superwomen for moving and lifting heavy loads. Sperry Gyroscope announced: "Women can and do work in every capacity possible." Tough individualized women, reflections of this stunning assessment, began to appear in the popular culture. *Wonder Woman*, after *Brenda Starr*, was the most popular cartoon strip of the period, and movie serials—the cartoonish and cheaply made "B" movies—tracked exotic creatures such as Ruth Roman in *Jungle Queen*, Kay Aldridge as "Nyoka," deeply embattled in the endless *Perils of Nyoka*, and Marguerite Chapman as *Spy Smasher*. For the first time since its intro duction in 1923, the Equal Rights Amendment was voted three times to the Senate floor.

Throughout the war years, an unusual number of actresses worked playing single women in films. Olivia De Havilland and Ann Sothern played aircraft workers in *Government Girl* and *Swing Shift Maisie*. Lucille Ball played a rich girl turned defense plant worker in *Meet the People*. Lana Turner played an unlikely war correspondent in *Somewhere I'll Find You* and an heiress turned WAC (the Women's Army Corps) in *Keep Your Powder Dry*. Movie girls also contended with what had become a housing crisis. In *The More the Merrier* Jean Arthur shared an apartment with two men. In *The Doughgirls* Ann Sheridan pretended to be married so that she could keep a Washington, D.C., hotel room. Ginger Rogers starred in *Tender Comrade*, as one of several women who chip in to share and fix up a large house. And they get along beautifully, with no trace of the competition and bitchiness of *Stage Door* (1937), in which some of the above-mentioned stars lived in a boardinghouse for actresses, battling one another for auditions, dates with producers, and walk-on parts.

But as early as 1942, a campaign was under way to prepare the workplace for men by planning—and I paraphrase an actual headline—how to get rid of the women. A *Time* story complained that women flirted at work and, as evidence, reported that Douglas Aircraft had been forced to close its Santa Monica bomb shelter due to "lovemaking" during the lunch break. It seemed that women wore transparent blouses and "peekaboo" sweaters that distracted men.

Other publications quickly leapt on the story. There was an excessive powdering of the nose on company time. Absenteeism due to menstrual periods or constipation or both. Rampant gossip. *Business Week*, once so enthusiastic about this addition to the workforce, reported in 1943 that single women had been caught "soliciting" for extra cash, although it was unclear where the alleged munitions-plant prostitution had occurred. WACs were the target of endless jokes and nasty cartoons. Suddenly everyone knew the acronym "PWOP" (pregnant without permission). The subject of their underwear, specifically, what color it was, became a conversational topic. There were more than 300,000 WACs, and not a week

passed without some newly invented scandal, very often involving suspected mass lesbianism. As if to purge the last impression, a 1944 Tangee
lipstick ad showed photos of seven uniformed women and this declaration:
"We are still the weaker sex. It's still up to us to appear as alluring and
lovely as possible."

The New York Times Magazine apparently agreed. In 1943 it ran a piece
called "What About Women After the War?" The question was answered,
primarily, by a female personnel manager who adopted the tone of an advice
columnist. "Different women want different things," she wrote. "I think most
of them—whether they admit it or not—want only to marry, have a home
and a man to do their worrying (and sometimes their thinking) for them."

The Labor Review for September 1945 casually reported that the Department of Labor was now "laying down recommendations on separation
of women from wartime jobs" and the "ways and means [to] cushion the effects of transition." The "transition" wasn't smooth; it was brutal. Several
states reinstated old restrictions that forbade women from lifting more than
twenty-five pounds in the workplace, to cite one of many examples, or
hired only "first-class" mechanics, when most women rated only third-class
status. Unions reinforced seniority clauses, and the GI Bill would give veterans preference in all government hiring; the civil service accepted appli-
cations only from veterans.

A little less than a year later, women had lost well over a million factory jobs, half a million clerical positions, 300,000 jobs in commercial service, and 100,000 in sales. Women's share of all jobs had dropped from 36
to 28 percent. Married women who could not coordinate the demands of
child care and household work, women who were chronically late or exhausted, became "voluntary withdrawals"—whether they wanted to leave
their jobs or not; single women rated no such sacrificial titles. They were
fired. Women who remained in the expanded postwar workforce—about
17 million, more than half of them single—found themselves seemingly
quarantined within a tiny range of jobs. During the first quarter of 1946,
writes historian Susan Hartmann, "government employment agencies
placed 40 percent of female applicants in household and other service jobs,
13 to 15 percent in semiskilled positions, and less than 5 percent in pro-

fessional managerial or skilled work. In June of that year, 70 percent of jobs open to women paid less than .65 an hour."

A 1946 survey of former WACs revealed that less than half of those employed had been able to find work that in any way related to their extensive wartime training.

Of course they had not really been expected to. In 1944, one radio executive had publicly predicted, "For nearly every man returning to his former job, there will be a woman returning to her former (or future) occupation—caring for the home." The chairman of the board of the National Association of Manufacturers urged women to leave "for the sake of their homes as well as the labor situation." The president of TWA reiterated what was fast becoming common knowledge: Most women in business had been there only temporarily. "They intended, and rightfully, to return home after the war or marry and make new homes."

HOMESICK

Immediately befor the war, marriage had undergone a mass revival due to the Selective Service Act, the 1940 draft law that raised bridal terror to new levels of intensity. (Will he come back, and if not, will I ever meet anyone else?) Among these rushed unions, there were many casualties— prewar, the divorce rate stood at 2 per 1,000 and by 1946 it had doubled. But many of these instant early weddings had been more like extended blind dates and the divorces that followed were as predictable and as unavoidable as schoolyard breakups. At war's end, marriage was still an essential and blessed institution. Whatever else you'd done—worked, begun to smoke, learned to drive—the next obvious and necessary step into adulthood was to wed.

"What else was this stupid war fought for?" asked an "engaged girl" in *Mademoiselle* magazine in 1945.

In a national poll conducted two years before, young women were asked to choose between three distinct life options: (1) home and husband, (2) the hard-to-imagine career/marriage combination, and (3) the single career woman. Three quarters of the participants answered "home and husband," while 18 percent sought having both the man and the job. Only one in nine envisioned an independent life and a career as opposed to a job.

There was, however, a problem, and that was the verifiable man shortage. It was drastically bad form to say so, but 250,000 men had died overseas, and—this part could be said—thousands had returned with foreign brides. Those who returned solo seemed "resistant" or "reluctant" to wed, or, more to the point, a little scared of the American women they'd found at home. A former correspondent for *Stars and Stripes*, the army newspaper read throughout the Allied universe, told *The New York Times Magazine* in March 1946: "Being nice is almost a lost art among American women. . . . After three months in the land of challenging females, I feel that I should go back to France!" That same year *Harper's* reported, "Many American war veterans are bearing some unexpected rehabilitation difficulties in coming home to what used to be a pleasantly pliable and even appealingly incompetent little woman and finding a masterful creature recognizing no limit to her own endurance."

That is to say, she'd had a job, she'd lived alone or with a group of other working women and had somehow mislaid her supply of charming helplessness.

One World War II veteran I interviewed recalled:

When we came back from the war, yes, my God, there was a sense that [even] if we'd changed, we hadn't expected women to change. . . . There were lots of women everywhere, very breezy, confident. It was . . . a little shocking at first, but not really a bad thing. I remember being on a subway and this woman just sitting down next to me and starting a conversation, and all I remember thinking is, she's not even going here for a pickup, she was chatting. Women didn't do things like that before. . . . Now they were different, more of a presence.

He might have added that there were just *more* of them. As actor Glenn Ford spat at Rita Hayworth in *Gilda* (1946): "Ha! . . . There're more women out there than there are insects!"

Cursory reports from the Census Bureau confirmed that women had become the majority sex in the United States. Obviously there'd been war losses. But medical data was also starting to show that men had a higher susceptibility to disease and infection and that women in general had stronger immune systems.

In the spring of 1948 *The New York Times Magazine* devoted a cover to the news that women were "The Stronger Sex." They had stronger hearts. They faced far fewer bar brawls, stressful commutes, industrial accidents, et cetera, but the news still was not good. Because of their newly discovered strength, women were more likely than ever to end up alone—widowed and unable to beat out the competition for a replacement—a condition that was made to sound far worse than that of all the many men who would simply be dead. (The piece led with an illustration showing buxom ladies with butterfly nets desperate to catch their weak, elusive prey.) The *Times* had in ways been covering this story since late 1945, when it first reported that because of war losses, population shifts, and female longevity, 750,000 women would most likely have to live without husbands. Three years later it was time to assess damages and ask the important questions: What was going to happen to all these women? What would it mean for society if there was suddenly a permanent single class? Would government, at the local or federal level, in some way be responsible for their welfare, and how would such women fare emotionally?

Everyone at least had an answer for that last one: very poorly.

This conclusion was rooted in a kind of pop-Freudian mandate that had evolved during the war. According to the tenets of this new "understanding," modern woman was no longer merely frigid or heartless; she was a full-scale neurotic. In *Modern Woman: The Lost Sex* (1947), a bible of sex-role hysteria, authors Marynia Farnham and Ferdinand Lundberg labeled the twentieth century a time of "epidemic neurosis" and characterized women as its most appalling victims. Theirs was an existential crisis, for they had lost their essential identity and purpose. That is to say, females had been torn from their place in the home, metaphorically removed from the hearth. As the two doctors explained in both the book and in a series of stern filmed lectures:

Thousands of women became deeply and genuinely uncertain about whatever they undertook. More and more conscious of themselves as "drags" upon their husbands in the competitive struggle for place and prestige, frustrated at the inner core of their beings, they proceeded to react in a number of ways—as male-emulating careerists, as overdoting, restrictive or rejecting mothers, or as a combination of career women and women suspiciously placing too much stress in one way or the other on the natural maternal function. In short, they became neurotics.

And those were the healthy married ones. The mid-twentieth-century single woman presented a scarier case. As the authors saw it, the country had already faced down the feminists, bohemian nuts, and, worst of all in retrospect, the suffragettes, whose "ferocity . . . led to property destruction on a large scale; damages ran into the millions. The government seemed powerless to deal intelligently with the situation. Women had truly gone berserk." And now came the lost woman, plagued by a "bundle of anxieties" all of which were grotesquely heightened in the unwed woman. "If she hasn't a husband and is seeking one she is fully aware that others of her kind have the same primal purpose. . . . She cannot help but observe [women] scattered about profusely . . . stenographers, secretaries, hat-check girls, models, fashion designers or female riveters . . . they are no longer secluded, hidden away, but out hunting, as it were, in packs."

These edicts had to be viewed in their proper Freudian context. As explained in numerous books but most forcefully in Modern Woman, all women had a biological and social imperative to mate, then to reproduce. Throughout her life, in other words, a woman was really no more than half of a human unit, who alone could not evolve and maintain her own superego. As a "half," she would not ever be able to make up her own mind—a primary trait of many fifties TV heroines. And never would she possess a fully formed conscience. Only a man could provide the already unsteady, unmoored modern woman with moral balance.

Of course women did not walk through life upset because their "primordial rhythms" had "broken," nor did they believe—not really—that

they inherently lacked some essential mental component. But many be-
leaguered single women believed they now had not only a personal but a
societal obligation to find a man. This led to an epic outburst of tension—
at least as it was reported in magazines—and especially between friends
who had come to share the same (nagging, anxious) suspicion: Wasn't
every woman a potential "other"?

Many books appeared to help her in battle—"finding," "attacking,"
"getting," "securing," "safeguarding." Reading about single life circa 1948
is like browsing through a collection of busy war strategies that alternate
with wordy, scolding conduct guides. A great example of the latter genre is
Anything but Love by Elizabeth Hawes (1948), a thick book that was to
serve as "a complete digest of the rules for feminine behavior from birth to
death, given out here in print, but also put forth by the author . . . over the
air . . . in popular magazines and on film . . . [advice] seen and listened to
monthly by some 340,000,000 American women."

A few of her dictates, all eerily reminiscent of the nineteenth century:

All girls want to be whistle-worthy, and that raises what is . . . the
biggest worry in your life: Does he see you as pretty? . . . One of the
miracles which mass production has wrought is that every single
American girl can be seen as pretty. Our ugly ducklings can be
turned into beautiful swans.

The main purpose of girls getting jobs is to meet men they may
subsequently marry. A girl may continue to hold a job and earn
her living in whole or part to age 23. Thereafter, only if she has
become a successful star of stage and screen.

Occasionally something appeared that addressed single female life as
pitiable, it went without saying, but manageable for a reasonable amount
of time. Jean Van Ever, in 1949, published *How to Be Happy While Single*,
a practical guide to living life alone before marriage. As she wrote: "Meal
planning, marketing, vacuuming, and the wear and tear of housekeeping . . . these skills are worth the struggle to master, so, while you have the

chance, practice up. Even if you have a job and you are tired at the end of the day. Practice."

But increasingly the "authorities"—and they were everywhere—didn't bother with the particulars of single life (the hunt, the frustration, the outfit changes). They cut to the point and the point was to marry. To reproduce. And, of course, to consume. In 1947 the Daughters of the American Revolution released a statement that echoed those issued by far less conservative organizations: "The social order must now reassert itself. That is our job. That is our purpose. Those who follow their own paths, no matter how worthy, those who do not participate in the reconstruction of the society, to marry, to bear American children, must be labeled 'Selfish.' "

In 1948 the U.S. Women's Bureau held a conference to celebrate the one hundredth anniversary of the Seneca Falls women's rights convention, calling it "The American Woman, Her Changing Role: Worker, Homemaker, Citizen." The keynote speaker was Harry Truman, who changed the order of the roles in the title; "homemaker" went first and "worker" last. It had been psychological doctrine. Now it was an executive order.

THE AGE OF ANXIETY

Despite the at times surreal amount of cheerleading for marriage, for home and "womanhood," the divorce rate was actually rising.

It had become much easier to accurately count the number of divorces nationwide. Before the era of Social Security numbers, driver's licenses, and primitive computerized records, the actual number of failed marriages remained hazy. A 1995 edition of the *Monthly Vital Statistics Report* explained that after the war—well beyond the initial 1946 surge—there was a steady rise in the divorce rate. Ultimately, between 1946 and 1950, the number of divorces and annulments would total 4,020,000.

Magazines, newspapers, dime novels, even newsreels were quick to jump on the rising divorce story. One anonymous woman interviewed for *Harper's Bazaar* in 1946 wrote, "It seems like everyone is getting divorced and, yes, that does scare a lot of women, including me on occasion . . . [but]

I think what it comes down to is keeping up an interest in all areas of your marriage. Even if you are dishwater tired."

But if a woman happened to be dishwater tired, how was she to recognize what the *Reader's Digest* called "separation signs"? And what was she to make of the sudden presence of so many obvious divorcées?

Suddenly, in good communities, in any community across America, there were newly divorced women seen committing basic acts of daily life—smoking, retrieving the newspaper or mail, putting out trash, shopping, chasing kids. Divorcées had always seemed a little tarnished and sad, but in a certifiable man crisis they took on new characteristics. They were now directly threatening. Sexual. (As the divorce rate began its brief but dramatic decline during the monogamous fifties, the divorcée portrait— floozy blonde; blinds down at 2 P.M.—would become more of a gross sexual parody.)

Alice Hoffman gives a superb recounting of divorcée paranoia in *Seventh Heaven*, a novel set in the early 1960s on suburban Long Island. At the start we meet several housewives attempting to place a new neighbor. Finally, after much speculation, they come to what must be "the only explanation," even though none can "bring themselves to say the word divorced out loud. . . . [But] the word was there, it had entered their vocabularies and now hung above them, a cloud over their coffee cups . . . they were all so completely married, and they were in it together. . . . And yet there it was, across the street, a hand without a ring holding a Windex bottle."

The married women swing into defensive action, and "by the end of October, every mother of every child . . . knew that Nora was divorced. . . . Billy [her son] was never invited over to anyone's house after school . . . she herself hadn't been told about the monthly PTA meetings. No one mentioned the Columbus Day Bake Sale."

Hearing about it, Nora stays up all night making a cake, a handcrafted candy-dotted castle, pink and voluptuous, a real Jayne Mansfield of a cake. No one goes near it.

In 1949 one society matron confessed to the *New York Times*, "I do not invite unattached women because it seems to me—I don't like to say this—but you know, Perry and I are so happy and these unattached women just envy the beautiful happiness we have. . . . They sit there, it doesn't matter where you put them. . . . they are so sad and distracted, that they have nothing of this. Frankly, it bothers me to be surrounded by such hungry devouring eyes."

And occasionally we witnessed the angry single sniper in action. In *A Letter to Three Wives* (1949), morbid suspicion of the other, experienced woman animates the entire film.

The story is this: Three wives each receive a letter from the town vamp, socialite Addie Ross. The letters inform them that Addie has stolen one of their husbands and plans to leave town with him that very day; one of them, in other words, is in for a nasty surprise at dinner. We never meet Addie; she speaks off camera in an alluring faraway voice, the siren song of the willowy bitch. The three women spend the day together, each dropping off into long spells of contemplation. How has her marriage, and how has she, been disappointing? The mood is thick with apprehension, ill ease, and finally paranoia until the moment we *know*. As it turns out, they all are safe. One husband had planned to leave with Addie but changed his mind. All is well and Addie and her giggly voice recede, though it's clear she's had a wonderful time torturing these three to the very core of their feminine souls.

Still, women were interested in reading and watching films about women in situations other than domestic panic. Some of the period's most popular films concern women who had jobs, and not only the Mildred Pierce psycho-careerists who haunted "women's films." Claudette Colbert played a haughty novelist in *Without Reservations*; Ginger Rogers played a tough editor in *Lady in the Dark*; in *Laura* Gene Tierney was a graphic designer, and Rosalind Russell in *Take a Letter Darling* had a male secretary (who eventually accused her of anti-womanhood as if it counted as an un-American activity). Most delightful was Bette Davis in *June Bride*, playing a top magazine queen who's got a bum but loveable writer fiancé in her past. During the course of one horrific wedding shoot, she's tossed back together with him and, ultimately, has to choose: power, top job perks, great apartment, or a loving if irresponsible man from the past.

They surrender, all, but with seconds to go before the closing credits, a holdout that is less a suspense tactic than a means for allowing female viewers two full hours of screen time to watch funny, smart-ass women brilliantly run the show. (A similar device operates in some of the era's most popular radio soap operas, for example, *Portia Faces Life* and *The Romance of Helen Trent,* each primarily about love relationships, the stuff of female life, but as experienced by, respectively, a lawyer and a Hollywood designer.)

This same kind of "holdout" was at the core of the bobby-soxer phenomenon. There were other elements, of course, namely, advertisers thrilled to have unearthed an independent peer group (pubescent girls) that ran a slice of underground economy (baby-sitting). Bobby-soxing further gave to Shirley Temple a mature but still cute persona to inhabit before retiring. But most important, to be a late-forties bobby-soxer was to be a young woman between girl and wife. Soon enough she'd emerge from the protective cocoon of rumpled jeans, saddle shoes, and daddy's shirts. Soon she'd begin her husband hunt in earnest. But just for the moment she was off the market.

Once-upon-a-time single women might have urged her to stay there, or at least not to rush.

In 1949 the *New York Times* interviewed female members of the college class of 1934 to see how their lives had played out during the Depression and World War II. Of the entire class, 82 percent were still married and only 12 percent worked "outside the home . . . the predominant experience of the class of 1934 was as housewife." We also learn that almost 90 percent had children, and that as of 1949 many of these kids were not yet in school. The story moves along to its point: "A strong note of betrayal runs through . . . the study. These women entered public life in a flush of post-suffrage optimism. They belonged to a generation of women which stressed and exalted in the importance of jobs for women." Real jobs. Not the kinds of jobs they ultimately found going through the "Jobs-Female" section of the classifieds. Some of them "understood the employment realities." Others were bitter, like the interviewee who concluded that her life had been worsened by having to work in a "lesser position."

But it would be far worse—and there was a consensus among the women interviewed—to go through life singly. To be single was to "experience the feeling of contamination," as one expert put it in *Ladies' Home Journal,* or as *Time* somewhat awkwardly described the single state in 1950: "pin-stuck with a cramp of isolation."

Of course there is a women's film that deals specifically with issues of singular contamination and isolation. It's called, appropriately, *Autumn Leaves* (1956), and stars Joan Crawford, as a spinster who marries a man she does not really know in order to improve a life spent inside her L.A. bungalow, where she types manuscripts with maniacal speed and efficiency. As it turns out, her husband, a younger man, is plainly maniacal—a kleptomaniac, a pathological liar, prone to crying and "shrieking like a woman," until Joan has no choice but to "put him away." At the home, he receives electroshock treatment, a procedure usually associated with snarly, uncooperative women. Joan, soon after, receives a jolt of her own. Seated on the edge of a straight-backed chair, hands mangling her purse, she confronts the psychiatrist, the authority figure who had replaced the preacher as the man who brings the bad news.

The diagnosis: As a late-marrying spinster, she does not represent to her husband an actual wife. Rather, she represents "neurotic need." If she had children or seemed at all a sexual creature, she might have been a mother figure; as it is she is more of an "aunt." It is clear that he will have to leave her because she is, in her tainted spinsterish way, as sick as he is. Still, there is some twisted hope for them both. The wounded man and his neurotic need walk together across the hospital grounds. He pauses at a point to examine her hand, which is bandaged. Once, before his commitment, as she lay sobbing on the ground, he dropped the typewriter onto her wrist, making it impossible for her to earn a living. In so doing, he had graphically demonstrated his desire to be a man. A starting point.

Anyway, at least, they were married. And nothing would have more social significance in the 1950s.

Sociologist David Reisman, author of *The Lonely Crowd* (1950), once remarked that in the nineteenth century the failure to marry was considered a "social disadvantage and sometimes a personal tragedy." In the 1950s, however, it would become "a quasi-perversion."

CHAPTER FIVE

THE SECRET SINGLE: RUNAWAY BACHELOR GIRLS; CATCHING THE BLEECKER STREET BEAT AND/OR BLUES AT THE BARBIZON

It may be said that she has learned by the use of her independence to surrender it without a struggle or murmur when the time comes for making the sacrifice.

—ALEXIS DE TOCQUEVILLE, ON AMERICAN WOMEN, 1838

The Single Career woman . . . that great mistake that feminism propagated may find satisfaction in her job. But the chances are that she will suffer psychological damage. Should she marry and reproduce her husband and children will be profoundly unhappy.

—LIFE MAGAZINE, SPECIAL REPORT ON WOMEN, 1956

Girl gets off bus in Port Authority Terminal, goes into Bickford's, Chinese girl, red shoes, sits down with coffee, looking for Daddy. Life. Something.

—JACK KEROUAC, "A BEAT TOUR OF NEW YORK," HOLIDAY MAGAZINE, 1959

I DO, I DO, I HAVE TO

I had a friend for a while when I was single who, between day jobs, worked as a performance artist. According to her self-produced catalogue notes, her art consisted of, or was "located" in, the re-creation of "aesthetic epochs," as they were "parsed out in the locution, Decades." That meant she continually redid her apartment according to themes such as "1922" and "1890." The 1950s, however, represented her greatest triumph—a live-action *tableau vivant* starring a single girl, living alone in a single-girl apartment that is outfitted with the perquisites, the furniture and clothing, of married life.

"Jill," as she was known within the installation, asked all visitors to leave their shoes at the door, directing them to period shoe racks that held all manner of appropriate footwear: bowling shoes, saddle shoes, impossible pumps, sensible shoes to look good beneath a gray flannel suit. If there were no shoes that fit, visitors walked in socks among the various pieces: the blond-wood Scandinavian couches and modular chairs, and the coffee tables—low and slatted or biomorphic—each stacked with amoebic ashtrays, old issues of *Life* and *Look*. A dwarfing hi-fi cabinet opened onto a tiny TV screen and turntable. The space was small, and because she'd made a breakfast nook and a sewing room and because there were filmy stockings everywhere on lines "drying," visitors selected decorative pillows and hit the floor.

During the run of this "show," Jill appeared in lima bean–green midriffs with striped pedal pushers. Or she'd whip open a door wearing mock Dior New Look tea dresses, squealing "hel—loow," Annette Funicello trying on a mid-Atlantic accent. Most all of this annoyed her boyfriend, Jim, a writer who lived in the space with Jill, whose name, he liked to remind people, was really Ann. Jill would French-inhale her cigarette and squeeze his arm sympathetically. She understood. Here was a man who every day for months had been asked to impersonate a "beat poet, struggling," when all he wanted to do was write or drink his coffee. But it was hard even for Jim to deny that life inside this made-up 1950s could be absurd and amusing. Jill served pancakes, fondue, and highballs all at once. And we all played a game she called Do the Dot. This required participants to gather around the ancient TV and stare expectantly at the tiny screen. Slowly the tiny white spot, the old TV warmup dot we'd all forgotten, would materialize at the center. It glowed there a minute, then expanded into a mess of bad reception. Everyone screamed for an encore and Jill would turn the TV on and off and then again—on and off—until she'd start to maniacally laugh and sometimes pretend to faint.

She'd get up, go on to the next activity, but the point, I always thought, had been made: Had she been a real fifties single, a bachelorette, alone, with all the perquisities of married life but no marriage, she might have gone crazy.

Simply stated, marriage in the 1950s was the absolute norm. In 1953, *Look* magazine rhapsodized: "Not since the age of Victoria has the idea of the happy home compelled such overt sentiment and general admiration . . . advertisements with their happy parents and rosy children in a setting of creature comforts and domestic bliss, the magazine covers with their warm scenes of family life . . . testify to the expectations with which men and women enter the blessed state."

Young women earned great praise for their compliance with the prerequisites and demands of this blessed state. Especially considering—and everyone had to concede the point—that some had once led different lives, lived at least a little bit like "Jill." As a 1952 *Good Housekeeping* guide to marital relations put it, "Having worked before marriage, or at least having been educated for some kind of intellectual work [the woman] finds herself in the lamentable position of being 'just a housewife.' . . . In her disgruntlement, she can work as much damage on the lives of her husband and children and her own life—as if she were a career woman and, indeed, sometimes more!"

But as it was expressed in almost every publication, public-service announcement, newsreel, and classroom lecture, a Female Miracle had occurred, resulting in the birth of a new "unique femininity." In reaction to the postwar man shortage, or to the pop–Freudian imperatives to "adjust," many women had abandoned their drive to work in the world of men. *Look* editors, as if celebrating a new-model car, wrote: "Forget the big career . . .

now she gracefully concedes the top jobs to men. The wondrous creature also marries younger than ever, bears more babies and looks and acts more feminine than the emancipated girl of the 20s and 30s . . . if she makes an old-fashioned choice and lovingly tends a garden and a bumper crop of children, she rates more loud Hosannas than ever before."

Single life more than ever stood out as a social aberration, what an old family friend of mine calls "living polio. Not married, you were in the iron lung. Paralyzed." And there was resolutely no excuse for it. One 1954 home-economics textbook spoke out harshly. "Except for the sick, the badly crippled, the deformed, the emotionally warped and mentally defective, almost every girl has an opportunity to marry." A popular female advice columnist seemed to feel even more strongly. "Every American girl must acquire for herself a husband and a home and children . . . any program for life in which the home is not the center of her living, is worse than death."

Occasionally, a writer broke ranks and published a story with a title like "There's No Right Time for a Girl to Marry" (the New York Times, 1952). But these were anomalies and served most often as dartboards for more conservative writers and for the corporate heads who felt moved now and then to speak out about the necessary place of the American female in the home. (The manufacture and sale of furnishings and cars had become huge business, and between 1950 and 1958 sales of major appliances alone would rise by 240 percent.)

It all sounds a bit crazy, I have to say, almost science-fictional. But the rhetoric is backed up by numbers. By 1951, almost 60 percent of all American women were married—one in three of them having wed by age nineteen. By 1957, 14 million girls were engaged at age seventeen and many more were married by age twenty, and most of them were mothers at twenty-one. In 1958, 97 out of every 1,000 girls between the ages of fifteen and nineteen gave birth. Betty Friedan would later estimate that the U.S. birthrate in the mid-1950s had come close to overtaking India's.

I interviewed one woman, a pediatrician, married at twenty in 1956, divorced in 1968 with four kids. She laughed, then deeply sighed as she recalled "the marriage-attack-from-Mars years."

If I tried honestly to describe it, I'm not sure my own four girls would believe it. One example, in high school, if you did not have a date for a Saturday night, that meant you stayed in, hiding out, and swearing your younger siblings to silence. And I mean you were HIDING. In your room, with the lights off, in the event a boy you knew passed in a car and saw your light on. That meant they would KNOW you were in without a date. . . . College years, it was all right to date around for a year or so . . . [but] if you weren't set by junior year, *and* there was another group of new freshmen coming, oh, that meant your life was slipping away. . . .Land[ing] a guy seemed like the only possible way you were going to survive economically . . .

It is hard to read a magazine or watch a movie from that time and imagine any woman living in peace by herself. Everyone in the culture seemed programmed to harangue her. The *Saturday Evening Post* warned in 1952, "It's harder than ever to snare a husband!" Unless, of course, one made sacrifices, for example, abandoning school. The writer, Rufus Jarman, speculated that the dreaded war brides, all 113,000 of them, had moved in on American women because too many of "these American dynamos had those three letters of doom—Ph.D., doctor—in front of their names." To the GIs, the American single had shown "superior airs" and no instinctive gifts for housekeeping. But now, he noted, "most girls who are doing post-graduate work for various high-flown careers would drop their studies and get married in a minute if the right man came along."

Some limited exceptions were made for artistic types—dancers, ac-tresses, fashion designers—and it further helped if one resembled Lauren Bacall or Audrey Hepburn. Later in the decade, exemptions passed to younger celebrities who had a tough kind of girl/boy quality—Shirley MacLaine (married, though her husband lived full-time in Japan) and Françoise Sagan, who, at twenty-one, had published a wild unapologetic mistressy novel called *Bonjour Tristesse*. Françoise instantly became an ob-ject of fascination to men and women both, who loved her short hair and red sports car and her way with a cigarette. Then, of course, she was

French, barely spoke English, and the French, as one commentator wrote, were born "astray."

But even here, in provincial married America, all sorts of girls went astray. Even if they did so very briefly.

DOWN THE UP STAIRCASE

The roots of the 1950s marriage mania reached back into the postwar culture: the GI Bill, which made low-income housing and other benefits available to veterans who married; the restrictions these same GI privileges imposed on women (fewer college openings; fewer jobs), and then all that pseudo-Freudian dogma demanding that real women seek out their male halves. But there were thousands who, setting aside domestic destiny, graduated or just left home with something else in mind besides a wedding. Stashing their marriage prospects into imaginary safety deposit boxes, middle-class girls traveled to Europe. Traces of these temporary runaways can be found in fifties films such as *An American in Paris*, *Three Coins in the Fountain*, *Funny Face*, *Marjorie Morningstar*, in some of the Gidget movies, and, most memorably, in *Breathless*, in the form of Jean Seberg's morally ambiguous girl/boy reporter.

Others left home for New York and jobs in theater, dance, publishing, or just to cut themselves off from suffocating fiancés, dull jobs, or like Holly Golightly in Truman Capote's novella, *Breakfast at Tiffany's*, lives so desperate and dreary one can only guess at the details.

Starting in about 1953, at the height of "togetherness"*—a magazine-inspired concept advocating the total centrality of nuclear-family life—there seemed to be a rise in the number of single young women settling in

---

*"Togetherness" grew from the work of famed sociologist Talcott Parsons who, along with other academics, wrote long tracts on "modern personality" as it related to the structure of families. As that translated, the modern family unit had to shed the old-fashioned day-to-day contact with the extended family. "No home is big enough for two families," Parsons wrote. "Particularly of two different generations, with opposite theories on child training." As one magazine put it in 1954, "The modern family, as a singular unit, pools brains, looks, activities and thinks like an army platoon and competes against other platoons in the neighborhood." Single women, through with school, momentarily adrift in life, were sometimes invited back to stay a while with the platoon. But like traditional spinsters, they were often given specific tasks to carry out in exchange for board.

New York City. The intensity with which reporters tracked this alleged rise, interviewing employment agents, Realtors, or clerks at all-girl hotels, demonstrates how terrorizing the single female was as mere concept.

"It was still such a radical notion," says one my subjects, Simone, now sixty-six.

> In fact, to get away was like testifying before a miniature version of the HUAC committee: Were we now and had we ever been inclined to hurt ourselves by deliberately ruining ourselves? . . . Leaving home was supposed to be very, very dangerous. . . . But we were girls who were not ready for the Donna Reed life. Poor Donna Reed! Even she wasn't Donna Reed! She was an Oscar winner! . . . At home, everyone, in that J. D. Salinger sense, was required to put up a false phony self and it just got so tiring. . . . So you confronted your parents, and they acted as if you'd just announced you'd become a Communist or a Nazi *and* a slut. But your bags were packed. Like a spy, you had the details worked out in advance. Now, you had to hold your ground under interrogation.

Many editors, professors, and psychiatric professionals fixated on this "lone female" escapee, studying her like a lab animal who'd been wired to do one thing and was now atypically doing something else. In the press there was the formal bow, or military salute, made to the good-sport all-American wife out in the 'burbs. But the real fascination was with these city types—the astonishing 34 percent who, by 1954, had made it to age twenty-four without marrying. She or "it" was debated, as an entity, in every publication from the *Reader's Digest* to the *Atlantic Monthly*. Sometimes she appeared as a caricature—a dazed-looking girl, hitchhiking, a bridal gown in one hand and a suitcase in the other (no one picks her up), or a young woman watering plants on a sooty fire escape juxtaposed with a woman, in sun hat, cutting flowers in a large country garden. Humorists created bestiaries of lone-girl types, for example, the "Can't-Help-It-Drabbie," "The Mammary-Deprived," "The Marginal Wallflower," the "Office Matron," "the Premature Auntie Griselda," "the Thespian Manqué."

The *Kinsey Report on Female Sexuality*, published in 1953, shocked readers as much as had the original male report several years before—and seems to have fed fears about these amorphous but threatening gangs of female strays. (One of Kinsey's troubling statistics: More than half of all college-educated women, plus 20 percent of noncollege girls, had engaged in at least one same-sex erotic experience. If that was true, what was likely to occur in "pervert's-ville" New York City?) Post-Kinsey, the language used to urge girls back into domesticity, into marriage (as if all that many had actually left!) turned apocalyptic.

For a while, in 1954 and '55, writers bypassed the gray and rainy adjectives common to sad-spinster stories and rushed on toward the nuclear arsenal: "Atomic Red Alert for Romance!" "From Here to Oblivion—Marry Now or Marry Never!" "Snag Your Space of Shelter, Girls, Before You're Crowded Out!"

Despite a birthrate like a third world country's—and despite the fact that more eighteen-year-old girls got married some years than went to the prom—the perception spread that Young White Single Females had to be reined in. In the form of the helpful how-to "service" story, magazines revived one of the world's older single propositions: to move single women in herds from dry areas (Washington, D.C., ranked worst overall; New York and Boston ran close seconds) to places where men were plentiful. In pieces that included maps, arrows, and literal directions, editors set out to pinpoint where on earth men were most heavily clustered.

Call it, after the movie, the song, the theory in general: *Where the Boys Are*.

According to the Census Bureau, UPI reported, women outnumbered men in every section of the country except in the wild "western" areas. Thus one typical newspaper headline read, "Go West Young Woman, if You Want to Wed!" The text continued, "Droves of bachelors are on the great open range begging to be roped and branded . . . in Wyoming and Nevada there are seven unmarried men for three single women . . . for the girl willing to migrate for marriage, the best trails lead west."

In "Memo to the Girls," *Look* undertook "a massive man-hunt missive," noting, "there is a surplus of bachelors . . . but husband hunters should know where to look." The winning locales were the same as those cited elsewhere, as if a consortium of media and governmental bureaus had conspired in a campaign to reinaugurate the mail-order bride.

Life editors found two bachelor girls who'd moved themselves to Caspar, Wyoming, then had them, for the benefit of the photographers, throw an impromptu bachelor-girl party. Panel by panel, we follow the action: The girls make last-minute "on-the-spot" calls to boys. The girls prepare the beverages and then, the triumphal sequence, "the boys respond to the call." Twelve men, big hefty guys, thirtyish and single, have all crowded into their living room. The caption read: "They bagged twelve!" But "bagging" out in Caspar didn't require throwing a "do." We also see the "lucky" Barbara Mills receive a "quadruple escort" just by walking through the business district. It was noted that had she lived in Montana, the number of escorts might have been up around nine.

GETTING THE GIRL BACK IN LINE

As in the nineteenth century, the plans for mass removal of single women to isolated areas did not catch on. Young women continued to move to New York and to Washington, and others—older women, especially—continued to express their concern. In 1956 *Mademoiselle* published a remarkably progressive piece, "What's Wrong with Ambition?" intended to highlight the views of young women who'd gone off on their own and were loving it. But the most shocking, radical aspect of the "Ambition" story was the response it provoked—both in letters and in stories published in other magazines.

"They make me nervous," said one married woman of girls cut loose in major cities. "I could shoot the first woman who went to work in a man's job. My ambition is to please my husband in every womanly way." Another outraged wife said, "These girls come back from a day in the outside world with something to talk about and what is that? Men. She's been out all day with men. Other women's husbands. . . . [she] is a threat to every self and

family-centered homebody." Another said that she'd "be content to liqui-
date [this] army of competitors who have forgotten the true functions, duties and gracious giving pleasures of the mature woman—creating for
others, not for herself. There is something unnatural and frightening in
this behaviour. . . . It is against order and I really think humanity."

Training young women to capture husbands now underwent a vast
CinemaScopic fifties-era renaissance.

In 1955 alone there were more than three hundred promarriage, antisingular tomes. From one foreword : "It would seem that some have come
to view marriage in its current state as . . . disappointing for women, and
especially those who have taken the higher degree." As if it was 1910, the
author concluded: "The lure of the city and its many pleasures will make
of many potentially fine and worthy wives unnatural defeated spinsters . . .
sick and lonely women."

As always, commentators dragged the discussion back to education
and the eternal topic—"what should we teach our women?" One home-
economics professor from a college in Virginia wrote in the *Reader's Digest*: "Unless there is a direct application to the home, or the conflicts
and issues that will confront her in the home, in [dealing with] her husband or children, it is not valid education; it is unfair to the girl and
confusing."

One 1956 home-ec textbook provided a quick-study list of thirty-five
tasks to perform before a husband returned from "his labors." Here's a small
sampling of what the fifties singles studied:

1. Have dinner ready: Plan ahead, even the night before, to have
a delicious meal—on time. This is a way of letting him know that
you have been thinking about him and are concerned about his
needs. Most are men are hungry when they come home!

2. Minimize the noise: At the time of his arrival, eliminate all noise
of washer, dryer, dishwasher or vacuum. Try to encourage the children to be quiet. Have them properly dressed to give their greetings.

3. Make him comfortable. Have him lean back in a comfortable chair or suggest he lie down in the bedroom. Have a cool or warm drink ready for him. Arrange his pillow . . . speak in a low, soothing and pleasant voice.

Whatever her interests, the single girl picked up a magazine, went to the movies—got into a conversation with just about anyone—and heard about what single girls had heard about since 1860: how to catch a man and make him stay. For example, a February 1952 issue of *Ladies' Home Journal* provided a "quick inventory for bachelor girls": "What about your . . . hair, complexion, clothes? Are you a good talker, dancer, listener? Do you have a sense of humor? Hobby? Outside interests? . . . If anything is lacking you must go to the hairdresser, psychiatrist, whatever is needed. Only then are you prepared to face the world."

These articles and books prescribed ways to achieve a kind of robotic period perfection, "a rigorous ideal that is . . . to be desired by any woman who cares about her future." But in fact the physical attributes of 1950s "perfection" were intensely difficult to attain. The dictates of the female ideal were repeated and reprinted as if they were a paper doll's mantra: "I am 5 feet 4 inches tall, 122 pounds, with brown hair, blue eyes, a 25½-inch waist, 34-inch bust, and 36-inch hips." Famed anthropologist and frequent commentator Margaret Mead found it startling—and not necessarily "good"—that the average 1956 girl was fifteen pounds lighter than her counterpart thirty years before.

New products appeared to assist in her transformation, most dramatically, hair dye that one could use safely at home without burning the scalp or turning hair purple (both incidents documented in a 1922 diary). Shirley Polykoff, a female advertising executive who, along with Estée Lauder and PR magnate Eleanor Lambert, were the professional "exceptions" to every rule, brought hair dye into the average bathroom or, for many single girls, into the kitchen sink. Her idea was to convince women that by changing their hair color they could change themselves. Wives would become more interesting to their husbands. Single women, suddenly more assertive *and* more feminine, would attract more men. As one promotional piece explained this proposed alchemy:

> By changing the color and hue of your hair, you can change your entire way of being. It frees you to behave and act in ways you would never have dreamed possible when you were your former self. . . . And you can do it in secret. People will notice you and think, "She seems different." "And her hair!" "How did she get it to look so lovely?" "Is it a wig?" "Is it dyed?"

Paraphrasing a question her mother-in-law once asked in Yiddish, Polykoff put forth her own query: "Does she or doesn't she?"

Playboy magazine, then in its mysogynistic glory days, was quick to point out that hair color didn't matter, not for a wife of all people, and certainly not for that inherently slutty single girl. In the "Playboy Coloring Book," a popular monthly feature, the reader was presented with three single chicks he might place inside his make-believe bachelor pad.

The only instructions: "Make one blond. Make one a brunette. And make one a redhead. It doesn't matter which." In the *Playboy* schematic, what mattered was mammary glands—bosoms, bazooms, jugs; only class-A breasts could really alter the average woman. Although, even then, she'd be a joke. One popular *Playboy* cartoon at that time was, in fact, called *The Bosom*. Here was the story of a woman who measured 43-22-36. In each issue, the Bosom tried, despite mighty gravitational pull, to walk down the street.

Because so many people thought and often talked about blondness and breasts, even the most highly educated single found herself forced to consider the merits of Clairol and falsies or, more bluntly put, peroxide and "stuffing." And she confronted an onslaught of beauty advertising—campaigns and strategies way beyond hair dye—that would have made a devoted flapper faint. In its 1956 issue on the American Woman, *Life* took great glee in itemizing the tricks and tools of the chase. That year alone American women had spent $1.3 billion on cosmetics and toiletries, $660 million on beauty treatments; $400 million on soap and electric grooming devices; $65 million on "reducing." And that leaves out of the calculations all the clothes that were purchased to allure what *Playboy* called "the female's permanent cash box. The hapless soon-to-be-broke American male."

If some single women were repelled by this competition, others were matter-of-fact. Wrote one woman in the *Life* extravaganza: "If the race is to continue, we like to provide a second parent. So we go about the serious business of finding husbands in a serious manner, which allows no time for small luxuries like mercy toward competitors. Nature turns red in tooth and claw, every method is fair and rivals get no quarter."

To say the least, this materialistic—and carnivorous—vision of the single world was disturbing. Columnist Anita Colby, a single working woman herself, wrote in 1956, "Emotionally we single women are at the greatest disadvantage of all women . . . we face a frightening world by ourselves. . . . Our enemies are loneliness and insecurity. Anxiety is a familiar houseguest." But she had some encouragement to add. "Don't go around feeling unfulfilled, jealous of your married friends, looking at every man you meet as 'game.' . . . You have a life of your own."

As early as 1957, there were 11.5 million single women over eighteen in the United States, compared with 14.5 million single males. Not all of them were updated Eve Ardens—self-deprecating, not quite beautiful, resigned to it—nor were they pathetic Miss Lonelyhearts, the name, in fact, of a character in the 1954 Hitchcock film *Rear Window*. In this, a bored wheelchair-bound photographer casually watches, and names, his neighbors, following a whole courtyard of minidramas and intrigue, including of course one nasty murder. Miss Lonelyhearts, in a subplot of a subplot, is a single woman who appears in a lone window frame, pacing in boredom. At one point she pretends to throw a dinner party for two when she is all by herself. Another time she brings home a man who attacks her. She breaks down. She takes too many pills. But the average young woman, if she lived alone, was not necessarily "playing dinner" or playing with bottles of miltown.

She was happily "astray." Or at least surviving nicely. And she wrote home to say as much on expensive stationery that had on it the word "Miss." One 1957 *Science Digest* survey of 6,750 single women, age twenty-five to fifty, reported, "We now seem to be in a nation with a certain group of females who do not look forward to getting married. . . . they keenly desire other experiences outside the normative marital pattern. They may not always understand why they feel as they seem to. Yet they nonetheless do."

From another report, written at the University of Michigan: "Whatever secrets they're not telling . . . we can now safely say that for certain of these girls, the search for a mate may take an entirely unpredictable path. They are waiting. Even if this, from any reasoned point of view, allows their options to give way."

One popular holding pattern was to take up residency inside a parent-approved, high-rise nunnery. The YWCA offered small rooms for rent, these regarded as a bit déclassé, and even less glamorous were the bare-bones old-style boardinghouses. Most nervous first-time émigrés fantasized about the exclusive all-girls hotels on Manhattan's Upper East Side, specifically the Barbizon, a serene Italianate landmark on Sixty-third Street that was to rooming houses what Smith and Wellesley were to colleges. As the familiar ads read, "Some of the world's most successful women"—and that included Grace Kelly and Gene Tierney—"have been Barbizon Girls."

The copywriters left out an essential word: briefly.

A nineteen-year-old resident explained to one of the many afternoon papers, for one of the many "Barbizon Life" stories: "It is the place where you go when you leave something—college; your immediate family; your old life. And for that it's perfect—as long as *you don't stay too long*." (The oldest resident, usually juxtaposed in photos with a young freckled preppy type, was in her eighties. She was famous for playing the house pipe organ at the afternoon teas.)

In 1958 Gael Greene, then of the *New York Post*, wrote an extensive ten-part series devoted to her twenty-three-year-old life at the Barbizon, attempting to do for the high-rise residence hotels what Dorothy Richardson had done for shabby lodging quarters fifty years earlier. Like so many other recent graduates, Greene had come to the city "seeking something indefinable—something to do. A rent-paying job, romance, the alchemy that will transform an ordinary girl into an extraordinary woman."

What she found at her first destination, the glamorous Barbizon, was an overheated planet of lonely women, spinning in an orbit that paralleled that of the city but did not overlap. As she wrote,

> . . . *a phone that does not ring. Tears of Homesickness. Gentle smiles of resignation* . . . these are the marks—worn bravely and bravely concealed—by girls and young women alone. There are thousands in every corner of every city. They have no one habitat. Many live in cells—at the "exclusive Barbizon Hotel for Women," at the Salvation Army's Evangeline House, at the YWCA. I have lived among them. Each cell is an island. Each island is surrounded by depths of fear:
> Fear of Failure
> Fear of Spinsterhood
> Fear of Sexual assault in a Subway station
> And those unknown, inexplicable fears that dull the complexion and glaze the eye.

The day Greene arrives, one floor mate warns, "It's not easy to make friends. Don't think you're going to meet just hundreds of boys or that you'll meet the One."

She doesn't. She doesn't really meet anyone, except Oscar the famous doorman, who gets her name wrong. She goes out for lone walks and contents herself with small gestures such as buying and polishing an improbably shiny red apple. She sits on her bed and brushes her hair or writes a letter. Her actions are in some form repeated in every small room around her, except in those where a drunken girl is crying or smashing glass objects. To escape the sound (they've learned from experience that going in results in one-sided four-hour conversations), residents leave the floor and wander off to do what Barbizon girls do when they haven't scored a date on a Saturday night. They sit in a room filled with young women wearing nightgowns and watch television. Sometimes, after stations have gone off the air, Barbizon girls, Gael Greene among them, watch the network's test pattern.

PLAYING IT SINGLE

On television during the mid- to late 1950s, single women showed up in the familiar guises. They were older widows saddened or made sarcastic by life; busybody aunts, maids, older sisters, teachers, or mistress-of-ceremonies types who sang and introduced guests or "gave testimonials," meaning they held and caressed the sponsor's product and spoke about it for up to a full five minutes. On commercials, single women were either invisible or ethereal, creatures disconnected from physical life. They never appeared in their apartments or houses or in their offices. We never saw their front steps, their kitchens, their cats. They were pictured only in fantasy scenarios—standing next to Chevrolets and gesturing, waving from magically flying Chevrolets, and dressed most often in evening gowns. The single woman had no place in a domestic scheme, unless she was a spinsterly grandmother or one of those ascendant female consumers, the teenager.

The single woman in 1950s television lived on the sitcom. Here, she almost always played a grown woman who behaved like a perky superannuated teenager. She lived at home, usually with a widowed parent, held a clerical job, and either matchmade crazily for everyone in the cast or became the subject of matchmaking by everyone in the cast. Consider three prime-time examples:

- *My Little Margie*. A precursor to Gidget, minus the surfing element and smirky cuteness. Margie, played by Gale Storm, whose name promised something slightly more dramatic, lives with her widowed father; although she is supposed to be twenty-one, she seems at times to be about twenty-seven and at others thirty-five. The plotlines can be reduced to two conflicts. First, Daddy can't control his overgrown baby as much as he'd like, and, second, Margie can't control Daddy. She doesn't like his girlfriends and often tries deliberately to spoil his dates. Gidget with a Freudian undertow.

- *Private Secretary.* Here we meet single girl Susie McNamera, the top secretary to important talent agent Peter Sands. Naturally, Susie is in love with Peter but not fully aware of it as she organizes every facet of his existence, including the arrangement of his paper clips and assessing the merits, so sadly few, of his dates. Eventually, she realizes that *she* wants to marry Peter and plots with the receptionist to change her image. No one, including a resident expert at the Museum of TV and Radio, is too sure what happened next because the show went off the air suddenly.

- *Meet Millie.* Secretary Millie Bronson lives with her widowed mother, whose job in life is finding Millie a suitable husband. Millie has a boyfriend, Johnny, who is the boss's son. But knowing what comes of such class-crossing arrangements, Mom is ever on the lookout, and so is the requisite house beatnik, Alfred Prinzmetal, an artist who does nothing but comment, often to Millie, whom he has deemed worthy of his erudition. This was one of the first shows to establish a principle that would long exist on TV if rarely in life: Everyone loves the single girl. She is the adorable needy human equivalent of a stray pet others want to domesticate.

In fifties films, the single woman turns up most often as a recognizable spinster (Kim Novak in *Picnic*; *The Rainmaker* with Katharine Hepburn) or as the exceptional quirky character, in the upper-class division Katharine Hepburn (*Desk Set; Pat and Mike*), and in the working-class, Judy Holliday. In *It Should Happen to You*, she's a girl—a "goil"—who becomes famous by advertising herself on a billboard; in *Bells Are Ringing*, she works for an answering service, playing a special part for all her clients.

But rarely is the spinster, the shy single sister, the center of the action. As in literature, the spinster serves to better set off the lustrous qualities of the married, engaged, or just physically beautiful star. Either that, or she's a witch (Kim Novak in *Bell, Book and Candle*) or a monstrous bitch (Joan Crawford in *Johnny Guitar* or just about anything else).

If a film had a single woman at the center, then the central question concerned sex and, specifically, whether or not she had any before marriage. One of the most popular films of the late fifties, *Marjorie Morningstar*, was based on a lengthy Herman Wouk novel set in the 1930s that told in excruciatingly minute detail the whole story of an aspiring actress from a traditional Jewish family that migrated "up" from the Bronx to Manhattan. Marjorie, part princess, part bohemian, struggles with everything—her mother's prudish interference in her career and snobbish views of boyfriends; the embarrassment and love she feels for her lower-class Jewish relatives; and then the boyfriends themselves, who are so numerous and detailed they need their own book.

But the movie reduces all conflicts to sex. And so it is centered on the novel's key story—the epic tale of Marjorie and songwriter/intellectual poseur Noel Airman. The film, starring Gene Kelly and Natalie Wood, streamlines the years-long affair—separations, rapprochements, Noel's impossible drunkenness and cruelty—and in the end marries Marjorie off to the wrong person, which is to miss the whole point. But who cares? It tortures with that core question: Does Marjorie ever break free of her strict Jewish upbringing and sleep with Noel?

In *Franny and Zooey*, the J. D. Salinger novella, the entire narrative is propelled by Franny Glass's faint in a restaurant and long, depressed recovery on the living room couch. She claims to have had a religious experience (a common enough occurrence in the Glass family), though young female readers were desperate to know if she was pregnant.

I think it's been fairly well established that she was. And in the book, yes, Marjorie slept with Noel after months of tortuous concerns about frigidity. In the film, though, as in any fifties film, it's hard to say. Any discussion of sex, any hint of two people possibly having had sex, was so oblique that the only way to really know was to go back to *Peyton Place* and *From Here to Eternity* and read them again. For many young women of the time, that constituted "close" reading.

Sex, and life generally, was even more tortured for the fifties widow. Jane Wyman plays a blind widow who must somehow "go out and meet new people" in *Magnificent Obsession*, then moves on to playing a lonely widow in *All*

That Heaven Allows. She is only in her forties, but her two grown children believe that Mother must now stay at home, mourning her loss. She tries, then slowly does the unexpected: falls in love with her young gardener, Rock Hudson, who takes her out driving and—very unusual for someone of her social standing—to lobster parties at the beach shacks of bohemian friends. She returns home to lectures on how she is maladjusted and possibly insane. In consultation with members of the family's country club, the children arrange a match for Mother with a respectable doctor. When she turns them down, they drive the gardener away in retaliation and disgust. Then, to make it up to her—to give her something warm and new in her life—they present her with her first TV. That will keep the old girl company! She sits there staring at it, unable to turn it on, her reflection staring back, a lone face trapped in a box. But then she's up! Breaking with all form, tradition, her entire life, she races out to find her gardener before it is too late.

Of course the most famous single-girl film franchise of the era belonged to Doris Day, as she played a series of working girls with nice apartments, wise-cracking maids, and careers in demanding but still feminine areas, usually interior decorating. She was always well dressed, articulate, and unusually happy with herself. Until someone started teasing her about her love life. Usually this came down to the question of whether she was a virgin. It's clear that the accusation bothers her—she probably *was* a virgin—but it's not something that, until now, she's felt badly about. To achieve the kinds of things she has achieved, she's had to live a disciplined life, looking after herself, part of which meant keeping in mind society's vicious sexual double standard. For the time period, this attitude seems less prudish and warping than it does practical. (For of course if she had *not* been a virgin, she'd have had hell to pay for that, as well.)

Unfortunately the issue would in short time make a joke of Doris Day. As comedies began their descent into so-called sophisticated sex romps, the Day/virginity factor became a repetitive gag. (As one producer famously quipped, "I knew Doris Day before she was a virgin.") She came to seem righteously wholesome. Dull. A too-chatty full-figured gal snobbish critic Dwight MacDonald once described as "bovine."

But the best of the Day characters were stalwart about sex for a reason.

They understood how easily it could be misinterpreted and used against a single woman. In *Minor Characters*, a 1983 memoir of 1950s Manhattan, Joyce Johnson wrote: "The crime of sex was like guilt by association—not visible to the eye of the outsider, but an act that could be easily conjectured. Consequences could make it manifest. . . . In the 1950s, sex—if you achieved it—was a serious and anxious act."

CROSS YOUR LEGS. DO NOT UNCROSS UNTIL WED.

By 1957, sex seemed to be everywhere—in magazines, novels, in the movies—and if you were single and living in the city, there was a sense that it might soon arrive in your very own apartment. The *Saturday Evening Post* was not alone in declaring, "There are new considerations a girl living alone must take into account."

In all the many etiquette guides, sex had been little more than a shadow presence, an issue alluded to but not directly addressed. Most of these how-to-live guides covered general comportment—how a woman should walk down or cross the street without seeming too "available"; how she should remove an apartment key from her purse, and how, if there was no doorman, one stood there seeming respectable while opening a door, on a city street, all alone. One could further study how to walk down the apartment hallway when putting out garbage; how to stand or sit while talking on the phone, including, in one book, some pointers on gracefully twirling the cord.

Sex, however, rated few paragraphs. Because allegedly there was no sex. Guides were there to help young women better avoid even the hint. A small sampling of postdate evasions from two books, circa 1953:

— (To be said just before reaching home, while yawning). "Gee, I wish I didn't have to get up so early—six A.M.! (checks watch) How did it get to be so late? I wish I could ask you up, but perhaps another time. I've had such a nice evening. Goodnight." (Girl then very quickly races up steps to house or out of taxi cab. She waves.)

—(To be said as she opens her apartment door and sees a suitcase, a prop she planted earlier). "Oh my, look! *Ssshhh!* She's here! My roommate! She's a stew! She just flew in from Japan. Oh, dear. I'm so sorry. We'll have to take a rain check on that nightcap, I think."

—(To be said if the man was already inside, drinking that nightcap). "Well, I do have to get up awfully early." If that didn't work, "I wish I could offer a refill, but (blinks, squints) I'm getting a migraine." In desperation: "My mother is here from Cincinnati. She'll be back any minute and so . . ." Sometimes a roommate might magically appear, or a neighbor who needed (female) help with "a very personal and *very upsetting emergency!*"

But it got harder to delete sex as a presence in one's living room and, generally speaking, in one's life. As one twenty-five-year-old told a Sunday newspaper supplement in 1957:

> I was involved in a . . . conversation with an unfamiliar young man . . . and I mentioned that I'd just moved out of my parents' home into an apartment of my own in Greenwich Village. The young man's ears perked up, his eyes took on a new gleam, his smile grew enterprising and his manner insinuating. "Oh-h-h, so you live *alone*, do you? And in the Village!?" I realized I'd apparently taken not a new address, but a new address that gave me a whole new character. . . . I could just see him at my place. We mix up some drinks and . . . so much for the conversation. You can imagine the rest.

Let's go back to that man, circa 1953, having his nightcap and listening to excuses in the living room. Here's how a 1958 guide updated the situation.

> From the moment he entered, he leapt to certain conclusions . . . the curtains are closed and there is alcohol out and on display. The girl has an obvious familiarity with mixing drinks. Note and note well: The way a woman handles . . . *the liquor question* is essential because men, except for an unusually sensitive minority, immediately assume that if a girl lives alone she is worldly and, especially if she drinks, she must certainly hope to use her freedom as fully as possible.

Many advice columnists counseled meeting men elsewhere—blocks, entire districts, away from one's apartment. One 1958 guide, *Today's Manners: Footloose and Fancy Free*, was devoted to this idea, providing many specific suggestions on how to manage oneself while entertaining in public. For example, if a single woman invited friends out for dinner, she would designate an escort for herself, first "making it clear to the management that she was the host, that she would sign the check, but that 'an escort' would handle the actual transaction." If there was no available escort, a man at the table could be "discreetly called upon to do the honors."

If the plans called for her to arrive at the appointed place alone, there were comparable instructions. According to *Footloose and Fancy Free*, "If a woman arranges to meet a man in a central spot, a hotel or a restaurant, for example . . . [and] she is the first to arrive . . . she should ask to be seated at a table. It is perfectly alright to order a cocktail or coffee while wait-ing . . . the man pays for it when he arrives."

But life was rarely that simple. Men came over. They often invited themselves or just showed up. And as much as no one wished to acknowl-edge the idea, men stayed over.

"My kids have the idea that nobody before 1960 had recreational sex," said Martha, a secretary turned travel agent, now sixty-four. "Oh, you tried harder in those days to push it back. You went to theater and made excuses after, tried not to have him see you home, or he came in and you tried to cut it off and it was *so* awkward. . . . Eventually, though, you're twenty-three, you're not married, and you're human. As they say, do the math."

Part of the math involves a consideration of the unpublicized figures. Between 1944 and 1955 there was an 80 percent increase in the number of white babies put up for adoption and an unspecified but noted rise in what were known as "homes for wayward girls," especially on the East Coast. While it's impossible to calculate the number of illegal abortions per-formed, coroner's and doctor's reports indicate that between eight hundred and one thousand women died each year from these procedures.

Other signs of sex in the culture were harder to miss. By the late fifties there was an increasingly visible sexual demimonde. As one *New York Tribune* columnist described it: "Movie stars who are idolized by millions jump in and out of bed on the front pages of daily newspapers. Celebrities and socialites return from trips to the Caribbean with 'traveling companions.' A celebrated romance finally culminates in a wedding and five months later a 'premature' 11-pound baby is born." And less celebrated young women became the subjects of stories typically entitled (this from the *Daily News*): "Bachelor Girls: Their Lives and Loves."

The bachelor girls in question were usually models or Rockettes; starlets, including Tina Louise; debutantes; the serious young career women "who work in the budding communications field;" and sometimes shockingly "open" rising stars. Like "Queen of the Bachelor Girls" Kim Novak. In two columns, she was pictured with four different men, including one South American dictator and a "Negro" entertainer (Sammy Davis, Jr.). She was also pictured all alone, sitting back in a chair, eyes closed, her bare feet up so that a reader had to remark both at her casual mien and her flaming red pedicure.

Bachelor girls like Kim, it was solemnly reported, "play by their own rules."

For example, good for three columns, they dated married men. "Sure, I mean, course we do," one BG told an eager reporter. "If only for the convenience! They don't stay. They don't make a fuss. In some ways it's the ideal date." One "Swedish girl" interviewed for the husbands series told the *News* that "other girls laugh at me because I don't understand why they would go with a husband. They can't see that it is a problem." The Americans defended themselves. They were not immoral but "regular" women "making the most of a difficult situation"—not meeting the right men, perhaps not yet ready to—and, as another put it, "We are not evil. We are tired of sitting home on the weekends. . . . What does it mean to be immoral? We are just living the lives we have and we happen not to have husbands. . . . I do not think that for this reason we are going to hell."

Surprisingly, the author of one 1959 story sided with them. Sort of. "Today in the midst of the rootless, unmarried groups that gravitate to a large city, a girl finds that it is often 'square' to be good. Besides, she herself isn't quite sure anymore what is good and bad, and neither is anyone else. . . . there is not a dropping off of morality. Just a shift in emphasis."

Others disagreed entirely. In 1959, the Juvenile Aid Bureau, a social agency that had previously dealt largely with runaways, was charged with "easing the flow of incoming girls to New York City." As one bureau official explained, "We spot a girl getting off a bus or a train and wandering the streets. We question her." Under an obscure piece of municipal legislation called "the Girl Terms Act," they could further "hold her until her family can be queried. If there is no family, or, as is often the case, the family does not want the juvenile back, and if the girl has no immediate relations in New York to claim her, we will send her back to the point of embarkation on her ticket." In 1959 the JAB reported returning 350-plus suspicious-looking girls (that meant oddly dressed girls, slutty-looking girls; those too young and those not white).

Everyone acknowledged that most of these girls would find their way back in. At best they'd get clerical jobs they'd quickly lose, becoming rootless "wandering types." Or they'd become prostitutes and drug addicts. Worse, they might become bohemians.

ON THE BEAT

The Beat generation is one of those mythical twentieth-century constructs that we associate with a loose conglomerate of crazy brilliant men. Jack Kerouac and his male muse, Neal Cassady; Allen Ginsberg, of course, and William Burroughs—and all the lesser luminaries who floated into and out of their lives, novels, and poems from their days at Columbia University, circa 1945 through the 1960s. But floating around in the background, handing out invitations to poetry readings, discussing art and writing, were a lot of intriguing young women—Hettie Cohen Jones, Joyce Glassman Johnson, Elise Cowen, and poet Diane diPrima, among many uncelebrated others.

These never quite became household names, but many of the onetime Beat girls went on to become writers and artists, just like the men. And some turned out to be chroniclers. It's these women who later wrote the best memoirs of Beat life in New York City and San Francisco. And as much as these stories and the memoirs—*How I Became Hettie Jones; Minor Characters; Beat Girl*—re-create the joy ride of Beat life, they are also historical documents of what it was to be young and single in the 1950s and to have blatantly ignored the rules. Many, like Joyce Johnson, began life as middle-class girls, from "decent" families who lived in Upper West Side apartments that had grand pianos, shelves filled with the "great" books, and well-kept furniture. In *Minor Characters*, her 1983 memoir, Johnson writes better than anyone, ever, about the female double life, the one that started for her at age thirteen, with furtive trips into the Village, and continued as she moved out of her parents' house at twenty-one, radically taking her own place.

"Everyone knew in the 1950s why a girl from a nice family left home," she writes. "The meaning of her theft of herself from her parents was clear to all—as well as what she'd be up to in that room of her own . . . On 116th Street, the superintendent knew it. . . . He spread the word among neighbors that the Glassmans' daughter was 'bad.' His imagination rendered me pregnant."

Actually, what she did was to live there (and in many other places), to hang around with important male artists who spoke mostly to each other, and to work. She supported her boyfriend, Jack Kerouac, when he was around, as well as anyone else currently in the Jack entourage. It's what the girls did. Every morning, long before the men were up, with their hangovers and artistic visions, supportive Beat girls left the confines of the Village, took a train, and, as Johnson writes, "emerg[ed] into the daylight at Fiftieth Street [where] I'd feel I'd been swept up into an enormous secretarial army advancing inexorably upon Madison Avenue . . . as part of this army, I typed, read manuscripts, answered the phone, ate egg-salad sandwiches in the downstairs luncheonette (I'd learned very quickly how to locate the cheapest item on a menu)."

Her own books and stories were published, although no one, including her, made much about it. The Beat girls who became famous did so for extreme and daring acts, like Elise Cowen's. Joyce's beloved and dearest

friend, she threw herself through her parents' living room window, a suicide at twenty-eight.

At about the same time, Rona Jaffe published her best-selling novel *The
Best of Everything*, the classic three-girls-come-to-the-city story, and fore-
runner of the Jackie Susann blockbusters. Her mother grieved. It was
1958, and a career put such a damper on a possible marriage! Then the
book was turned into a film with Hope Lange as the aspiring editor and
model Suzy Parker as the second of her roommates; Joan Crawford even
put in an appearance as the bitch spinster boss who keeps them overtime
at the keyboards. It was a huge hit. But "poor Rona!" as a family friend
said to her mother. "With the film sale . . . all that money, now she'll
never get married."

A popular magazine feature during these years—adapted as a late
newsreel short subject—was the photo essay I think of as "Girl Comes to
the City." Panel by panel, we watch the new girl arrive and get settled. She
meets her roommates, gets a job, fights for a stool at the pushy luncheonette counter, and accepts that she will not find a seat on the subway. These
features always included a shot of the girl in a bathrobe, hair twisted up in
a towel, as she prepared for a date. No one has ever looked so excited while
painting her toenails.

In other shots of her at a desk, or stopped on the street, waiting to
cross, she looks sad. Months have passed and she's learned a few things—
about married men, wolves, loneliness—and she wonders perhaps if she
shouldn't just pick herself up and go home. Then the last panel. Girl in the
tiny shared living room, staring out at the skyline or, more realistically, at
fire escapes and squat brown water tanks. The scene is so hypnotic that she
has the essential epiphany: There is so much here to see and to learn that
to return home, where she's seen and learned all there is to know, would be
a kind of death.

I'm sure some looked at these pictorials and saw a titillating but point-
less risk. Others saw a travel poster on which a special message had been
engraved for them in invisible ink. It said, "Come join us!"

CHAPTER SIX

THE SWINGING SINGLE: CAREER GIRLS, THE AUTONOMOUS GIRL, THE PILL POPPER, AND THE LONE FEMALE IN DANGER

I used to pick out the people who lived alone—on the subway, the street. Every time they had these glassy eyes, like nothing's living in 'em. Dead.
—NATALIE WOOD TO STEVE MCQUEEN, *LOVE WITH THE PROPER STRANGER*, 1963

Whatever your age, your single state is nothing to be ashamed of. Let the girls who marry at 18 or 20 defend their position. They're the ones who are missing out.
—REBECCA E. GREER, *WHY ISN'T A NICE GIRL LIKE YOU MARRIED?* 1969

We have a message for the men here today: FUCK OFF FUCK YOU. You have caused enough grief humiliation for centuries . . . Leave your lie-wives and girlie-friends. Give us back the names we came with. Go!
—A BROCHURE I FOUND IN A PARK, SPRING 1970

THE SECOND COMING OF THE SINGLE GIRL

Images of the 1960s have been so long in circulation that someone born in 1984 could easily assemble his or her own timeline or montage: JFK and Jackie; the Zapruder film; Martin Luther King and Malcolm X; Vietnam (with asides for the Beatles, the Apollo missions, LSD), and, depending on one's mood that day, conclude with Woodstock and microminis, or Kent State and My Lai.

In most schematics, single womanhood as a significant phenomenon does not make the charts alongside the antiwar crusade or the blossoming of the counterculture. It bubbled along throughout the sixties as a bright and sexy trend, a magazine story or pictorial that could also be played as maudlin or scary. As a serious, permanent social fact, it would emerge with the women's movement of the early 1970s. And the early women's movement was the last and, as many, many frightened people viewed it, the least serious of the uprisings. Who was being hurt, exactly? Was the phrase "white middle-class woman" next to the word "oppressed" an oxymoron?

One "then girl" explained: "Nobody took you seriously if you were married and presumed to be a housewife—you were just another married speck. What were your problems—and who cared? If you were single, even if you were wearing bright yellow vinyl boots like I was, you were still just a girl who was going to become a housewife. No great tragedy. . . . As someone who might have a complicated political or social situation—forget it. You were invisible."

By the mid-1970s, however, single women would emerge as among the most economically and socially significant of all the onetime shadow population groups. Being single, like being openly gay, would finally lose any lingering taint of ugly character weakness, any hint of pathology, and come to seem an entirely viable way to live—what someone back in 1925 had first called a "lifestyle."

Traces of this new single appear as if on cue in 1960. First, the 1960 census reported that 9.3 million households, about 18 out of every 100, were headed by solo women. (And the dramatic rise—more than a million since 1950—was genuine; it did not reflect the fact that there were simply more households overall.) More women, it seemed, earned their own money, and because there was more readily available housing, they did not have to live with relatives if they chose not to. True, most of these women were safely identified as widows, but close to 2 million were divorcées, 900,000 were separated from their husbands, and most shocking of all, 1.4 million of these women had never wed. "Who Needs a Man Around the House?" asked the *New York Mirror Magazine* in spring 1960. Beneath the enormous headline we see a Grace Kelly blonde, stretching as she gets out of bed wearing a negligé. We next see her pictured seated serenely with coffee and newspaper, and in another frame she is casually repairing a broken cabinet all by herself. It's threatening, but for safety's sake, a cat has been included in one photo and a caption reassures readers that she used this pet as an "outlet" for expressing affection.

By the early sixties, marriage as a national ideal, an enforceable teenaged daydream, had lost some of its hypnotic force. The number of divorces nationwide had doubled in the ten years since 1952. Thousands of housewives, already identified as "miserable" and "suffering," were sending rescue notes to magazines, begging advice. *Ladies' Home Journal* launched the famed, long-running feature "Can This Marriage Be Saved?" *The Feminine Mystique* came out in 1963. "Togetherness," that byword of 1950s normalcy, began to sound ominous. Among the most popular films of 1962 was *Days of Wine and Roses*, starring Jack Lemmon and Lee Remick as a couple free-falling into mutually supportive alcoholism. The film seems microscopically focused on alcohol abuse, complete with a Twelve Step savior who appears at the end, to explain Important Facts about The Issue. But it may also be seen as a portrait of midcentury marriage as claustrophobic nightmare—"togetherness" as the theme for a monster movie. Here, in a small apartment, live a devoted modern couple who have dutifully excluded their closest relatives. In their isolation, their willingness to get or do *anything* for each other without question, they slowly poison each other.

By far the most controversial element of an evolving single consciousness was the introduction in 1960 of the Pill. All over the country, college-aged girls, "nice" girls from "fine" schools, began taking it en masse and saying radical things about sex—or so it seemed to a population unaccustomed to this open public discussion. More alarming still, they sounded very blasé about the things they said. These young women "assume that [sex] is a possible and probable part of a single girl's experience," wrote young reporter Gloria Steinem in *Esquire* in 1962. As one graduate student told her, "Lovemaking can be good outside marriage and bad in marriage just as easily as the other way around. Sex is neutral, like money. It's the way you use it that counts." One national magazine polled four hundred college students on "chastity." The findings: Nearly "all respondents . . . virginal or no more . . . said . . . sexual behavior is something you have to decide by yourself."

Many young college women used their training in logic to support this newly constructed morality. One of Steinem's subjects had affairs out of marriage because, in her considered view, women were meant for lots of sex. As she reasoned, females were the only mammals capable of orgasm during times they were unable to conceive, therefore orgasm must have served some other purpose, namely pleasure. Another argued: "I'm not preaching against the institution of marriage by having affairs beforehand and I'm not going to produce illegitimate children for society to take care of. People who have no share in the consequences should have no share in the decision." A companion of hers solemnly concluded, "With one hundred percent birth control you are not running the risk of hurting anyone by your behavior and therefore it is not immoral." Others were more practical: "If I'd known, I might have postponed my wedding and had premarital relations instead." (One campus student board declared that by 1984 "women will be 100% unchaste.")

Within two years of its introduction, at least 750,000 American women were on the Pill and an estimated 500 more began taking it every day. *The Complete Book of Birth Control*, published by the Planned Parenthood Federation, reported on who they were and went on at some length. I quote it briefly: "More education and better income . . . tend to shift the responsibility for birth control to the wife. Informal studies indicate the same shift among unmarried girls." Unlike the diaphragm, the Pill could be prescribed for a number of nonsexual causes—menstrual irregularities, control of ovarian cysts—and thus there were convenient excuses for anyone to take it.

Gloria Steinem, starting here to sound like Gloria Steinem, wrote that "the development of a new autonomous girl is important and in numbers quite new. . . . She expects to find her identity neither totally without men nor totally through them . . . She has work she wants to do and she can . . . marry later than average, and have affairs if she wishes, but she can also marry without giving up her work."

This new female "type"—still, of course, years from reality—so excited authors and sociologists that they began to examine the possible specimen right away. What many saw was a normal girl, a future wife who had, amidst this onrush of divorce, become cynical, a wary spectator at what Phyllis Rosenteur in *The Single Woman* (1961) called the "quickie in-and-out affairs that often masquerade these days as marriage." She called her the "intuitive woman" and charted her development in this way:

> Out of childhood, into adolescence, a girl begins observing for herself, and what she sees and hears and feels runs counter to conditioning. Many become confused and, more than that, suspicious. . . . Nothing is accepted as blindly as before and some may even actively rebel against some of the rules. Others merely back away from both the "normal" path to marriage and the ranter's route to stormy singleness; in some private corner of themselves, they plot an independent course, and then pursue it just as silently as people will permit.

The following year, researchers at Stanford announced that women with deep insight into established male/female roles were less likely to make an early "uninformed" marriage. *Science Digest* reported that a University of Michigan study of twenty-five hundred singles had found unwed women to be happier overall than their male counterparts—no matter the

persistent belief that men idealized their bachelor years and left them re-
luctantly. With the exception of divorced women, who were uniquely stig-
matized, researchers concluded, "the single woman who lives alone . . .
[was] not usually a frustrated old maid. And among those who live alone,
women are not the weaker sex. Generally, single women . . . experience less
discomfort than single men. . . . They are more active in the working
through of the problems they face and appear stronger than single men in
meeting the challenge of their position."

Helen Gurley Brown, newly appointed editor of a revivified *Cosmopolitan*, hated that language—"discomfort," the "challenge" of one's
sadly "compromised" position, or the word *frustrated* as it applied to anyone single. She had just married for the first time at thirty-seven. And,
using her own slang ("mouseburger," for example, meant a quiet, spinsterish girl) and dousing it with exclamation points, she'd published the best-
selling *Sex and the Single Girl* (1962). Here we meet a new variation of the
single girl, this one a tornado of competence—pretty, slim, but also
smart, "up" on the news, well-read, and given to sewing and cooking
while at the same time cramming in some art history or Russian literature. She worked hard at a job in the arts and lived by herself in a sleek,
sexy apartment. She was enormously popular but seemingly choosy, selective; very hard to get.

As Helen Brown says of her own single days, "The phone just rang in-
cessantly. It was terribly annoying if you were trying to get something done.
There were nights, I tell you, when I just carried the phone over and *put it
into the freezer*."

She'll go on to tell you of the radical impact she made with this vision
of a single aristocrat. ("It was the first time anyone suggested that being
single was not the same thing as having a social disease!!") But even
though this girl "lived by her wits . . . sharpened . . . honed . . . coping with
people trying to marry her off," she was still an elaborately decked-out slab
of bait. Brown devoted whole chapters to mascara, clothing, and bizarre se-
ductive technique ("any unusual jewelry is a come on, but it should be
beautiful or you'll look *too Ubangi*!"). Just as nineteenth-century girls had
been encouraged into smashes, their affectionate behavior good practice

for the marital arts, so this new single girl was honing herself to be a unique modern wife or, in the spirit of Helen Brown, a delectable, frothy, and fabulous wife!

Still, all silliness aside, Brown was advocating a time-out for self-improvement before marriage. Gloria Steinem's autonomous girl calmly went out, or so it was said, and had sex. And the vision of all those cabinet-repairing amazon divorcées! Put together, the new sixties singles began to sound slightly alarming.

Esquire in particular became obsessed with a female uprising. There were long essays on ball-busting new types, for example, the "American Witch," a spoiled, selfish bitch who deliberately failed to share male enthusiasm for football and did not leap at commands for food. One parable told of a distant time when little Caroline Kennedy, grown and now president, oversaw a program that allowed every American woman to grow a penis. Men, psychological eunuchs, took refuge in bars.

Others objected along more familiar lines. Author Pearl Buck, returning to the States after years abroad, wrote that of all changes "the new ethics of sex" was most amazing, "so abrupt, so far reaching that we are all dazed by it." But she believed that an insufficient few had stopped to consider the consequences—the many unwanted children that would still, even with the new "technology," result in "rows and rows of tiny unattended cribs."

Several professors from universities such as Stanford, Princeton, and Tufts foresaw in these loosened sexual constraints a dissolving national morality. If women, like men, could engage in whatever sexual practice they chose, when they chose, in short, without any external controls, they were more likely to develop a reckless spontaneity in other of their actions. From a letter to the *New York Times*: "Women, like some men, now find it fashionable to behave and conduct themselves in whatever way they choose, in consideration only of their own feelings. Too bad if there are children." To quote one Harvard psychologist, "This sudden emphasis on individual choice, a morality of one, is . . . dangerous."

Occasionally one heard a measured voice. Sylvia Porter, in her *New York Post* column, "Your Dollar," took on the new female single as a social development that required a practical, not moralistic, response. She called on manufacturers to package smaller meals and scale products down to suit the family of one. The housing industry, she believed, would need "to develop centrally located . . . inexpensive, small apartments." As she reported, "According to a census spokesman . . . there will be more and more [single women] as the years go on."

In fairness, one professor who'd expressed concern about a relative female morality also urged caution in too quickly judging women. Considering female freedom, he had found at least one "salutary" side effect. "A woman free to find fulfillment in marriage *and* work" was far more likely to "be self-motivated. Autonomous . . . *This* is the kind of woman who makes the ideal teacher."

It was, after all, still 1962 or 1963. Most of the single women inspiring such terrorized discourse were still in fact teachers, secretaries, or something else safely within the canon of female careers. A 1960s board game for girls, "What Shall I Be: The Exciting Game of Career Girls," laid out the possibilities. Along with teacher and secretary one could work toward "stewardess," "model," "nurse," trying to avoid two old-maid-ish cards known as the Duds, either a fat middle-aged actress with runny makeup or else an unmistakable spinster.

Interestingly, the spinster as a type had floated back into the national discourse, this time as the subject of an obituary. So many millions of girls automatically married that the society for some time had lacked traditional spinsters. But lamenting the lost spinster—that toothless, brutally bunned stick in black—was actually a handy way of denouncing the new single. In cartoon panels and staged photos, our suddenly beloved spinster was juxtaposed not with the baby housewife who had replaced her, but with a Pill-taking stew or a wealthy single babe, a socialite with décolletage stretching down to her navel. In 1963 *The New York Times Magazine* ran a spinster eulogy that refined the identity of the primary "spinster killer," who was none of the above—not the baby bride, the pill-taking girl, or the rapacious socialite. She was, rather, the average unmarried working girl who could easily beome any one of the above. She applied cosmetics, hair dye, and as one caption put it, "overnight, she's a new girl, with a new look, a new personality, a new life." Whatever direction it took, she was very unlikely to end up a traditional and suddenly beloved auntie spinster.

I'M FEMALE, FLY ME

According to the Labor Department, single women in the sixties worked in greatest numbers as secretaries, titles that after several years might be renegotiated, fluffed up, and rechristened "assistants to." That is, if the girl in question remained a girl and didn't marry. There was still a deep mistrust of the married working woman, who would, wrote one insurance-company employee in *Glamour*, "naturally get herself pregnant at the first opportunity and abandon her precious files one afternoon, just like that." (United Airlines enforced what were perhaps the most blatant restrictions. Until 1969, all stewardesses had to be provably single; if they married, they "retired.")

But the finest of the young career breed—the white, the virginal, the unwed—were often canonized in *Look* and *Life* spreads, as they had been twenty years before. The jobs, or the companies at least, had cachet—CBS, the UN, Christian Dior. The girls, however, still took shorthand.

As *Life* exclaimed in 1962, "Glamor, Excitement, and Romance and the Chance to Serve the Country—How Nice to Be a Pretty Girl and Work in Washington!" And there she was—Nancy Becker of Columbia, Missouri, at her desk, chin at rest on manicured hands, her pearls, her pencils precisely arrayed, her eyes "full of stardust." She worked, filing, for the Justice Department. On the following pages young women with similar jobs were seen at Georgetown dinner parties, playing touch football (just like the Kennedys!), and shopping for antique rocking chairs. "It's the perfect opportunity and so honorable to be here," said a twenty-three-year-old interviewed for the piece. "But I think we most all agree, most of us are going to be marrying and seeing where that takes us, even if that's Kansas." They'd always have Washington.

In New York City the working girls weren't so sure. In a 1961 *Made-*

moiselle piece, "The Great Reprieve," young Joan Didion wrote of Manhattan as an Emerald City that held out to its most tentative residents

> this special promise—of something remarkable and lively just around the corner. . . . They do a lot of things but girls who come to New York are above all uncommitted. They seem to be girls who want to prolong the period when they can experiment, mess around, make mistakes. In New York, there is no genteel pressure for them to marry, to go two-by-two. . . . New York is full of people on this kind of leave of absence.

By 1963, the year *The Feminine Mystique* crash-landed, many reported "feeling bugged," bothered about "all the intense spying to see what I am up to," to quote an airline ticketing agent in *Glamour*. "I expect to look up and see my brother standing there, 600 miles from home, just dropping by to examine my ring finger." One of Didion's subjects refused any longer "to parry delicate questions about my *plans*." They had left home, gone off, transformed themselves. They were trying.

"It was an outrageous dare," says "Sally-Jo," age now "fifty-plus."

> I remember getting off the bus from Wisconsin. It was in 1964. Beatles time. And I was waiting for my luggage—I'd brought a big round hatbox and a big suitcase-sized makeup kit—and I was standing right by the exhaust pipe. I remember feeling dizzy and thinking—Yes! This is it! I inhaled deeply. That's how thrilled I was! . . . Asphyxiated, wandering off to find a subway, not a clue where I was going, holding a freaking hatbox.

Just as they had in the fifties, and in the thirties, and in the time of the Bowery gal, officials likened these "girls" to unwanted immigrants. It was as if the shirtwaisted shop girl had reemerged in Marimekko separates, gotten drunk at lunch, and been spied on her break doing the Watusi. No one knew what to do about her or it or *them*: gangs of fully developed females who'd finished at school and now seemed to be on quixotic scholarships of their own design. An excerpt from a 1964 inquiry published in the Sunday *New York World Telegram*:

> Every day they come. They come from Oregon and Iowa, from Utah and Illinois, from Ohio and California. The come from small towns and medium-sized cities . . . from colleges and communities where they were important, special, secure. They come to a city that is dirty and difficult and massively indifferent to them. A city that will charge them outrageous rents and pay them shamefully small salaries at first . . . it is a city bursting with thousands who are equally talented and gifted. Who are they? These women ignoring the fears of parents, the advice of friends, the gloomy prediction of city planners? . . . How many will there be this week and the next? How many will there be in five years?

One soothing remedy from the past was to count them. According to New York's YWCA, there were about 100,000 more in 1964 than there had been the year before and an employment agency specializing in the now popular "communications" jobs (advertising, TV, magazines) reported its "applicants from out of town going up, up, up—8 percent more this year [1964] than last." There were 350,000 total, reports read. One heard that 25,000 were hiding out in the Village, 300 of them appearing semiweekly in Babe's Beauty Shop and close to 400 working or volunteering in museums. Odd random surveys, to cite one, revealed that 500 girls interviewed on the subways had once been Girl Scouts, though most—93 percent—did not think their scouting skills helped much in their lives as city girls. And it seemed they now wanted jobs that demanded more than a proven ability to whip through "A-S-D-F-J-K-L-semicolon." *Glamour* in its 1963 "Happiness Index," reported, "Happiness is an $8 raise; the boss's compliment; not having to shave your legs." A contemporary issue of the *Saturday Evening Post* proclaimed: "The girl who comes to New York is no longer just the young actress or ballet dancer yearning for a chance . . . Madison Ave. has replaced Broadway as the street of dreams . . . the new girl is more likely to see herself writing sparkling copy or holding a clipboard for a television producer."

By the mid-sixties, young single women had begun to appear in ads and fashion spreads as busy TV-set assistants, lone car drivers, career girls holding blueprints with pencils tucked behind their ears. Although these were models, human props, it's hard to imagine anything like it—discernible professional tracings—even five years before. Lone girls were also shown doing unlikely things. (One 1965 Goodyear ad showed a woman in standard sensible dress changing a tire. Read the caption: "When there's no man around, Goodyear should be.") Even tampon ads featured actual photos of young singles with names like Deborah or Patty. Dressed crisply in white, they were "stepping out" on their own. Tampax, say what you will, was another sign of their "independence!"

There were also certifiable single working girls on TV—Marlo Thomas as *That Girl* in her yellow-striped chain-belted minis; Honey West, girl detective—as well as clever dare-taking teenagers (Patty Duke; Sally Field) and magical creatures beyond male control as on *Bewitched, I Dream of Jeannie,* and the little-remembered *My Living Doll,* in which Julie Newmar, prior to Catwomanhood, played a beautiful robot who goes her own way. Real life provided even more exotic singular oddities (Joan Baez,* Gloria Steinem, Barbra Streisand, Renata Adler, Shirley Chisholm, Diane Arbus, Jane Fonda, Anna Karina, Suzanne Farrell, Twiggy). Even the singles featured in the long newspaper stories ("Why?" "For how long?" "What about those babies?") seemed more stylish, daring, and accomplished. One *World Telegram* Sunday section, circa 1965, featured young, pretty, and, for a change, serious professionals. They interviewed a twenty-five-year-old woman who designed furniture. Another worked at *Mademoiselle* and also freelanced for a magazine called *In: A Guide to the Swinging Single New York.* There were real estate brokers. Broadway production assistants. Former civil rights workers hoping to get involved in politics.

Of course at least one among the young professionals questioned it all.

Time put Joan Baez on its cover in 1962, featuring not a picture of Joan but a painting, a dark Modigliani-esque blur (her features are so crooked she seems as if she might fall apart). Details from the story: "She walks straight to the microphone and begins to sing. No patter. No show business. She usually wears a sweater and skirt or a simple dress. . . . She is 21 and palpably nubile. But there is little sex in that clear flow of sound . . . it has in it reminders of black women wailing in the night. . . . She is a lovely girl who has always attracted numerous boys. But her wardrobe would not fill a hatbox."

Here that was a thirty-two-year-old advertising account executive who, pictured chewing a pencil, admitted, "I want a career, but I don't want to be the kind of woman men talk about as career women. I'd like to keep at least a few shreds of my femininity."

Single-girl stories always included such confessions, worries, or an authorial caveat, as if it was the writer's responsibility to list all contraindications for this radical trial drug called independence. Most of the pieces concluded with a haunted question: "Even now, in black moments, they ask, 'What am I doing here?'" or "Why should I stay? Who'd notice that I was gone?" "What if there is no one here for me?" or "Is this . . . it?" But there were also breakthroughs. Entrée to a key social circle. A new man. Better, several men. And there were always the women who—damn it all!— went out and battled to become the serious "girl" who did not type. (Typical tale: As late as 1968, famed NPR correspondent Nina Totenberg was told by a potential employer, a friend, "Nina, you know we have our girl already." Nina, successfully, went and became the Girl somewhere else.)

Even the average single woman now had, as the *Reader's Digest* said, "a shot at life previously unimagined. Today's plain Janes have opportunities their spinster aunts never did—trips to Europe, a Peace Corps assignment in Asia, interesting jobs in research or government. And in all these places they have a chance to display a mettle that may attract a man who might otherwise have been addled by a momentary attraction to a dumb blonde."

They also had a bit of fun. Many became expert at blowing off whole afternoons at foreign films or in Lord & Taylor's. And gradually, whether they liked the idea or not, young single women began to go out in mixed groups. When asked where they were going, no one said, "On a date." The new reply was "Just out."

THE SINGLE STRIP

The "swinging" singles scene began with a simple and unglamorous realization: Young people were lonely. Families had begun their slow dissolve, shown the first fresh results of divorce, corporate transfers, migrations south and, of course, the familiar, now more frequent announcement "I'm off to the city, Ma, bye!" Many magazine stories and essays began this way: "The girl or boy who lived next door or two towns over has gone, off to school in the East, to Europe, or New York City." It was a cliché—any reference to a girl next door had long been a cliché—and yet it was in some undeniable way true. "Anonymity" replaced "togetherness."

In his 1965 book, *The City Is the Frontier*, Dr. Charles Abrams, the head of Columbia University's urban-planning department, warned that the city was unprepared for the "convergence" of all these anonymous strangers. How would people meet? Not on the street, where a strict taboo prevented eye contact and conversation. The city, Abrams advised, would have to open to singles, to build special housing, unique public meeting places, become in some sense what he called a "trystorium." Thus began a small singles industry. At the start there were simple "pay parties," mimeographed telephone lists, and gimmicks—restaurants with phones at the tables so that if a girl wished, she might call a man seated elsewhere, or "wash-a-terias," Laundromats that served Cokes and played records. In late 1964 Mike O'Harro, an ensign who had founded a private dating "association," organized a computerized list of forty-seven thousand singles nationwide. "I had the idea at a party I threw in Virginia," he told *Newsweek*. "I realized that every person at this party, everyone did different things, and they were all lonely. I was lonely, and it occurred to me that it had to be true in other places."

Along with others who'd had the single epiphany, he began to stage regional activities. To be single in Denver at the time might have meant attending a "woodsie," a weenie roast and dance party up in the Rockies. In New York, couples met at rooftop "drinks parties"; roofs had been declared among the "new mating frontiers." "Causes" were also big—work for a candidate, attend many fund-raisers. Single visionaries took it further, plotting apartment complexes for singles only, miniresorts that would include pools and tennis courts, bars and lounges placed everywhere for optimum mixing.

Grossinger's, the venerable Catskills resort, had held its first singles weekend in 1961. By the mid-sixties there was barely a resort or a cruise

line that had not imitated the package. By 1965, single life was said to generate somewhere between twenty and fifty million dollars per year. And
those figures grew as whole neighborhoods "went single." Manhattan's East
Side, starting at East Thirtieth Street, heading up to Ninetieth and stretching from the East River all the way to Fifth Avenue, was christened "the
singles ghetto," a minicity of new high-rises and older buildings where girls
learned a few quick rules about real estate. ("No one wanted to rent to
three girls—three girls was a brothel," says one marketing analyst, now
fifty-six. "You claimed two and kept the third as a constantly recurring
cousin from home. Or a stew.") Thousands of actual stews, secretaries, ad
copywriters, sports columnists, "just regular guys with jobs" filled out the
area—780,000 of them, according to one insurance company. (There was
in fact a real "stew zoo." The address, as well known as the Barbizon
Hotel's, was 345 East Sixty-fifth Street. During the mid-1960s, the building was 90 percent stewardess-occupied.)

On weeknights residents filled the restaurants and movie theaters;
on weekends, they filled the bars—Maxwell's Plum, Mister Laffs, TGI
Friday's—a collection that stretched out along five crowded blocks of
First Avenue. By midnight on Saturday, it seemed that someone had
thrown a frat party without realizing a street fair was already under way.
Newsweek called it "the body exchange." Others likened it to a zoo, a
"place made up of hands, hands, HANDS grabbing at you." Or waiting
on you. It became one of the city's much-repeated mating tales that J.
Walter Thompson employees actually competed for waiter and bartend-
ing jobs after hours. As one explained, "Where else am I going to meet
chicks?"

The bar strip was also ground zero for journalists assigned to this generation's singles beat. The standard device was to catch bits of conversations between couples who'd "connected," as if on *The Dating Game,* and
had invariably misheard each other's names. The strategy, then, was to
follow the strangers—one long-haired eyelinered female, one preppy male
wearing bell-bottoms—as they moved in on each other and, if the reporter got lucky, left the bar together. But there were other scenes and
other stories, and many girls could not stand the meat market that was the

Upper East Side. Some preferred Village bars or jazz clubs or the scenes at Max's Kansas City, Cheetah's, or the Electric Circus, where there was less date making than dancing and for the shy a lot of visual distraction— Warholian performance art; the first of the sparkly-ball light shows—also much potential single-girl sex. Sometimes right there.

"Wherever you went out in the 1960s, and I went, just went, wherever—it was very dark," says Julie, now forty-nine, divorced, and the mother of two kids she adopted on her own.

> It was the bars that were labeled "singles" bars that were the creepiest, I thought. Little red candles, all those guys with the open shirts and this glob of hair sticking out. People dressed alike. I liked places where there was more of a circus-y diffused scene . . . these bars really *were* meat markets. . . . I can remember at Maxwell's, or one of them I got dragged to this one time, being afraid of going to the bathroom because I had inadvertently made eye contact with this manly-man kind of guy at the bar and I was afraid he would misinterpret my walking toward the bathroom as a cue. . . . It seemed so predatory.

WHERE HAVE OTHER SINGLES GONE?

At the time, of course, an enormous slab of the American single population was not in singles clubs of any kind, but still in college. Some would avoid the singles scene by getting married the day after graduation. But the MRS. degree had already begun its slow fade from the curriculum. "When I started school in 1965, we wore plaid skirts and had proper dates and had parietals," says Sally Hoffe, a fifty-four-year-old lawyer, never wed and now a single parent. "By the time we left we were dressed in flowing scarves and ragged jeans and many of us had no makeup on except maybe a crescent moon on our forehead. We had thrown out hair dryers. . . . Sex—we just had it. And unless you got pregnant or caught VD, the tone—at least with certain people anyway—the whole subject was casual as can be."

In March 1966, *Time* devoted its Education section to a story on the younger "free sex movement," what was largely a Berkeley phenomenon that had been around in some form since 1960. Printed below an extremely dark and blurry photo: "As they do at countless collegiate parties everywhere, the couples wriggled to the watusi and gyrated to the jerk, while recorded drums and saxophones resounded in the dimly lit apartment of a University of California student in Berkeley. Unlike most parties, however, the boys and girls were naked."

"That sounds about right," says Sally Hoffe.

> Very Berkeley, but I'd be lying if I said in the Midwest I did not attend my share of like events . . . there was a lot of loosening-up of what you wore and *who* you *were*. Or who you thought you were that week . . . [but] not everyone participated. There were many girls who still had on the sensible Butterick sew-it-yourself shifts. . . . There were the wedding announcements and the "bride elect"! I always remember that phrase, bride-elect, the chosen. But what was it she chose? . . . My radicalization was to see this engagement ritual as a kind of sleepwalking. . . . Did they really want to get married, or had they run out of ideas already?

At about this point in time it becomes more difficult to write about single women as a unified class. There were so many variations on the single state, so many stops along the singular spectrum. For example, in 1967 half of all women in their thirties were married mothers who remained at home full-time. But of these women, 17 percent were legally separated, or temporarily apart from their mates due to the Vietnam War. Thousands of women were already choosing to keep rather than give away out-of-wedlock babies—and to live with friends, sisters, boyfriends. The number of women who reported cohabiting or "having recently cohabited" was at about 550,000. Some single women lived in Upper East Side apartments or at the Y. But an equal number lived in communes or feminist collectives or in coed group housing. And many were developing unique new views of singularity. A graphic artist and illustrator recalls life on "the commune of the Feminine Mystique, Brattleboro, Vermont":

> Everyone was equal and everyone was beautiful and cooked. Of all the memories of that time, I still see mostly the bowls and bowls of spaghetti. And I remember what they looked like the next morning, when I came down and, as one of two women, found them waiting for me . . . I was never really able to have roommates after that. If there was one night and things didn't get put away, I became this insane despot. . . . I think it's true about a lot of single women—they have their weird baggage. They're pretty much always there, living alone, for a reason. And that reason is usually other people, no matter how many times they make the mistake again and again. . . . I think most of us end up where we want to be.

In Mary Gordon's first novel, *Final Payments* (1977), we meet a young woman who's devoted her entire adult life to caring for a pious father. Like a nun, she leaves the house for a walk just once a week; the rest of the time she organizes his papers, infuriating the local widows who desperately want the job. After his death, the widows seek their revenge, joining with the church leaders of this small Catholic community in trying to sell her off to some other old person in need of a secular nun. They manage to give her a hideous spinster haircut. But she is rescued by a trio of childhood friends who have watched over this stunted single life for years. One day they force her into the car, into the city, into a life of her own.

One asks if she wants to get married.

No, she doesn't. "I want a terrific pair of high-heeled shoes . . . like Rosalind Russell . . . I want a very small apartment and I want people to refer to me as a bachelorette."

"The term now is swinging single," one of them tells her.

"And they call that progress," she responds, knowing that they could have called it anything and called it an improvement.

SINGLE SLASHING

If singles were an increasingly diverse group, there was still one stereotype that reporters loved most of all—the "swinger"—that college grad with fake eyelashes and daiquiris or the faux hippies holding joints and daiquiris. By 1968, New York's famed "singles ghetto" had been renamed the "girl ghetto." And its residents came under unkind, often vicious, scrutiny. Tired of writing about bar etiquette, reporters began to meet subjects at their apartments to get the inside view, often the morning after a singles night out. Many of these apartments were in upscale buildings— three and a half rooms, the rent at about $225 per month, making a three-way share just affordable. No matter how lucky they might have felt, whatever it was they'd got away from, girls could never quite convey to male reporters just what it was they found so thrilling about their own interpretation of single life. That's because reporters did not want to know.

These pieces ("Living It Up on Broadsway") always began with an inventory of the girl's appearance. She was usually dressed in a bathrobe or some kind of unflattering caftan or muumuu, one shoulder forward, so that it formed a bony shelf for messy hair. Mascara was always smudged and eyelashes glued together in tiny triangles. Here was the perfect way to survive articles you didn't really want to write: Apply New Journalism techniques to an otherwise dreary scene. Stories told of freshly washed coffee mugs that "still had on them lipstick traces" and, once, brilliantly, a lipstick-stained school-size milk carton. They noted what was on the couch—a heart-shaped pillow, cat-shredded tasseled pillows, teddy bears—and what was under it (always a cache of cigarette butts, magazines, a shoe). These sorts of stories often included tours of the refrigerator, where some vegetable had metaphorically dried and shriveled. And they had a real time of it when it came to the medicine chest. Tranquilizers? Laxatives? And "depending on the carefulness of the housekeeping" . . . the Pill?

Occasionally, very occasionally, a woman wrote about the new single life for herself. The only prerequisite seems to have been that she find it, with six months' retrospect, disappointing and scary. In 1966 *The Washing-*

ton Post Magazine ran an unusual parallel assessment of the city's single life, from the point of view of a white writer, Judith Viorst, and a black writer, Dorothy Gilliam. The lead paragraphs:

> Judith Viorst: Washington is full of single girls between 20 and 30 who are having a ball, cracking up from loneliness, being mistresses, living in deadly fear of rapists and purse snatchers, trying to decide which man to marry, or trying to face the dismal fact they never will.
>
> Dorothy Gilliam: There are single Negro women all over Washington who live and breathe and laugh and weep and take tranquilizers and fret that there are too few men and too little culture. They aren't poor or on welfare. Their lives are parallel to white working girls' but with exceptions—exceptions that extend from the fact of their being Negro.

As the sixties wore on, the reporting moved from "realistic" to what may safely be called "hostile." Writing about a bar in Washington, D.C., another *Post* reporter lightly described the patrons, then got down to it.

> To walk into Wayne's Luv is both an admission and an assertion. She is admitting to anyone who cares to notice that she has not been found attractive enough to have a date that night; and she is asserting that she is realistic enough not to worry with the mundane games of dating propriety that were encountered by an earlier set of singles. In a sense, she assumes a more active role of enticement, hoping in her own mind that somehow he will saunter out of the amber haze and notice and speak and want Her. . . . it beats the Great Grey Tube.

No stories ended without a reference to television. In Washington, D.C., clerks were stuck at home watching *Get Smart*. (Although Agent 99 had a fairly exciting single-girl life.) Secretaries in Chicago all had colds in the winter and nothing but *Gilligan's Island*, *The Beverly Hillbillies*, and *Lost in Space* reruns to keep them company. Some stuck in their mate-meeting high-rises might have tuned in to one of the popular doctor's shows, many of which carried a special message for uppity single women. In a 1989 essay, academic Diana Meehan relates the sad fates of three single-girl guest stars on these 1960s hospital dramas. First, on the popular *Marcus Welby, M.D.*, Welby protegé Steven Kiley makes an advance on a nurse and she rejects him. Within hours she is thrown from her horse and paralyzed. On *Dr. Kildare*, a "No, thank you" to an internist seems to lead right away to a leukemia diagnosis. On the precursor to *E.R.*, *Medical Center*, the one who says no, in the span of twenty minutes, contracts breast cancer.

During the early seventies, there was a popular Friday-night show called *Love, American Style*. According to *TV Guide*, more people were likely to see it in a given week than to experience anything like love of any genuine style in their lifetimes.

DAYS OF MACE

Back on August 28, 1963, a petty thief named Richard Robles broke into an Upper East Side apartment and killed the two young women who lived there. Years later, when such single killings had become commonplace, *New York Times* reporter Judy Klemesrud wrote with complete accuracy: "The brutal slaying of a young single girl . . . probably causes more shock and public horror than any other."

But the "single girl murders" as they became known across the country that fall, were a shocking devastation. The perpetrator had chosen the address, 57 East Eighty-eighth Street, because he'd seen an open window, there was no doorman, and he thought no one was home. When he got through it, intending to steal jewelry or money, Janice Wylie, a blond twenty-one-year-old *Newsweek* researcher, ran in from the other room. Robles grabbed a kitchen knife and raped her. Emily Hoffert, a new roommate, entered the apartment, shrieking that she would remember his face, identify him—and something snapped. Robles began clubbing both girls with glass soda bottles, then for an hour slashed and stabbed them with knives.

The case is remembered now as the one that led to passage of the Miranda rights legislation; the wrong man, not properly questioned, spent years in jail before Robles was apprehended. But what remained in consciousness, of course, was the girls. Emily had just started work as a teacher. Janice wanted to be an actress and looked so hopeful, ready to go!, in all her pictures. Her father, Max, a well-known adman and writer—who, with a third roommate, found the naked bodies—later committed suicide. (An ironic footnote: It was his brother, Philip Wylie, who wrote such misogynist tomes as *Generation of Vipers*, the World War II diatribe that accused those neurotic "Lost Sex" women of ruining men, killing them, destroying their souls.)

An entire litany of single female names would follow, perhaps most famously Kitty Genovese, a twenty-nine-year-old bar manager who'd decided, in a highly unusual move, to stay in the city when the rest of her large Italian family made the move from Brooklyn to Long Island. She was stalked at 3 A.M. after exiting a Queens train and stabbed repeatedly en route to her apartment; notoriously, neighbors all around the complex heard her shrieking but none called the police. The one man who considered it later confessed that he'd seen her stumbling and, thinking her drunk, changed his mind.

Two years later, in Chicago, Richard Speck pushed his way through the front door of a student nurses' dorm, dressed like a disheveled James Dean—a tattoo, BORN TO RAISE HELL, on his arm—and demanded money. No one, he swore, would be hurt. Twenty-four student nurses lived there, most of them Filipinas. About half were home at the time and he forced them all to a room, had them lie down, and tied them up with strips of torn bedsheets. Girls were returning home every few minutes, and as each came in, he tied her up. Then he lifted one or two at a time and dragged them into another room. He'd return, take another five. Another three. Until the room was empty, and he fled. He'd missed one, however, a small young woman who had managed to roll herself under a bed and stay hidden. She's the one who found the carnage—her friends, strangled, mutilated, stabbed in the eyes and breasts. Somehow, still tied up, she crawled out onto a fire escape shrieking.

"The nurse under the bed" became a set piece in scary games girls played during my childhood. The message was clear: If you live by yourself without a husband, you'd better learn how to hide.

By the seventies, and the full blossoming of the bar scene, single murders began to fall into a category of their own. This kind of dispatch was commonplace: In October 1973, Carol A. Hoffman, thirty-one, a publishing assistant, was stabbed and then brutally strangled with panty hose in her apartment. The most shocking aspect of the Hoffman case was that she had let the killer into her apartment because she'd *felt sorry for him*. He had appeared at her door in distress and told her he was looking for another resident of the building who'd raped his wife. While the man was there, elaborating on this story, Ms. Hoffman's boyfriend happened to call. He advised her to get the guy out quickly and even spoke by phone to the distraught visitor. He raced over, but by the time he arrived she was dead. Building residents were horrified—but not, it seemed, all that shocked. Here was a "mostly singles" apartment, no doorman, with a history of muggings. One neighbor, identified as Marti, a graphic designer, recalled bringing home a strange man who, after three hours of conversation, attacked her. She'd escaped by racing down the hallway, banging on doors. "How could I report it?" she asked the reporter. "What was I going to report? Oh, hi, I brought a man home with me, and look what he did!"

The women who wrote these stories—Gloria Emerson, Judy Klemesrud, Charlotte Curtis, Nan Robertson, among others—were on their own emerging as singular voices. They had come up the usual journalistic route: from file clipper or researcher, then moving, after a few years, to the 4F sections or pullouts. (4F: "food, furnishings, fashions, family" was still the journalistic female ghetto). Some of them had been quiet forces in the sex desegregation of the *New York Times* help-wanted ads in 1967 and had been active in the landmark class-action sex-discrimination suits brought against the *Times*, *Newsweek*, and other news corporations during the early seventies. (Without these actions, it's unlikely their bylines would ever have appeared anywhere outside the 4F cookie/sweater slum.)

Their stories of singular peril began to take on an eerie similarity. Imagine modern Bowery gals, a group of friends dressed up to go out one weekend night, to a place that seemed like a wild carnival midway. It was loud and friendly, but there was also an unmistakably dangerous undercurrent. Patrice Leary, Roseanne Quinn . . . their names blurred with their stories and photos. Just regular young working girls, in their twenties, hair parted down the middle, found dead after leaving a bar alone or with a man they did not know. Their friends, who resembled them, would be photographed huddled together outside the bar. Sometimes their words made up the captions: *"There is no such thing as too cautious." "To be realistic in this city means to be paranoid." "I sleep with a baseball bat next to my bed." "The uglier I look, the safer I'll be."*

An acquaintance of mine recalls:

In the early to mid-seventies—that was when New York made its big turn. . . . It was not just edgy in some places, but filled with drug addicts and people who weren't wearing shoes and talking to themselves. . . . It seemed very dangerous all of a sudden. . . . I remember the week I was flashed by three guys, once right in the subway and, I swear, he was looking straight at me; once when I came home—I lived in the Village—and found a guy on the steps with his dick hanging out, and once as I waited to be buzzed in at a friend's. . . . I had been at the bar [W.M. Tweed's] where Roseanne Quinn disappeared, I still remember that, and I left and walked over to this apartment and there was the man with his dick out. . . . That's when I got a purple belt in karate.

As journalist Lucinda Franks wrote of young women in the early seventies, "Anxiety had slipped around their lives like a back brace."

It seems in the spirit of the times that Jane Fonda won the Oscar for *Klute* (1971), in which she played a prostitute stalked by a crazed john. Another hugely popular film, *Play Misty for Me*, flipped the roles, updating the noir B movie *Detour*, in which an inexplicably demented woman stalks a man she's casually met, here a radio deejay played by Clint Eastwood. *Looking for Mr. Goodbar*, based on Judith Rossner's 1975 novel, concerned a seemingly plain Irish-American schoolteacher who, in response to upsetting events in her past, starts to pick up men in bars, night after night, year after year, until finally one of them kills her.

But despite its seeming death sentence, single life in New York City continued to thrive. New Yorkers, after all, like single women living any-where, had been forced to cultivate and maintain a sense of humor— satiric, or sardonic, and that adjective so often stapled to the single woman, masochistic. The most perfectly preserved example of sardonic fe-male masochism may be found in the Gail Parent novel *Sheila Levine Is Dead and Living in New York* (1970). Sheila, who'd moved from Franklin Square, Long Island, to the city, has, after several years, decided that she has no hopes of marriage. Every girl in New York City has the same apart-ment she has, the same hairstyle, has read the same books and has the same recipes and goes to the same kinds of events to meet the same men. In the movies, Doris Day had moved to the city and day one found a spacious brownstone she paid for with her unemployment check. The next day she ran into Cary Grant, who accidentally spilled coffee on her, gave her a job, and eventually married her. As Sheila observes, her life has taken a slightly different course. Thus she's decided to kill herself and spends most of the novel both looking for a mate and shopping for a nice, reasonably priced coffin.

But let's put aside all the feelings of terror and doom and look at some of the more common low-grade anxieties that plagued the 1970s single pi-oneers. The best depiction of this ill ease, the widespread state of singular dislocation, may be found in a little-known film called *T. R. Baskin* (1971), starring Candace Bergen. Here is a young single woman, well educated and interesting, ready to experience life, yet self-protective and a little shy. Her circumstances, that is, the 1970s, don't favor the self-protective and slightly shy. She has just moved alone to Chicago, has her own apartment, works at an anonymous office job, and on the weekends attempts to go out with her friends—but it's always a struggle. In groups they go to restaurants and clubs or to apartments far more garishly decorated than her own. The parties always start up quickly. Never is she really a full participant.

By the early seventies, the singles culture had reached the point where men very often assumed that single women they met wished to have sex with them. That's the atmosphere here—uninvited male hands suddenly everywhere. Men attempting to feed our heroine Kahlúa, whiskey sours, and spilling the drinks down her shirt. More than once we watch T. R. struggling out of a male hold and explaining to friends, who tease her, call her a prude, so *uptight* (then practically a curse word), that she must go. Like a lot of reserved young women, T. R. is uncomfortable in the anonymous new single world. I think of the old shop girls and how the same questions applied: Will the heroine maneuver out of the dreary job and away from all those awful people? How can she avoid parties like sexualized rackets if they scare her? And what about the friends determined to find her a one-night guy? Why, as T. R. might have said, do I have to be this age and single right now?

THE BIONIC SINGLE

In many ways it was an excellent time to be young, single, never-married, or even divorced. Penny, a science writer, now forty-nine, says,

> People don't understand that the 1960s progressed very slowly in terms of actual change. On tape, it all looks like a . . . colorful streak! But for a long time girls had helmet hair and pleated skirts on, stockings with garters, *not* panty hose, plus squishy-toed heels. To go out, you prepared for upwards of two hours. You went out "put together" or you—my mother said this—"put your face on" and then, all "faced up," you could face the world. Even though the fashions had this baby-doll quality, the little dresses and booties, you still had on so much makeup and support garments that you kind of looked armored. . . . Most girls, remember, got married—that's what you did; you got married and that was the progression. A lot of people lived through all the weirdness of the 1960s in a married couple. But when things really crashed—in 1969 and I'd say 1970—they really crashed. The changes started seeping out from there, and there was no going back.

Consider that in 1957, 53 percent of the American public had believed that unmarried people were "sick," "immoral," or "neurotic," while only 37 percent viewed them neutrally. During the early seventies, a similar study found that just 33 percent of a large sample group had "negative attitudes and expectations" of the unmarried. Fifty-one percent viewed them "neutrally" and 15 percent approvingly.

There was even a weak but nonetheless official endorsement of single womanhood from the *New York Times*. In August 1970, the *Times* ran an editorial announcing the emergence of "the Liberated Woman." It began by providing necessary context.

> Because western societies are increasingly rich, they can afford to educate more of their women and provide them with leisure. Because science has eliminated most of the drudgery if not the tedium of farm [and] . . . household work, millions of women are free to leave the fields and the kitchens and work beside men . . . those women who have no taste for marriage or childbearing will feel less constrained by society to adopt roles which are uncongenial. . . .

That was not to incite all solo girls to rush out and change. As the authors went on to note: "The family has proved to be a durable human institution in many social settings. . . . The revolution in the status of women will change much and will leave much else unaltered."

One of the biggest changes would be in mass perceptions of unwed women.

During the next few years the single woman would enjoy her own widely endorsed public honeymoon. *Newsweek* reported the following year that "singlehood has emerged as an intensely ritualized—and newly respectable style of American life. It is finally becoming possible to be both single and whole." There were stories on dropout wives, and some sociologists and economists predicted that we would eventually find ourselves in a "totally singles-oriented society." Frozen dinners for one. A rebellion against the terms "double-occupancy" and "family discounts." *The Mary*

Tyler Moore show was in its prime, Rhoda and Phyllis still popping in to complain before fleeing Minneapolis for their own single sitcoms. In 1974 the *New York Times* wrote, "In all respects young single American women hold themselves in higher regard now than a year ago. [They are] self-assured, confident, secure."

For the first time in decades, perhaps for the first time ever, single women began to think about establishing adult, fully furnished lives by themselves. Landlords, who'd clung to the image of stewardess-with-dead-plants (or, not that it was said out loud, "dead stewardess"), began to see a new kind of single female tenant—older, meaning thirtyish, more established and serious. In the words of one young woman, "Do not dare call me a swinging single. I'm an unmarried grown-up."

"Women's lib," as it was still called, had started to change things. "I never in a gazillion years thought I would rent, much less *buy* a house without being married or at least living with someone," says one never-wed art appraiser, "age—deliberately vague." But, she says, by the time she'd reached thirty, "I was tired of living out of the big version of a suitcase—not having the nice things in the style I wanted them in because, goddamit, I was supposed to have these things selected from my registry, or to pick them out together with my husband, with whom I was to establish a real, permanent home. . . . I didn't even have a nice car. Everything was on hold and I was just too far along in all the other areas of my life to live without a decent shower curtain or wineglasses."

One marketing executive called it learning to "think singly." And everyone, even the very married, was advised to learn the dance steps.

By 1975, one in four households were headed by single women, the combined results of so many women waiting to wed and so many others having their marriages unexpectedly end. The Equal Credit Opportunity Act of that year made it much easier for women to buy condos and entire houses and to have aligned in their wallets as many credit cards as they chose. (Before that, in many states, it was impossible for a woman to get credit except under her husband's name.) And many were using them "to buy very 'nice things' like Limoges china and Baccarat crystal," as *The Christian Science Monitor* reported in 1975. "They don't feel that a woman's home life begins when she marries."

"It's hard to imagine attaching much importance to an ashtray, or to even now believe you owned an ashtray, but I bought a Steuben ashtray," says "Jo March," forty-six, special-events manager for a large department store. "It was so clear and heavy and big it took over the room. I saw it that way, anyway. Because it was 'real.' Because it didn't fold up or come in garish colors. I'm not sure I even liked it, I just wanted to have a Something that told people I was living in that place for real, that I was a big girl, and that I had taste."

The other enormous change in single lives was the addition of children.

Back in 1960 an approximate 10 percent of all unwed mothers had kept their babies; ten years later that number had climbed to 45 percent, and in 1975 fully half of all unwed mothers—in most major cities in the Western world—kept their babies. When interviewed, most of these women said they'd like a mate and a large number indicated that they had wanted to live with the baby's father. Then they'd go on to explain why, for many complex reasons, it was not possible. But that didn't change a thing about the baby. He/she was hers and belonged to her alone (not in any way to her parents, spouse, priest, "society," or the baby's father), and she planned to raise him/her on her own. Starting in 1970, more young mothers every year would never marry.

It had also become easier for a single woman to adopt. In 1968 New York City officials had looked at the "staggering illegitimacy rate" and decided, according to one city-administration official, that "half a home would be better than none." Borrowing from a Los Angeles program, New York social services offered to qualified singles "children termed hard to adopt," meaning over the age of three, handicapped, or mixed-race. The adoptive parent had to meet specific criteria—have a steady income and a college degree. It was important that they have primary family members nearby. As it happened, all of those who qualified were women, former or full-time social workers, either widows or divorcees.

The most visible symbols of change were not these sudden mothers minus fathers but the outspoken and very cool-looking single celebrities. The best example of the breed was without a doubt Gloria Steinem. Steinem began her public life during the early sixties as a hardworking journalist, who happened to be very pretty and went to A-list parties and dated famous men. She hated being referred to as a "woman writer," which of course meant the secondary, soft kind of reporter. But from the start of her writing career, she'd been drawn to women as a subject. To mass changes occurring in women's lives. And to situations that exposed what was not yet called sexism. She also chose female subjects who seemed to have much stifled anger and no voice, most famously Pat Nixon, who managed to express much outward public rage at Steinem's perceptive and honest portrayal.

The details of Gloria's life intrigued people. She'd grown up poor and neglected, then won a scholarship to Smith and spent a year abroad as a Neiman Fellow in India. She returned to New York and settled into an Indian-themed studio in the East Seventies that she kept filled at all hours with interesting people—politicians, reporters, actors, and, increasingly, prominent women. Over the years, Gloria was most frequently pictured out dancing with her wealthy, good-looking beaux. But by the early seventies, once she'd been declared the new voice of feminism, magazines like *Newsweek* stopped the dance-party photos and went with long vertical shots of her giving speeches, the sort where the viewer begins at the shoes and works up the long, long legs to the incredibly short dress, to the famous hair, and then, lastly, the microphone.

No matter what Gloria Steinem said or did, no matter whom she interviewed—and she was for a long time a political columnist for *New York* magazine—it would be noted only that she "did something for clinging dresses," thanks to legs "worthy of mini skirts."

She was described as "the thinking man's Jean Shrimpton." Even after she'd founded *Ms.*, turned her apartment into a sort of women's shelter, and become the women's movement's most important player, its secret weapon—the one not perceived as ugly, angry, or cranky—here's how people wrote about her: "She stands there, striking in hip-hugging raspberry Levi's, 2-inch high wedgies and a tight poor-boy t-shirt. Her long blonde-streaked hair falls just so above each breast and her cheerleader-pretty face has been made wiser with the addition of blue-tinted glasses; she is the chic apotheosis of with-it cool."

Gloria Steinem liked to state that "young girls were refusing to be blackmailed into domesticity." But no matter what she said, the ultimate question for Gloria Steinem was always *What about you?* She was gorgeous, though well into her thirties, and so what was she waiting for? When all was said and done, people wanted to know When Would Gloria Settle Down?* Otherwise put, when would she shut up and get a man?

She married for the first time at age sixty-five.

THE SINGLE TAKES A SLIDE

The 1980s, by any estimate, marked a low point in the public accord between single women and men, each side accusing the other of roughly the same crimes: insensitivity, dishonesty, stupidity, and sometimes martyrdom. It was during the late 1970s that this public mudslinging got under way. In newspapers and books and on TV talk shows, the women—"liberated," successful, often divorced—suddenly began to lament a shortage of intelligent, sensitive men. And it was more than mere numbers, more than the well-known fact that so many men were gay. It was the quality of the men themselves. As *Mademoiselle* had put it with great prescience back in 1955, "Perhaps there is only a shortage of *desirable* men—men who are not too fearful and too repressed or too smug or too uninteresting."

In stories typically entitled "Where Are the Men Worthy of Us?" prominent women denounced the single-male population—those "guys" hunkered down in dated bachelor pads, who readily lied and preferred jail bait or the standard fuck-and-run. Reporters in cities everywhere gathered groups of men in bars, apartments, offices, and asked them to answer the charges. Sessions sometimes lasted well into the early morning. Christ! Weren't these bitches just spinsters-in-training? Victims of women's lib? They were probably dogs. There were references to dry vaginas.

---

*No matter how radical you were, it was hard to get a break. Feminist Kate Millet, author, bisexual, artist, and one of the few women to have it out publicly with Norman Mailer, was promoting a book. Her mother, who approved of her daughter's work, or at least some of it, nevertheless had to express herself defiantly in 1971: "Kate is really missing the boat if she appears on the *Mike Douglas Show* without washing her hair."

And the conclusion: If there was a shortage of men, it was only be-cause so many women out there were female losers. As one man, forty-one, told the *New York Times*: "All these intelligent, articulate frank strong women . . . [who are] attractive, beautiful and who now feel so much bet-ter about themselves, now look around only to find men suffering from var-ious sexual and psychological dysfunctions? Who's jiving whom? If you're not turning us on, baby, check your assets. You really haven't come a long way. You are boring us."

On it went, from 1974 to 1980:

Women: "I have lost all patience with men who like little girls."

Men: "Women want to see your pay stub and your investment portfo-lio before accepting a drinks date."

Women: "Aging bachelors can age all on their own, without my assis-tance."

Men: "What do women want? They want to be free to do whatever they want, as long as a man pays for all of it."

Both: "It's just too hard . . . I think I'll stay home . . . I got an answer-ing machine!"

Columnist Russell Baker, in 1978, questioned the value of so many staying home alone.

> The women's movement attempts to lionize the female bachelor. Newspapers, books, and magazines recite happy tales of women who, having successfully skirted the perils of husbands and nest-building, have found contented anchorage in private harbours alone with their TV sets, their books, their wine, their pictures, their telephones, and their self-fulfillment. . . . you wonder whether we are becoming a race that is simply afraid of people.

There were many women out there in other parts of the country who were not afraid of people, not angry, and not included in this press cover-age of the single and her minidramas. Single life as presented in the mass media was a phenomenon of the big cities and the affluent areas in partic-ular. Said one woman in the mid-seventies:

I just laugh when I read about the exciting single life . . . what wonderful chances there are for a girl alone today. That Cosmopolitan Girl! Wow! I'm a secretary to a man who owns a liquor store—the only other men I meet are married liquor dealers. If it hadn't been for my kids, I would've moved to a bigger town— maybe Detroit, when my husband took off. But I bring home ninety-five dollars a week—before taxes, get that—and my mother takes care of my two little girls while I'm working. . . . Where is my wild single life? And I am twenty-eight, thank you.

At the same time, no matter their circumstances, all single women had many unlikely things in common.

To speak of the very tangible, unmarried women's household incomes averaged 60 percent less than two-income (usually married) households; unmarried men, however, maintained household incomes just 15 percent less than those of married couples. Single women paid more taxes than married women—as much as 20 percent more ("America has a severe case of the singles," said *Money* magazine in 1976). And there was also the bizarre single world of insurance. For a long time it was hard for single women to buy homeowner's insurance: because there was likely to be no one home during the day, she was considered a bad risk.

And they shared less tangible things.

Most significant was the fact that women, even if they loved their single lives, were not accustomed to spending so much time by themselves. In *Toward a New Psychology of Women* (1979), Dr. Jean Baker Miller, a feminist and psychiatrist, addressed this absence of "connection." She described one subject, a "bright career woman" about twenty-seven or twenty-eight, who was "very active and effective" but essentially depressed. As difficult as it was for her to believe, this woman had found that she could not feel happy without a man around, even briefly, to watch her and approve her efforts. After many years of training to perform in front of or manipulate men—not that she would have put it quite that way—she found that she needed the affirmation, if not the security of a regular relationship. As quoted in a story on the book:

I know it's bullshit . . . but what if there isn't a man there, watching me? Then it's like this moment—whatever it is I am doing—
doesn't matter. . . . Of course I really care about my girlfriends;
that's a given in my life. But those bonds can't really ever develop
into what I'd call the fundamental thing. To make it real, or meaningful, or whatever, there has to be the sound of one man clapping.
I know this sounds totally sick.

Miller argued that such women—and there were a lot of them—suffered less from father fixations or advanced insecurities than they did problems of "affiliation," what Miller called the learned overemphasis on
connections to men. As she wrote, "They lack the ability to really value
and credit their own thoughts, feelings and actions. It is as if they have lost
a full sense of satisfaction in the use of themselves and of their own resources or never had it to begin with." One single woman, thirty-one, put
it bluntly: "There's the sense that there has to be the other person there."

There was also the shared sense that the singles scene, or culture, or
business was becoming an embarrassment. "I went, I swear, once to a 'singles fair,' " says a bonds trader, forty-eight, married now but at the time the
kind of woman who had "affiliation" issues. ("I always sat on my couch fac-
ing kind of sideways, with my legs curled up, as if I was having a conversation with someone. I wasn't.")

She recalls leaving the fair after one group exercise: To walk out of the
hotel hosting the event and into a nearby "department store and to walk
out with the names and phone numbers of three single men. I would rather
have risked the humiliation of being rejected at Studio 54 than have had
to do that," she says. "This was the key to my future?"

Singles expos, singles magazines (*Your Place or Mine?*), and humiliat-
ing gift books (*How to Make Love to a Man*, with chapter headings such as
"Wash the Dishes Nude") made single life seem sleazy. And it was still,
more so than ever, a dangerous way to live.

City cops and social workers routinely made statements to news-
magazines such as, "Young unmarried women are destroyed by seeing liberation strictly in terms of sexual freedom." They referred to the fact that

the single murders so common in '73 and '74 had continued and now most often had a drug connection. And they didn't mean the much beloved Quaaludes. (Just to give some sense of how "beloved": In 1979, Edlich's Pharmacy at First Avenue and Fiftieth Street reported filling eighteen thousand prescriptions for methaqualone, generic for 'ludes, more than half the entire state's total and more than half went to young women.)

"Nice" girls were found in motels far west on Forty-second Street, overdosed on heroin, and others OD'd from the lines of cocaine that were passed around on party platters. Girls from the suburbs were found in Central Park, unconscious or dead. Rape attacks were up or just reported more consistently.

The head of the New York City rape squad very memorably put it this way: "Single women should avoid being alone in any part of the city, at any time."

And there were deeper, less immediately palpable terrors still.

In January 1979 the *New York Times* reported, "Hospital at last identifies its shopping bag lady." Pictured was an old Hungarian woman who'd been found a while back wandering, stupefied, her possessions—old photos, letters, postcards, canned soup, pretty scarves—neatly arranged inside Bloomingdale's and Macy's shopping bags. The director of the Human Resources Administration's Office of Psychiatry noted that "there are probably a couple of hundred shopping bag ladies in the city." (If you had looked up the very first reference to "shopping bag lady" in *The Reader's Guide to Periodical Literature*, 1977, you'd have found "see tramps.")

Her cheeks had collapsed around her gums. Her hair was gray and spongy, and she wore whole sets of clothes on top of other clothes as if she were her own personal closet. She looked like a character summoned to the present from an old fairy tale, only the summoning spell had played a trick. She was not the pretty, wide-awake heroine you'd been expecting. She was the embodiment of all that can go wrong to the pretty and wide-awake heroine. Hers was one of the classically awful female fates—the hideous hag—and there was nothing comfortably mythic or metaphorical about her at all.

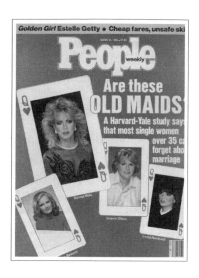

CHAPTER SEVEN

TODAY'S MODERNE UNMARRIED—HER TIMES
AND TRIALS: ICE QUEENS OF THE EIGHTIES AND
NINETIES, BABY BRIDES, SLACKER SPINSTERS,
AND THE SINGULAR CRY OF THE WILD: "HEY!
GET YOUR STROLLER OFF MY SIDEWALK!"

There is a thin and pretty woman in New York who thinks that Bloomingdale's is the loneliest store in the world because, on Saturdays, so many couples shop there.

—THE NEW YORK TIMES, 1974

There is a single woman in New York, bright and accomplished, who dreads nightfall, when darkness hugs the city and lights go on in warm kitchens.

—THE NEW YORK TIMES, 1987

I am so lonely I could die. I wake, realize I don't have a boyfriend and put my head in the oven. . . . I go to parties, night classes, museums, various clubs and mixers with my eyelashes curled hopefully and am

*wracked with disappointment to find only more hopeful women with
curled eyelashes. I go to dinner parties and my throat seizes up with envy
as I watch the happy couples, who are my friends. My nights are long
with longing. Grief. Also, I have a large bridge in New York to sell you.
Ho. Ho. Ho.*

—CYNTHIA HEIMEL, PLAYBOY, 1997

To close this book, I naturally set out to identify the preeminent single
icons of the moment, and to analyze how they had evolved out of all the
many preceding incarnations. Most important, I needed to know if "single
icon" as a term was still culturally relevant. The work itself at least seemed
easier. After months of handling frail brown-edged magazines and fifth-
generation copies of out-of-print books, I enjoyed arriving at my Internet
portal of choice and typing in *single women*. As it turned out, that was like
typing in the name of a continent: an entity so massive and complex that
thousands of possible routes crossed any small section.

After several hours spent on-line I changed my metaphor. Single life
seemed more like a huge, overcrowded refugee camp, the refugees desperate for help in escaping.

Here is the world's most extensive catalogue of single life and thought,
and it is dominated by a highly particularized collection of personal ads, and
popular e-dating services, interspersed with creepy bride-buying offerings.
("Bulgarian girls! Russian, as well as from the Belarus and Ukraine! Also
beautiful girls who will make fine wives from Greece and Turkey!") Hoping
to find less depressing expressions of single life at this point, I hung around
in the ubiquitous chat rooms. But these "rooms," with their cheesy masquerade-
ball requirements, seem as awkward and unnatural a place to communicate
as the sixties-era "trystorium." (That included, as you may remember, rooftop
daiquiri parties and go-go coed Laundromats.) The singular Web sites and e-
zines ("Leather spinsters on the Web—the e-zine for the Happily Unmarried
Woman"; "Young Spinster—No Marriage Prospects, No Apologies") seemed
more promising. Here was a new forum for the sardonic, faux-masochistic
single sensibility—the self-deprecating jokiness of female stand-up comics—
but mixed with fairly serious tables of contents.

Unfortunately, these sites are infested, as are the personals and chat rooms, with intrusive pop-up windows, the first and highest form of Internet graffiti. Some of these ads are for personal services ("alluring" hair braids; all-over body waxing; phone sex to aid in masturbation), while some hype "reconstruct-your-entire-self" kinds of books accompanied by inspirational CDs. A subcategory of these single books—a specimen rampant on Amazon.com—is the wiseass advice manual or what I think of as the clever novelette. The tone is sarcastic and funny, and each comes with lots of reassuring space between the paragraphs and a shiny "cool-girl" cover. (Cool-girl covers are all alike: They feature a skinny, dark-haired, red-nailed cartoon girl wearing a little black dress. Either her arms are folded, or she is smoking. The titles, in retro fifties-era fonts, announce the *Go-Girls Guide* or *Grrrrrl's Rules for Love and Life*, although some titles are long and have a kind of Borscht Belt cuteness, recalling *Sheila Levine Is Dead and Living in New York*. My favorite in this category: *Even God Is Single, So Why Are You Giving Me a Hard Time?*)

After touring the cyber singles world, I happily returned to the land of live subjects. But this last round of interviewing mirrored my experience playing around on the Web: Conversations were so digressive that in the span of minutes the person, talking about workplace dynamics, was very, very angry at some man she had not seen for several years and also, it seemed, if you asked her, that her nieces were the only sane or attractive thing about her sister. A number of women in their twenties talked for a very long time about the fun of writing and posting personals on various agreed-upon "cool" Internet sites. Many of them did it for the "hits," the number of responses they got to the descriptions they'd written of themselves. Often they did not actually go on these dates. But the hits were a way of "moving self-esteem" and "keeping up." Other women just stared at me and after checking messages and retracing lipstick wondered what I could possibly have to ask them. In fact, some women over thirty-five seemed to suffer a kind of celebritylike ennui, as if they had heard all the questions before and didn't really need to hear them again before answering.

Here, a random sampling from my notes:

1) Dates with men are more annoying than ever because many men are either divorced or widowed or just too young and believe it is the "point" of the evening to sit down and talk at length—often "through the entrées"—about themselves. On the other hand, dates are great for just this reason because they're over quickly and do not require any chancy emotional interest, nor even that one pay attention. Then, from other points of view, that's not the way it is at all; it's reverse sexism by horny disappointed women to say that men hog conversation. There is also the view that this is an inaccurate scenario because no one has a date of such length without a less risky meeting for drinks or lunch or on an airplane first.

2) "Older" single women are, in the span of one afternoon and three conversations, first cool pioneers figuring out how to live singly, or make communities, and have children, or else they are unbelievably pathetic losers. People who waited. People who were deluded by feminism. People who will have nasty experiences with Pergonal and Clomid. And depending on the circumstance—the speaker—"old" can occur at 30 or 35 or 40, 50 or 27.

I tried to find a clear passage, a defining subject line, through my notes. Margaret, forty-two, a talk-show booker who's twice divorced, said, "Forget it. . . . the single world is teeming." She did not view it as a continent or a refugee camp. As she saw it, "What you have here is a swamp."

If distinct single archetypes seem for the moment to have blurred, the conviction that single women are social outcasts—odd women who require constant translation—remains intact. Wherever she is, perhaps in a waiting room or on an airplane or lost in the morass of the Internet, she'll eventually find a story about her uncertain future and her inevitable regret. As always, the story will include picture of a lone single woman holding a ginger-colored or Siamese Pywacket cat. I've got a picture in front of me now as I write, part of a recent *Daily News* special on women who insist (again and again) that they don't want to have children. The caption beneath a photo of a long-haired woman with her stretching cat: "Her cats are enough, says busy film-maker Donna Gilardi, 35, about her decision not, ever, to have children."

But if one stays with it, ignores all the ads and distractions and contradictions, there are discernible single icons for the new century. To bring them more fully into focus it's necessary to look at those immediately preceding—the single types that were introduced and viciously attacked during the 1980s and '90s.

THE BIG CHILL: THE ANTISINGLE EIGHTIES AND NINETIES

During the 1980s bookshelves were crammed with punishing tirades: *Otherwise Engaged: The Private Lives of Successful Career Women; A Lesser Life; Smart Women, Foolish Choices,* and many tomes that featured the words "biological clock," a phrase repeated so often I began to think of it as a body part, perhaps a moody colon or a giant cyst. I include as an adjunct to this sad single genre the *Cathy* cartoon books, which seem innocuous enough until, on the fourth or fifth volume, the self-deprecation starts to seem like a pathological tic. In retrospect, I also think the most popular cat book of the era—and at the time "cat" was its own publishing category—played on stereotypes associated with single women. *Garfield* was a male cat, but his primary characteristics were borrowed from traits commonly ascribed to single females: he was fat, eccentric, sneaky, and lived in constant anticipation of food because there was nothing else in his life.

These books had various points to make, but the primary conclusions were always, however expressed or disguised, that women had paid an enormous personal price for the successes of feminism, in particular the demands and sacrifices required by their jobs. Married women with children, those said to "juggle"—the euphemism for impossible trade-offs between work and family—were well known to confront physical breakdown if they did not ultimately choose the part-time "mommy track," meaning the relinquishing of their career goals to work a nontenured, nonpartner three-day week that allowed them to leave at five.

The single woman confronted different kinds of possible and likely breakdowns. One of these, as described by a USA *Today* reporter in 1989, was "an O.D. of Machisma." The other can be summarized as a kind of all-new quiet spinsterly death by pathos.

This last was best described in a 1991 story, "What About Alice?," that appeared in *The Washington Post*. The piece, written by a man, began, "I shall invent a woman." And he did. A prototypical lawyer, good salary, fairly attractive, and, at thirty, still unwed. As the story begins, it was "dawning on Alice that she [might] never get married. And the same thing seemed to be occurring to many others she knew." Nobody understood why, but that's how "things were working out" and it was becoming frustrating. And expensive. Her creator explained:

> Alice is tired of celebrating the milestones of others. Sometimes her life is a wearying round of parties and weddings, showers and more parties. She is asked to celebrate what she is coming to see as reminders of her own failure: The engagements, weddings and babies of others. Each invitation is like a flunking report card. These events are not only emotionally draining. They are costly as well.

"Alice," he wrote, as if addressing all the unmarried law-school grads and unattached MBAs of the universe, "my heart goes out to you. You are the grim smile of every Academy Award loser." And he concluded by reminding us that Alice did not exist. Had she been real, she'd have "broken your heart." For all those like her—those contending with their non-chance of marriage, all those still forced to argue (years later!) about *Fatal Attraction*—it sounded grim. The *San Francisco Chronicle* summarized the dating climate, circa 1990, as an anti–greeting card: "Modern romance is a mess. To enter this magic land, one must maneuver through a gantlet of expectations, confusing miscommunications, desperate avoidance of intimacy and fears of everything from rejection to sex disease."

The professional woman "O.D.ing on Machisma" was just as sad. Older than Alice, this single character had spent years struggling against sexism, suppressing anger, and she was thus in her dealings with the world and men especially a brittle and sarcastic presence. The essential icon in this category was TV journalist Murphy Brown, as played by Candace Bergen on the long-running TV series. Murphy was known for many things, but I remember most the dresses that had openings at the shoulders, as designed specially for the show by Donna Karan. These "cold-shouldered" outfits were the power look of the moment, I always thought, because the metaphorical chips on Murphy's shoulders were so huge they mandated special tailoring. It seemed that women who'd worked their way to a position like Murphy's were just as pathetic as the Alices, if in a different way. They were tougher, more accomplished, richer, and had fabulous perquisites, all to cover unsuccessfully for the fact that they had forfeited their ability to do anything "female" in life. The macho career woman was depicted as an update on the harsh 1930s career woman, that intersexual, mannish, possibly lesbian postwar working bitch missing a heart. As it was most often expressed in the late 1980s and '90s, this woman had some kind of cerebral and/or neurological inability to deal with children. (Other people's children, of course, for it was presumed that she wouldn't have any of her own.) For example, if there was a baby in her apartment, how was she, a person with important work to do, supposed to know what it wanted?

Movies, again, form an excellent primer. One precursor to this 1990s archetype is Elizabeth Lane, the Barbara Stanwyck character in *Christmas in Connecticut* (1946), an early Martha Stewart kind of columnist who writes of her farm and her fabulous meals and her babies, although the entire thing is made up. She lives in the city and can't boil water. At Christmastime, the great Mrs. Elizabeth Lane is asked to play hostess to a war hero. On her farm. With her cows and antiques and babies and all the rest, including a husband, and so the panicked Stanwyck promises to marry a man she detests in order to borrow his farm. She also "borrows" a baby. At one point we hear the baby crying in the other room. Everyone looks at Mrs. Lane. Finally she understands! It's the baby! "It's crying!" she says, looking panicked. "Oh, um, I must *go to it!*" Forty years later Diane Keaton, the harried "tiger lady" in *Baby Boom* (1987), is not even capable of lifting the infant that's been left to her by a relative. Even with the improvements since Elizabeth Lane's day, "J. C.," the MBA and brilliant marketing executive, cannot get a diaper on the baby. A diaper is not within her conceptual framework.

A related example from real life: When the late film executive Dawn
Steel had a baby, people in the Hollywood community asked, jokingly,
"Who's the mother?"

But life among single professional women, or any other single women,
simply was not all that harsh. In 1986 the government funded a large six-
state study of single women's sex habits. It turned out that a third of all subjects at one point had cohabited because they did not feel "ready" to get
married. With more than half of all marriages failing, and a hefty percentage failing during the first two years, some felt no rush to marry. And, for
many women, the question was, "Marry who?" ("All the men I meet are either gay, married, crazy, or just plain boring," went the popular lament; if
it could have fit onto coffee mugs and bumper stickers, it would have.)

Research also showed that women in the eighties and nineties were
not as depressed or as suicidal as others liked to think. It had long been a
truism, for example, that single women were twice as likely to suffer from
depression as married women. But a 1992 study of 18,600 professional
middle-class white women and men, single and married, showed that the
difference in rates of depression was pretty low. Of all the married women
interviewed, 3.5 percent had been diagnosed with major depressive disorders, compared with 4.1 percent of the single women; after divorce, the
transition back into singlehood, the rate flew up to 9 percent, then
dropped down within eighteen months.

But the results of these surveys, and others like them, were lost or entirely unknown to a generation of younger women, born in and around
1970. The image of highly successful single career women dragging all
these personal crises through their lives seemed slightly ridiculous. In many
ways, this older generation of women seemed to have handled their lives,
especially their personal lives, irresponsibly. I read the following two paragraphs to all women I interviewed who were under thirty-two. The first, as
reprinted from a major newsweekly, circa 1990:

> With a bulk of baby boomers entering the final stages of their fer-
> tile years, the sound of several million biological clocks has be-
> come as loud as Big Ben on steroids.

I alternated this quote with that of an excerpt from *Salon*, 2000:

I did a year of unidentified inseminations . . . that's "donor-deposit" or "DD," where the donor remains anonymous. (If it's "DI," that means the donor is willing to be identified later.) . . . I carried my sperm home in a dry ice cooler that's called a "mini-mate."

After reading one or sometimes both quotes, almost all of the young women expressed disapproval that ranged from pity to physical disgust.

"No offense to you," one twenty-three-year-old subject told me firmly, "but I would not want to be your age and not have these ends tied together. That's really a hopeless way to build a life. . . . "a mini-mate"? This is so pathetic. . . . How low can you go?"

It is this generational contempt that gives us the first single archetype of the 1990s and the new century: the young, defiantly post-feminist woman who believes she must take care of the "single situation" in a prompt and businesslike fashion. Before she turns twenty-seven. Or else.

BABY BRIDES AND BABY BOOM BUSTERS

If you suffer, as I do, from a lifelong tendency to listen to three conversations simultaneously in public, "graduate-level eavesdropping" as I think of it, then you must have noticed, circa 1998, a shift in lunchtime conversations and those of women friends out for drinks and dinner. Suddenly they weren't just discussing men. They were discussing marriage. And they seemed young. I'd gotten married in 1989 at age thirty, and was one of the first of my peers to do so. (Two friends, separately, had spoken to me, asking if I would promise not to have a baby right away; it was too much, too distant and unthinkable; I'd . . . disappear. And besides, I was too young.)

For the generation below me, all those for whom "women's lib" is as archaic a term as "abolitionist" or "freedom rider," postponed marriage and childbearing is a laughable notion. It has been a long, long while since men were legally empowered oppressors and wifery the well-traveled path to madness. The conditions that made marriage so difficult for women—and spurred the protective notion of waiting to develop one's "full self" before leaping—had disappeared. There were more reasons to marry young, or whenever one could, than to wait. Many young women had lived what Rose, twenty-eight, a book editor, calls

> a totally new untraditional life featuring the whole range of expe-
> riences starting from a very young age and your parents separating.
> I mean we had step-siblings on top of step-siblings. We had pot
> and drinking and sex, even if that was deemphasized because of
> disease. There was a lot of worry and denial. Oh, I mean, by
> twenty-one you had done . . . everything. . . . And I think every-
> thing was too much for that age. I think our view was—I mean,
> my friends—if the opportunity was there, why not get married? . . .
> No, I'm not married, but I would definitely like to be married. A
> lot of my friends are married. . . . To be honest, I'm tired of being
> the odd girl out. It's a big pain in the butt.

During the early nineties the short-lived *Married Woman* magazine ran a story called "Old Friends, New Friends." The subtitle read, "Don't Feel Guilty if You Want to Put Your Single Friends on Hold and Reserve a Table for Four"; elsewhere in the piece we learned, "It's only natural to feel a strong urge to edit your address book."

This might have been written in 1953. But to intended readers, the total-itarian marital outlook of the fifties—an all-new "togetherness"— had noth-ing at all to do with their own lives in the 1990s. They were, to quote many TV commercials and newsmagazine segments, free single women devising cre-ative solutions to their lives and problems, primarily to the unsettling state of "singleness" in such an unsettled world. They were not "slaves to societal cus-tom . . . and not cruel to our friends who are not married yet," explains Tara, who did not get engaged until twenty-six. "I thought through my options and waited. . . . No one was pushing me to do it. Well, perhaps a little, because that's what society expects. . . . But what I wanted was someone in my life to go out with, permanently, and what is wrong with that? Someone to take with you out into life? Just think about what life is these days. Why wouldn't you want a partner? . . . Having your friends goes only so far."

More than one million young couples between the ages of twenty-two and twenty-five, last year agreed.

"There's just something so very right about confronting the world and your job and the hostility of everything, knowing that there's someone who is legally and emotionally attached to you," says Mrs. Caitlin Cardozo, the only young subject who did not wish to have her name changed. "I'm proud of what I've achieved in my personal life," she says. Although she admits that there is "a tiny bit of a stigma connected to marrying at a young age," she thinks "the people who object or have a problem with this are people in their thirties who have put a lot of emphasis on career, and now don't know what to think or do about marriage." She speculates, "Maybe someone like me is threatening to them. Maybe I make them concerned that their own way of doing things, all that cool late-night-at-the-office life, was not very well thought out."

This view is most wonderfully captured in a 1997 piece in *New York* magazine about young wealthy girls racing around to weddings as if it were 1952. The piece begins on Park Avenue and features young college gradu-ates, onetime private-school cliques, in Vera Wang's and Bergdorf's, look-ing impatient with the women crouched on the floor fixing the hems of their gowns. One young woman, twenty-one, explains, and I paraphrase, We're city-bred girls and we've had our share of wild times and drugs and fooling around. Getting married is a way to move beyond that phase in life and not to get stuck, in another one, alone.

And as author Sara Bernard assesses things, "The circle of women who seem to be skipping their Mary Tyler Moore Murphy bed phase . . . is bigger than just the waspy-preppy circuit." Many others out there had upsetting per-sonal histories that read like that of Rose quoted above, the "untraditional . . . range of experiences starting . . . [with] your parents separating." Many want to marry early or whenever it's right and, like Mrs. Caitlin Cardozo, believe that it is only older Others who have problems with this scenario.

But now and then someone acknowledges the unique tensions and am-biguities of younger wifehood, many of these conflicts directly related to youth—to the inescapable feeling that a twenty-one-year-old wife has in some sense skipped out on a vital part of her young life. These tensions seem to simmer and sometimes explode when doing housework. As one twenty-four-year-old puts it, "Others are having TGIF-fucking Friday and I'm having to vacuum—rugs and the floors and tiles—because, look, I'm not fucking mopping, thank you, and his parents are coming over in twenty minutes and we both work."

Vacuuming. Dishes. Laundry. Many younger married women say it seems to be more difficult to do housework as a married person than as a single. "I'll be vacuuming or changing the beds or the sheets and I'll get this creeped-out feeling," says "Jennifer," twenty-three. "When I was doing those things for myself, I did them because I wanted to, not because I had to—it felt like part of the fun of living on your own, out of your mother's house. Now there is a sense of 'I have to do this,' like there's something instinctual in my doing this, and I don't like it. Even if my husband helps, I don't feel comfortable with it."

An acquaintance of hers, "Veronica or Betty," agrees. "I have this strange antipathy to housework, which seems to have to do with this 1950s notion of what is a wife. . . . I'm really very surprised by this, but it's almost like I have this Stepford Wives fear of deep cleaning. That's the true reason I got a maid to help. It wasn't because I was too busy. I was wondering, What am I doing?"

Part of this discomfort is the natural adjustment to plain life after weddings that are only several steps removed from the grandiosity of Cher in Las Vegas.* And part of it is a genuine ambivalence about so huge a commitment coming so soon after another major life event—graduation—and with very little time off between.

But ultimately housework is a small and manageable part of the bargain.

---

*A random excerpt from one recent bridal publication on the subject of a "budget-conscious but still gloriously Luxe event." We learn, for example, that a 750-milliliter bottle of Moët et Chandon Brut Imperial costs $45.50, if you know where to shop; 100 guest invitations, depending on paper weight and calligraphic style, cost a minimum of $1,000, although that's conservative and does not take into account, in some stores, the envelopes and reply cards. The catering for 150 guests, as estimated by three much-in-demand New York caterers: $25,000; tux rental: $170; bridal gown, $1,800–$2,500, although there's a lot of latitude here; some go as high as $3,500. Then flowers. All we learn is that the floral package—bouquets, arrangements, boutonnieres—starts at $1,000 for "a small wedding party." Pictures, unless you have a talented and friendly relative, will run $4,500–$5,000 and the his 'n' her 18-karat-gold rings will cost upward of $800. Finally, the cake, or what were formerly cakes and now look like little Busby Berkeley sets with twirling staircases lined by cherubs and angels instead of girls with harps, begin at $5,000.

There is only one word that comes up again and again during conversations with baby brides, and it is not *dishes* or *vacuuming*; it is *safe*. *Safe* is a shorthand way of saying, "Go out into the world two by two." And it's the desire to consecrate and guarantee this safety that lies at the heart of monster weddings. The bigger and more complicated the official ceremony, the more tangibly serious and safe the marriage.

Go into any Barnes & Noble, find the display coffee-table wedding books, and take a look at how many pages are stained with coffee and/or greasy pastries. Last year, based on research at three separate branches and two independent stores, I determined that a special significance had been attached to page 127 of the original Martha Stewart wedding book. Always folded back and/or heavily smeared, the double spread shows a bride, all complex white angles, rushing across a busy Tribeca street holding calla lilies. In ways, it's just a typical fashion shot—fabulous dress stands out on dingy street. But this picture tells another story. At the moment of the photo, the single woman is outside, alone, dodging trucks on a filthy street. But up ahead is the restaurant—a chic sanctuary, where she will be "the star of her own wedding," to quote 1960s author Rebecca Greer. She will also be safe. If she doesn't scurry off to that wedding, however, if she *waits*, whether intentionally or because her life moves in other directions, she may confront obstacles beyond a lack of desirable partners. No longer scared and unsafe, she may develop a chronic marital ambivalence.

In a 1999 *Esquire* piece, "The Independent Woman and Other Lies," Katie Roiphe wrote about young independent women attempting to reconcile their longing for a traditional man and a free life of their own. She envisioned this male savior as "the Man in the Gray Flannel Suit," or any suit, a gentleman lawyer who'd instinctively pay for her drinks and bring flowers to the brownstone he'd bought for her, where she was at work on her novel and, alternately, taking bubble baths. It's a fantasy that anyone could pick up and play around with. But Roiphe herself, a published author and Ph.D., already had a great apartment and a life that allowed her to run around New York City at all hours and come home when she felt like it. And, as she thought about it, it was actually difficult to imagine sharing the space, and the life, with someone else. She realized that she had been indoctrinated into the Cult of Independence (my phrase). "It may be one of the bad jokes history plays on us," she wrote, ". . . the independence my mother's generation wanted so much for their daughters was something we could not entirely appreciate or want. It was like a birthday present from a distant relative—wrong size, wrong color, wrong style." And the "dark and unsettling truth" was that the gift could not be returned. The situation would forever be difficult to reconcile: the Man in the Gray Flannel Suit versus Her.

THE SPINSTER AS BEMUSED SLACKER

The premiere single archetype of the new century is someone who, like Roiphe, probably assumed in college she'd get married, then had a serious career, then had relationships, then . . . well, it gets hard to say, exactly, in a day-to-day recounting, but one *can* say life seemed to get very busy. Many boyfriends. Many major projects. Many drinks and events and then, oh, well, you know, it gets to be Christmas and, now, oh, God, not again, she's sort of rambling . . . but, hey, she's a cleverly scripted fictional single who, an amalgam of many real thirtyish never-weds, stands as the latest in singular icons.

There are two primary exemplars of this highly competent but still dithering archetype: Ally McBeal (of David Kelley and former Fox-TV fame) and Bridget Jones (of British journalist Helen Fielding/Renée Zellweger fame). To sketch them, let's borrow icons from the 1970s, first decade of the modern single working woman. Specifically, imagine cross-pollinating the hyper TV executive Faye Dunaway played in *Network* with Woody Allen's Annie Hall.

That's just a cartoonish idea. What makes Ally and Bridget special types, the essential single icons of the moment, is their ability to find the humor—corny as it sounds, the "humanity"—in some fairly unbearable social situations. Deadpan and highly self-aware, they can laugh at themselves without becoming self-deprecating and/or snide. They can be sad, sob at their desks, and it's never pathetic because they get over it and go back to work. Emotional states that women are usually punished for—rage, pathos, lust—are here just naturally occurring parts of the character and, by extension, parts of life.

The recently departed Ally McBeal was not terribly appealing at first, with her micromini suits, improbable Gumby body, and the supposed Harvard law education we never actually saw in evidence. But she grew on you. She was beautiful, successful, she could sing, but there were also the basic and unglamorous facts of her life.

She worked horrible hours, during which she tried, without great success, to be one of the guys. She worked, knowing that she also had to share the bathroom, aka "the unisex," with these guys. Some of whom she had slept with. While they'd been involved with her colleagues. Of course she met men elsewhere—in court (one of them accused her, loudly, right there, of treating him as a sex object), while out buying coffee (one of these, much later, told her he was bisexual), or at the car wash, where she dreamily followed a cute guy inside . . . the car wash itself, where he happened to work. She arrived at her own office soaking wet. Once she arrived in court with a bowling ball stuck on her finger. Once she was arrested for tripping a woman in a supermarket. And on and on.

As much as she looked like an *L.A. Law* alumnas, she had distinct elements of Lucille Ball, or Lucille Ball on LSD. As part of almost every script, Ally hallucinated. For a while she saw singer Al Green in many peculiar situations; of course there was the dancing baby, the diapered metaphor of female failure that appeared in her living room. (She was a good sport and danced with it.) Her sex fantasies took up most of her mental life—a much more realistic approach than the *Sex and the City* model, in which professional single urban women have sex at least four times a day.

Women loved Ally because she tried yet couldn't pull all of this together, couldn't make herself any emotionally or intellectually neater, resolved. She was always in flux—as if flux were a physical condition—and she couldn't imagine, like most women, what personal earthquake might occur to make it better.

Her British counterpart, Bridget Jones, is less professionally accomplished; in fact, she hasn't done much to speak of at all, but she has the ability to see and understand every nuance of single social life, and to record her observations in the now notorious diary. Women love her slangy comments on "smug marrieds" and "fuckwit" men. And they love that she can't *do* anything more to change the social order than can Ally McBeal. And Ally McBeal is *cute*. Bridget Jones is overweight. But unlike previous chubby single icons, for example, Rhoda Morgenstern, Mary Tyler's Moore's old housemate, she doesn't work the obvious fact into every sentence (the Phyllis Diller school of self-appraisal). Bridget simply records it, along with her cigarette and alcohol intake, and gets on with her life, which often consists of sorting dirty clothes in order to find clean ones. Like Ally, she is self-possessed and funny about her singleton status (an eighteenth-century term updated). She also defends it. One of my favorite scenes in the recent movie adaptation occurs when after a wretched workday Bridget has to attend a dinner party with a horrifying posse of "smug marrieds." That means a long table full of couples pressed up next to each other in units of two. She's placed at the head—the evening's sociological specimen. A man points to his wife's pregnant belly and makes a tick-tock sound; another man asks why so many career women in their thirties are still not married. She says (I paraphrase), "Maybe it's because of the fact that their bodies are covered in hideous scales." No one laughs.

I use the term "slacker spinsters" because these two, like so many women I know in their thirties, seem to be kind of hanging out in the lives that have evolved around them, making sporadic efforts to connect with men, then retreating back to the couch, the TV, or the phone or into an elaborate fantasy. They believe in the possibilities of love, though it's not clear they fully believe in the beautiful possibilities of marriage. They've lived through the same kind of chaos that baby brides list on their résumés. But they've come to different conclusions. Primarily, getting married will never guarantee a feeling of safety.

Not that they won't try. Try hard. Christ, in a desperate situation, they might even read *The Rules*, or its sort-of sequel, the new "Surrendered Single," conduct guides for the twenty-first century, as if interpreted by Helen Gurley Brown. But chances are they'd just crack up and throw those books across the room. Where they would land either on the dry cleaning or on a pile of unsorted clothes.

A SINGULAR FURY

Many real-life single women have read *The Rules*, and now *The Surrendered Single*, if only from an "anthropological" point of view, or else as a kind of joke. Because how could *any* intelligent life-form take this best-selling advice as less than hilarious?

> Act as if you were born happy! . . . don't leave the house without wearing make-up. Put lipstick on even if you're jogging! If you have a bad nose, get a nose job! Grow your hair long. Men prefer long hair. . . . Men like women. Don't act like a man, even if you are the head of your own company. . . . Don't tell sarcastic jokes. Don't be a loud knee-slapping girl.

The Rules and *Rules* mentality—manipulate, grovel, and lie to get a man—or the Surrendered Single stance—no control, give in, just lie there—does not strike everyone as hilarious or even mildly funny. It makes some women angry. And this angry woman—a New Mad Woman for the Modern Age—gives us a final, more decisive if less adorable archetype than the bemused Ally/Bridget slacker spinster.

"The concept of a person who is out to land men in a deliberately manipulative manner, suggests a frightening dream world," says Marjorie, twenty-five, unwed, and "seriously not sorry. I'm a documentary filmmaker. I travel all the time. And as a woman I couldn't take the time out to plot 'Getting Men.' This isn't junior high. Wear lipstick when you are jogging? If this is to be the basis for a relationship, then you might as well not bother. . . . At least you'd better stop reading. It is so sickening and unfair."

For these women—the documentary filmmakers, med students, marketing executives, serious artists—dodging the media has become a task as basic to everyday life as recycling plastic seltzer bottles.

For example, there is nothing on the single calendar more irritating than holidays, with all their attendant advice about what it is the single person should do to "survive" them. At least as far as other people are concerned. One particularly annoying festival is the national day of single dread, Valentine's Day. How many times can a grown woman be expected to read (and I quote from last year, a major newspaper): "Single in New York and Looking for Love: A Special Report on Dating in the New Century," which here sounds remarkably like the old. A small excerpt:

> Looking for love in New York City is harder than finding a seat on an F train to Queens at rush hour. You can get swamped on the platform. Somebody can cut in front of you. The train can go out of service. When it comes to finding that special person—and we're talking about relationships here, not just sex—a lot of New Yorkers never leave the station. . . . [these] are a complicated time for singles, between crushing work obligations and confused notions of how men and women should relate to each other.

"It really makes me want to puke," says Helen, twenty-six, a currently unemployed copywriter who has lived through many Valentine's Days and found them "more oppressive than Christmas." She continues:

> There is always the huge Valentine story—about how the creative guy proposed to his girlfriend by glueing letters to a Scrabble board. And they are as a couple so urban chic. They are only twenty-three, and yet they live in some amazing loft in TriBeCa and the skinny-girl delicate little bride-to-be is called Amelie or Chantal and she designs, oh, laced gloves or petite evening bags for dogs. And He, the man, wears those nerd glasses and has on a tie for some reason. . . . You think, these aren't real people, or these people are models. And of course they *have* been styled. To get your attention. And to get your goat. TO PISS YOU OFF. I shouldn't let it happen, have that response, but it's just very effective advertising.

There's a kind of story, a series of images, even more bothersome than the corny all-alone holiday story. That is the thousands of stories, in every known form of media—"the relentless hailstorm," as one former colleague put it—all about having babies and raising kids.

"I think it started with *thirtysomething,* in the eighties," says Gail, thirty-nine, a nature photographer.

> It was that horrible Hope character bouncing around with a baby in a forty-room house. . . . I don't dislike children, please! I just can't stand the way you are forced to "react" to them in a way that somehow expresses wonderment with a hint of jealousy because you don't have any. It's so sad! Another sad reminder. . . . I feel like I'm watching [on TV] old fifties footage of the baby boom in the 'burbs only it's set in the present. . . . You walk down the street, you're late and rushing, but wait, you can hear it in the distance getting louder—it's a stampede! Strollers. And these women never think to move their triplets' stroller. It's like, okay, I obviously have the right of way, and the culture supports that. You are just a woman who does not have children, is not married, and either you move or you will get run over.

Some, like Gail, call this confrontation "pure arrogance on the part of anxious younger women . . . the there-but-for-the-grace-of-God shit." Some wish only to clarify their own views on the child issue. Martha, forty-four, says:

> I'm not childless, I am child-free. And neither is my dog a substitute child. My dog is a fine dog. I am not confused on this point. . . . It's hard to believe, but I like my life. . . . I feel like I earned my life and my feelings about it. Because believe me, living in this culture, it is hard not to feel horribly about yourself when you are young and not following the feminine script. . . . I write nothing permanently out of my own personal script! I'm ready now to do these things, if they come up. I just wasn't before

and that doesn't make me a monster or a rule-breaker or a bitch who just, obviously, doesn't like kids because she complains when she is nearly flattened by strollers on Seventy-second Street. . . . Mothers take a perverse pleasure in punishing nonmothers. "How dare she speak that way? Oh, that hostile body language! *She* must not have any children!" That's the refrain of our age.

The media refrain has variations, but in essence it remains the same: No matter what the single woman says, she can't really be happy. Her life is barren and disappointing. Friends consider her a social exile. She is in danger at all times when on her own, and she could miss out on becoming a mother. She is, as Anthony Trollope wrote of his thinned-out, run-down Lily Dale, "blank, lonely and loveless." She is living the "long afternoon of unmarried life." I quote from a classic 1930s spinster novel: "Librarians never marry. And they never die."

Repeat.

Well, it makes for terrifically grim and sorry copy. And for a long time, I think, women believed it. Or at least they understood there were restrictions, a unique system of singular Jim Crow—unwritten laws concerning where they could go, when, for how long, and with whom. Through the 1960s these matters were actually spelled out in terms so precise the syntax and wording seem borrowed from Deuteronomy.

But though still misunderstood and—thanks to writers and directors—still so often maligned, single life is no longer what we for years have enjoyed calling a half life. There are still archetypes, easily applied methodologies for organizing and controlling the way we think about single women. Then there are the unavoidable live women themselves as opposed to the images.

During the nineteenth century, many real women (as opposed to spinsters and shrews) found it easier and more satisfying to choose women friends over men and/or family for their essential life "partners." And it's this long-discouraged practice that accounts for the true appeal of *Sex and the City*. A simple reading presents a very clever, witty drama concerning a variety—almost every variety—of relationships with men and sexual issues (premature ejaculation; strange bathroom habits; trying to make lovers out of sex toys and humans out of men who are angry, et cetera). But the real action and pleasure and love is among the four girlfriends, who spend all their available time together, discussing all of these other relationships. It's like life on an imaginary cruise ship—the four separate briefly, go off and have their various trysts in their various rooms, then return to the dining room, where they review the day, drink, and split dessert four ways. The real conflict occurs right there, among the women; it's in the way they push one another, tell one another the embarrassing absolute truth, hitting on weak spots and self-defeating patterns. And the amazing and perhaps fantastic element is how they don't walk out on one another. If they do, if there are hurt feelings, everyone participates in the reunion, which will typically involve baskets of homemade muffins and/or blender drinks and new shoes.

And it is now distinctly possible that another generation is going to miss the cues of single-illness, or uncomfortability, altogether. Recently I took a bunch of ten- and eleven-year-olds to see the movie *Kate and Leopold*, starring Meg Ryan as a thirty-fivish career woman who dresses like and has the body of a good-looking young man. In fact, her boss at the marketing company to which she's devoted her life compliments her by telling her that she's not really a woman. She's like, and this is the good part, she's like . . . a man. Her ex-boyfriend, like that of every other alleged spinster character—like Bridget Jones and Ally McBeal—has let her down. She gave him "the best seven years of her life." He replies: "Those were the best?"

He's much too preoccupied, anyway, with finding fissures in the space/time continuum and, as the movie starts, has found a portal into the nineteenth century. A handsome duke and inventor somehow follows him back into the present and home to his apartment. Two hours later, Meg, who still lives upstairs from this unfortunate boyfriend, is given every single working woman's dream choice: Go back in time and be rich and beautiful and beloved by a handsome duke, or stay here and be great at your job. Of course, she goes, by throwing herself off the Brooklyn Bridge, the site of the portal, and landing in the nineteenth century, wearing a blue dress.

I asked the ten- and eleven-year-olds what they thought about it, assuming they would vote for portals and dukes and fancy dresses and any way out of wearing those blah "work clothes" plus having a horrible boss. But they surprised me. One told me there were no "jobs for women except secretaries" and so who would want to live then? Although, hedging, she added that Kate's life "now" was "totally boring" and her blue dress was "extremely pretty." A girlfriend of hers suggested that Kate could move to a better apartment and, because she'd been promoted, she could buy all new clothes! She could get "someone who wasn't a weird geek for a boyfriend!" The first girl then added something that she'd learned in school: "Most people in those times didn't even live to be thirty."

Which led to a moment's reflection. Another girl who had favored Kate's going back now said, "If she really went back to *then*, then now, when it's time for her real life, she'd already be dead."

She should live well in her own time and, as they said when I was single, "On her own terms." And no one should say anything more about any of it. There have been too many epitaphs for the single woman, and almost every one of them is pathetic. She is not.

BIBLIOGRAPHICAL NOTES

A study of single women relies heavily on the accomplishments of women's historians. These academics and agitators have taken what was, twenty-two years ago, during my student years, a loosely organized post-sixties discipline and turned it into a recognized field of remarkable scholarship and theory. The body of historical works is at this point so vast that it is physically impossible to list all the books and articles I have consumed over the years and that have influenced my thinking about single women. But I include in the following notes the primary texts I consulted for each section of Bachelor Girl, any document I've quoted from, and a few related works that I think, or hope, will be of interest.

There are many excellent overviews of women's history. I used the following: Sarah Evans, *Born for Liberty: A History of Women in America* (New York: Free Press, 1989); Mary P. Ryan, *Womanhood in America: From Colonial Times to the Present*, 3d ed. (New York: Franklin Watts , 1983); William Chafe, *The Paradox of Change: American Women in the Twentieth Century*, a 1991 reworking of his earlier *The American Woman: Her Changing Social, Economic, and Political Role, 1920–1970* (New York: Oxford University Press, 1972); Nancy F. Cott, ed., *Root of Bitterness: Documents of the Social History of American Women* (New York: Dutton, 1972); Renate Bridenthal and Claudia Koonz, eds., *Becoming Visible: Women in European History* (Boston: Houghton Mifflin, 1977); Nancy F. Cott and Elizabeth Pleck, eds., *A Heritage of Her Own: Toward a New Social History of American Women* (New York: Oxford University Press, 1984).

A few more finely honed time periods: Mary Beth Norton, *Liberty's Daughters: The Revolutionary Experience of American Women, 1750–1800* (Cambridge: Harvard University Press, 1980); Margaret Fuller, *Women in the Nineteenth Century* (1855; New York: W. W. Norton, 1971); Elaine Tyler May, *Great Expectations: Marriage and Divorce in Post-Victorian America* (Chicago: University of Chicago Press, 1980).

On the history of feminism:

The standard reference and most frequently assigned women's history text is Eleanor Flexner, *Century of Struggle: The Woman's Rights Movement in the United States* (1959; New York: Atheneum, 1970); Rosalind Rosenberg, *Divided Lives: American Women in the Twentieth Century*, American Century series, Eric Foner, ed. (New York: Hill and Wang/Noonday Press, 1992), is invaluable for its analysis of the parallel struggles of black and white women, individuals, and activists; Nancy F. Cott, *The Grounding of Modern Feminism* (New Haven: Yale University Press, 1987); Elizabeth Cady Stanton, *Eighty Years and More: Reminiscences 1815–1897* (1898; New York: Schocken, 1971); *Elizabeth Cady Stanton/Susan B. Anthony: Correspondence, Writings, Speeches* (New York: Schocken, 1981); William P. O'Neill, *Everyone Was Brave: A History of Feminism in America* (Chicago: Quadrangle, 1969); Mari Jo Buhle, *Women and American Socialism, 1870–1920* (Urbana: University of Illinois Press, 1978); Linda Gordon, *Woman's Body, Woman's Right: A Social History of Birth Control in America* (New York: Grossman Publishers, 1976). And for all those ages twenty-one to twenty-eight who, like my research assistants, never took a women's history class (usual recollection: It was "gay"; "it had this stigma"; "it was passé"), here is a brief beginner's reading list of the second twentieth century feminist outburst, a movement that, like it or not, continues to shape all female lives.

Kate Millet, *Sexual Politics* (New York: Ballantine, 1969); Mary S. Hartman and Lois Banner, eds., *Clio's Consciousness Raised: New Perspectives on Women* (New York: Harper & Row, 1974); Vivian Gornick and Barbara K. Moran, eds., *Woman in Sexist Society: Studies in Power and Powerlessness* (New York/London: Basic Books, 1971), (see especially famed sociologist Jesse Bernard's "The Paradox of the Happy Marriage"); Susan Brownmiller, *Against Our Will: Men, Women and Rape* (New York: Simon & Schuster, 1975); Shulamith Firestone, *The Dialectic of Sex: The Case for Feminist Revolution* (complete with diagrams for the revolution) (New York: William Morrow, 1970); Michele Wallace, *Black Macho and the Myth of the Superwoman* (New York: Dial, 1979); the brilliant but scattered opus by "individualist" and celebrity feminist Germaine Greer, *The Female Eunuch* (New York: McGraw-Hill, 1971); Juliet Mitchell, *Women's Estate* (New York: Vintage, 1973); Robin Morgan, ed., *Sisterhood Is Powerful: An Anthology of Writings from the Women's Liberation Movement* (New York: Vintage, 1970); Mary Wollstonecraft, *On the Vindication of the Rights of Woman* (1792; New York: Harcourt Brace Jovanovich, 1974); Charlotte Perkins Gilman, *Women and Economics: A Study of the Economic Relation Between Women and Men* (1898; Berkeley: University of California Press, 1998); Betty Friedan, *The Feminine Mystique* (1963; New York: Laurel/Dell, 1983), and Simone de Beauvoir, *The Second Sex* (1952; New York: Vintage, 1989).

Major cultural overviews:

There are a few academics who break through and, without sacrificing the beauty and complexity of their argument, write their studies in colloquial English. To put single women in context I relied on three scholarly works. First, Carroll Smith-Rosenberg's erudite and imaginative essay collection, *Disorderly Conduct: Visions of Gender in Victorian America* (New York: Oxford University Press, 1985). Another essential work is Ann Douglas, *The Feminization of American Culture* (New York: Anchor, 1988). And Lois Banner's *American Beauty* (New York: Knopf, 1983) is a well-researched and amusing book on beauty culture and a must-read for anyone with an interest in the tangled evolution of female style.

Image and advertising:

For advertising in the nineteenth century, Ellen Gruber Garvey, *The Adman in the Parlor: Magazines and the Gendering of Consumer Culture, 1880s to 1910s* (New York: Oxford University Press, 1996); Roland Marchand, *Advertising the American Dream* (Berkeley: University of California Press, 1985); Stuart Ewen, *Captains of Consciousness* (New York: McGraw-Hill, 1979); George Burton Hotchkiss and Richard B. Franken, *The Leadership of Advertised Brands* (Garden City, N.Y.: Doubleday, 1923); John Berger, *Ways of Seeing* (London: Penguin Books, 1972); Erving Goffman, *Gender Advertisements* (Cambridge: Harvard University Press, 1979); Martha Banta, *Imaging American Women: Ideas and Ideals in Cultural History* (New York: Columbia University Press, 1987). The best and most amusing feminist media survey of the postwar years is Susan J. Douglas, *Where the Girls Are: Growing Up Female with the Mass Media* (New York: Times Books/Random House, 1994); also Joan Brumberg, *The Body Project: An Intimate History of American Girls* (New York: Random House, 1997).

On film:

The two best books on women in film, both published in 1973, approach the subject from differing perspectives. Marjorie Rosen's *Popcorn Venus: Women, Movies & the American Dream* (New York: Coward, McCann & Geoghegan, 1973) is a thorough sociological and historical accounting of women's roles in film from the silent era through the 1960s; Molly Haskell's *From Reverence to Rape*, 2d ed. (Chicago: University of Chicago Press, 1987), takes a psychoanalytic approach to the female characters and film tropes of the same period. Two period studies that attempt to assess the effects film had on young women are: Herbert Blumer and Philip M. Hauser, *Movies, Delinquency and Crime* (New York: Macmillan, 1933) and Henry James Forman, *Our Movie Made Children* (New York: Macmillian, 1935); Kate Simon's memoir *A Wider World* (New York: Harper & Row, 1986) is one of many memoirs and stories of taking refuge, and plotting out a life, at the movies. As she writes, "The brightest, most informative school was the movies. We learned how tennis was played and golf, what a swimming pool was and what to wear if you ever got to drive a car . . . and . . . we learned about love, a very foreign country like maybe China and Connecticut." Also: Tania Modleski, *The Women Who Knew Too Much: Hitchcock and Feminist Theory* (New York and London: Routledge, 1988); Robert Sklar, *Movie-Made America: A Cultural History of American Movies* (New York: Vintage, 1976); John Margolis and Emily Gwathmey, *Ticket to Paradise: American Movie Theaters and How We Had Fun* (Boston: Little, Brown, 1991).

On New York:

Kenneth T. Jackson, ed., *The Encyclopedia of New York City* (New Haven: Yale University Press, 1995); Lloyd Morris, *Incredible New York: High Life and Low of the Last Hundred Years* (New York: Random House, 1951); Hank O'Neill, *Berenice Abbott: American Photographer* (New York: McGraw-Hill, 1982), on the premiere photographer of the city; Mary McCarthy, *Intellectual Memoirs: New York, 1936–1938* (New York: Harcourt Brace Jovanovich, 1992); Mary Cantwell, *Manhattan, When I Was Young* (Boston: Houghton Mifflin, 1995); James McCabe, *Light and Shadows of New York* (Philadelphia: National Publishing Company, 1872); Dan Wakefield, *New York in the Fifties* (Boston: Houghton Mifflin, 1993); Elizabeth Hawes, *New York, New York: How the Apartment House Transformed the Life of the City* (New York: Knopf, 1993); Luc Sante, *Low Life* (New York: Vintage Books, 1991).

ON THE PRESS:

American journalism:

Frank Luther Mott, *A History of Newspapers in the United States Through 250 Years, 1690–1940*, 3d ed. (New York: Macmillan, 1962); *Single Blessedness, or the Single Ladies and Gentlemen Against the Slanders of the Pulpits, the Press and the Lecture Room* (C. S. Francis and Co., 1852); Don C. Seitz, *The James Gordon Bennetts: Father and Son* (Indianapolis: Bobbs-Merrill, 1920); Horace Greeley, *Recollections of a Busy Life* (New York: JB Ford, 1868); Hans Bergmann, *God in the Street, New York Writing from the Penny Press to Melville* (Philadelphia: Temple University Press, 1995); Paul H. Weaver, *News and the Culture of Lying* (New York: Free Press/Macmillan, 1994). *Godey's Ladies Book*, founded in 1830, became the premiere women's magazine, the model for all others, throughout the nineteenth century. Stories, lectures, allegories, storiettes I used in research: "Woman" (1831), "An Old Maid" (1831), "Husband Hunters" (1832), "The

Bachelor's Dream" (1832), "Mary, the Prude" (1832), "Female Accomplishments" (1835), "Female Education" (1835), "Women at Twenty-one" (1835). Books on Godey's include: Ruth Finley, The Lady of Godey's, Sara Josepha Hale (Philadelphia: J. B. Lippincott Company, 1931). Also, on magazines: Frank Luther Mott, A History of American Magazines (Cambridge: Harvard University Press, reprinted and updated, 1938–68).

CHAPTER 1: THE CLASSICAL SPINSTER

Martha Vicinus, Independent Women: Women and Community for Single Women, 1850–1920 (Chicago: University of Chicago Press, 1985), a wonderful study of women in England and their attempts to live communally in the mid to late nineteenth century; Nina Auerbach, Communities of Women: An Idea in Fiction (Cambridge: Harvard University Press, 1978). Working from four famous novels the author charts a fascinating and original thesis on societal responses to women living in groups. See also: Pauline Nestor, Female Friendships and Communities: Charlotte Brontë, George Eliot, Elizabeth Gaskell (London: Oxford University Press, 1985).

Sheila Jeffries, The Spinster and Her Enemies 1880–1930 (London: Pandora, 1985), is the best work published on 1920s-era sexology and its long-term detrimental effect on single women. Lee Virginia Chambers-Schiller, Liberty, a Better Husband: Single Women in America, the Generations of 1780–1840 (New Haven: Yale University Press, 1984) stands as the pioneering and intensive work on early single revolutionaries dubbed "the Singly Blessed"; Susan Leslie Katz, "Singleness of Heart: Spinsterhood in Victorian Culture" (Ph.D. thesis, Columbia University, 1990).

Dorothy Yost Deegan, The Stereotype of the Single Woman in American Literature: A Social Study with Implications for the Education of Women (New York: Farrar, Straus & Giroux, 1951), is the seminal work on the spinster in novels. The book received much popular attention because of what I'll call its news peg: There were, or so it seemed, a large number of single women in the population, and one had to study them in historical context and, with an unavoidable 1950s bias, determine what they might do to "adjust" to their status. The author concluded there was much a spinster might do in modern society, as opposed to most of the sad women she wrote about. Sandra Gilbert and Susan Gubar, The Madwoman in the Attic: The Woman Writer and the Nineteenth-Century Literary Imagination, 2d ed. (1980; New Haven: Yale University Press, 2000); Susan Koppelman, Old Maids: Short Stories by Nineteenth-Century U.S. Women Writers (London: Pandora, 1984); Laura L. Doan, Old Maids to Radical Spinsters: Unmarried Women in the Twentieth-Century Novel, (Urbana: University of Illinois Press, 1991); Mary Russo, "Female Grotesques: Carnival and Theory," in Teresa de Lauretis, ed., Journal of Feminist Studies/Critical Studies Bloomington: Indiana University Press, 1986).

On Florence Nightingale:

I. B. O'Malley, *Florence Nightingale, 1820–1856: A Study of Her Life Down to the End of the Crimean War* (London: Thornton Butterworth, 1931); Nightingale had the distinction of being the lone woman included in Lytton Strachey's *Eminent Victorians* (New York: G. P. Putnam, 1918) and the far more unfortunate distinction of being viewed in it as a repressed sexual hysteric. *Florence Nightingale to Her Nurses: A Selection from Miss Nightingale's Addresses to Probationers and Nurses of the Nightingale School at St. Thomas's Hospital* (London: Macmillan, 1914). There is an excellent discussion of Florence Nightingale in Nina Auerbach's *Woman and the Demon: The Life of a Victorian Myth* (Cambridge: Harvard University Press, 1982); Sir Edward Cook, *The Life of Florence Nightingale*, 2 vols. (London: Macmillan, 1913); Cecil Woodham-Smith, *Florence Nightingale* (New York: Atheneum, 1983). Myra Stark, ed., *Cassandra* (Old Westbury, NY: Feminist Press, 1979).

On Louisa May Alcott:

Ednah D. Cheney, ed., *Louisa May Alcott: Her Life, Letters, and Journals* (Boston: Robert Brothers, 1890); Sarah Elbert, ed., *Louisa May Alcott: On Race, Sex, and Slavery* (Boston: Northeastern University Press, 1997).

On Clara Barton:

Elizabeth Brown Pryor, *Clara Barton: Professional Angel* (Philadelphia: University of Pennsylvania Press, 1987); William E. Barton, *The Life of Clara Barton, Founder of the American Red Cross*, vol. 1 (New York: AMS Press, 1969).

Conduct books and nasty warnings:

Ann Judith Penny, *The Afternoon of Unmarried Life* (London: Brown, Green, Longmans and Roberts, 1858); Mrs. Ellis (Sarah Stickney), *The Daughters of England, Their Position in Society, Character and Responsibilities* (New York: D. Appleton and Co., 1842); Myrtle Reed, *The Spinster Book* (New York and London: G. P. Putnam/Knickerbocker Press, 1905); Susan C. Dunning Power, *The Ugly Girl Papers, or, Hints for the Toilet* (New York: Harper Brothers, 1875); Robert Tomes, *The Bazar Book of Decorum* (New York: Harper Brothers, 1877); Eliza Leslie, *The Behaviour Book: A Manual for Ladies* (New York: Willis P. Hazard, 1854).

"Muzzles for Ladies," *Strand Magazine*, no. 8 (1894); W. R. Greg, "Why Are Women Redundant?" *Literary and Social Judgments* (London: Trubner, 1868); Daniel Defoe, "Satire on Censorious Old Maids," in William Lee, ed., *Daniel Defoe, His Life and Recently Discovered Writing*, 3 vols. (1869; New York: Burt Franklin, 1969); Mary Ashton Livermore, *What Shall We Do with Our Daughters?* (Boston: Lee & Shephard, 1883).

Spinster novels:

Eighteenth and nineteenth centuries: Tobias Smollett, *Humphry Clinker* (1771; New York: Penguin, 1967); Jane Austen, *Emma* (1816; London: Oxford University Press, 1971) and *Sense and Sensibility* (1811; New York: Penguin, 1976); Charlotte Brontë, *Shirley* (1849; New York: Penguin, 1974), *Jane Eyre* (1847; New York: Bantam Classics, 1988), and *Villette* (1853; New York: Bantam, 1986); George Gissing, *The Odd Women* (1893; New York: W. W. Norton, 1971); Charles Dickens, *Great Expectations* (1860–61; London: Penguin, 1965) and *David Copperfield* (1849–50; London: Oxford University Press, 1983); Anthony Trollope, *The Last Chronicle of Barset* (New York: Penguin, 1981); Elizabeth Gaskell, *Cranford* (1853; London: Penguin, 1976); Nathaniel Hawthorne, *The House of the Seven Gables* (1851; New York: Buccaneer Books, 1982).

    Twentieth century: Edith Wharton, *Sanctuary* (New York: Scribner's, 1903); Edna Ferber, *The Girls* (New York: P. F. Collier & Son, 1921); Anne Parrish, *The Perennial Bachelor* (London: Harper Brothers, 1925); Margaret Ayers Barnes, *Within This Present* (Boston: Houghton Mifflin, 1933) and *Edna, His Wife* (Boston: Houghton Mifflin, 1935); Josephine Lawrence, *But You Are Young* (Boston: Little, Brown, 1940), a novel on the "new dependency," a trend also known as "the piggy family," and *The Tower of Steel* (Boston: Little, Brown, 1943), the story of four single girls in the city, an early version of this familiar genre (one is in flight from her piggy family—"the indecent demands made upon her spiritual privacy"—one commits suicide, and so on); Sophia Belzer Engstrand, *Wilma Rogers* (New York: Dial Press, 1941) and *Miss Munday* (New York: Dial Press, 1940); Zona Gale, *Faint Perfume* (New York: D. Appleton and Co., 1923); Fanny Hurst, *The Lonely Parade* (New York: Harper Brothers, 1942); Dawn Powell, *A Time to Be Born* (New York: Scribner's, 1942); Edith Wharton, *Ethan Frome* (New York: Scribner's, 1911); for the Lily Briscoe character, Virginia Woolf, *To the Lighthouse* (New York: Harcourt, Brace & World, 1927); Charlotte Perkins Gilman, *Herland* (1909–1912; New York: Pantheon, 1979) and *The Yellow Wallpaper* (1892; New York: Bantam Classics, 1989); Betty Smith, *A Tree Grows in Brooklyn* (New York/London: Governeur, D. Appleton and Co., 1943), for the two spinster piano teachers who live off the snacks brought to them or accidentally left by their piano students. Esther Forbes, *Miss Marvel* (Boston: Houghton Mifflin, 1935); Sylvia Ashton-Warner, *Spinster* (New York: Simon & Schuster, 1958).

    Theodore Pratt, *Miss Dilly Says No* (New York: Duell, Sloane and Pearce, 1945), a little-known spinster novel about a movie-company secretary who writes terrible scripts no one bothers to finish—they're as dull as she is! Then she writes a memoir of her life as a movie-company secretary, never thinking it might be published. It is. Becomes a best-seller. And so the film companies, her own especially, fight over the rights to make the movie of how idiotic they all are. Miss Dilly, locked up in a hotel room with a starlet bodyguard, repeatedly says "no."

    Muriel Spark, *The Girls of Slender Means* (New York: Knopf, 1963) and *The Prime of Miss Jean Brodie* (New York: Dell, 1966); Mary McCarthy, *The Company She Keeps* (1942; New York: Harcourt Brace Jovanovich, 1970) and *The Group* (London: Weidenfeld and Nicolson, 1963); Alison Lurie, *Foreign Affairs* (New York: Avon, 1985); Anita Brookner, *Look at Me* (New York; Pantheon, 1983), *Hotel Du Lac* (New York: Pantheon, 1984), *Family and Friends* (New York: Pocket, 1985), and *Brief Lives* (New York: Random House, 1990); Brian Moore, *The Lonely Passion of Judith Hearne* (Boston: Little, Brown, 1955).

Periodicals:
"The Old Maid of the Family—A Sketch of Human Life," *Atheneum*, no. 3 (January 1830); J. A. Turner, "Link Not Thy Fate to His," *Peterson's* (Apr. 1859); "A Woman Alone: Catharine Maria Sedgwick's Spinsterhood in Nineteenth-Century America," *New England Quarterly*, vol. 51 (1978); Elizabeth Meriweather Gilmer, "The Unglorified Spinster," *Cosmopolitan* (May 1907); Francis Power Cobbe, "What Shall We Do With Our Old Maids?" *Fraser's*, no. 66, (1862); "Why Is Single Life Becoming More General?" *The Nation* (1868); Molly Haskell, "Paying Homage to the Spinster," *The New York Times Magazine* (May 1988).

The cult of true womanhood/domesticity:
Barbara Welter, "The Cult of True Womanhood, 1820–1860," *American Quarterly*, no. XVII (1966); Nancy F. Cott, *The Bonds of Womanhood: "Woman's Sphere" in New England, 1780–1835* (New Haven: Yale University Press, 1977); Kathryn Kish Sklar, *Catherine Beecher: A Study in American Domesticity* (New Haven: Yale University Press, 1973); Susan Strasser, *Never Done: A History of American Housework* (New York: Pantheon, 1982); Glenna Matthews, *Just a Housewife: The Rise and Fall of Domesticity in America* (New York: Oxford University Press, 1987).

Memoirs and essays:
Marian Governeur, *As I Remember: Recollections of American Society During the Nineteenth Century* (New York: D. Appleton and Co., 1911); Domingo Sarmiento, Michael Rockland, ed. and trans., *Travels in the United States in 1847* (Princeton, N.J.: Princeton University Press, 1970); Elizabeth Lynn Linton, *The Girl of the Period and Other Social Essays* (London: Richard and Bentley, 1883) and *Modern Women and What Is Said of Them* (New York: Redfield, 1868); Natalie Dana, *Young in New York: A Memoir of a Victorian Girlhood* (Garden City, N.Y.: Doubleday, 1963); Hazel Hunton, *Pantaloons and Petticoats: The Diary of a Young Woman* (New York: Field, 1950); Edith Wharton, *A Backwards Glance* (New York: D. Appleton and Co., Century, 1934).

CHAPTER 2: THE SINGLE STEPS OUT

On working women in general and their economic status in the United States:
Lynn Y. Weiner, *From Working Girl to Working Mother: The Female Labor Force in the United States, 1820–1980* (Chapel Hill: University of North Carolina Press, 1985); Alice Kessler Harris, *History of Wage Earning Women in the United States* (New York: Oxford University Press, 1982); Claudia Goldin, *Understanding the Gender Gap: An Economic History of American Women* (New York: Oxford University Press, 1990). On male attitudes about organized female labor, specifically the idea that men, not women, had to support what would be recognized as a "family," see Martha May, "Bread Before Roses: American Workingmen, Labor Unions, and the Family Wage," part of the larger, very useful *Women, Work and Protest: A Century of U.S. Women's Labor History,* Ruth Milkman, ed. (New York: Routledge Publishing, 1985); Barbara Mayer Wertheimer, *We Were There: The Story of Working Women in America* (New York: Pantheon, 1977).

On immigration:
Hasia R. Diner, *Erin's Daughters in America: Irish Immigrant Women in the Nineteenth Century* (Baltimore: Johns Hopkins University Press, 1983); Sidney Stahl Steinberg, *The World of Our Mothers: The Lives of Jewish Immigrant Women* (Chapel Hill: University of North Carolina Press, 1988); Hutchins Hapgood, *The Spirit of the Ghetto: Studies of the Jewish Quarter in New York* (1902; Cambridge: Harvard University Press, 1967); Maxine Seller, ed., *Immigrant Women* (Philadelphia: Temple University Press, 1981); portions of Susan Ware, ed., *Modern American Women: A Documentary History* (Chicago: Dorsey, 1989); the classic, still viable New York story, Jacob Riis, *How the Other Half Lives* (New York: Scribner's, 1890), and Robert Hunter, *Poverty* (New York: Grosset & Dunlap, 1904), about Chicago; Henry Roth, *Call it Sleep* (New York: Random House, 1937).

Factory life and domestic service:
An extraordinary overview of women working in nineteenth-century New York is Christine Stansell, *City of Women* (New York: Knopf, 1986). The book tracks the long climb up from piece or "out" work to factory work (and includes a fascinating discussion of how one patriarchal system—in the home—was simply substituted with another in the factory). It is invaluable as a study of Bowery culture, the rackets, prostitution, and attitudes about domestic work. Virginia Penny's original *Employments of Women, A Cyclopedia of Women's Work: How Women Can Make Money Married or Single* (Boston: Walker, Wise, 1863) literally lists the thousands of jobs a woman did or might do during the Civil War era. If a woman earned a dime doing it, it's in here. Kathy Peiss,

Cheap Amusements: Working Women and Leisure in Turn-of-the-Century New York (Philadelphia: Temple University Press, 1986) is the best overall examination of the "culture of commercial leisure" (her phrase) and the dangers of the new, unsupervised world of dance halls and amusement parks and the practice of treating.

"The Story of a Sweatshop Girl," originally printed in *Independent*, no. 55 (1902) and reprinted in David Katzman and William Tuttle, eds., *Plain Folk: The Life Stories of Undistinguished Americans* (Urbana: University of Illinois Press, 1982); Benita Eisler, ed., *The Lowell Offering: Writings by New England Mill Women 1840–1845* (Philadelphia: J. B. Lippincott, 1977); Lucy Larcom, *A New England Girlhood* (1889; Gloucester, Mass.: Peter Smith, 1973); Bessie and Marie Van Vorst, *The Woman Who Toils: Being the Experience of Two Ladies as Factory Girls* (New York: Doubleday, Page, 1903); Alvin F. Harlow, *Old Bowery Days* (New York: D. Appleton and Co., 1931); David Katzman, *Seven Days a Week: Women and Domestic Service in Industrializing America* (London: Oxford University Press, 1978). In Clara E. Laughlin, *The Work-a-Day Girl: A Study of Some Present-Day Conditions* (New York: Fleming H. Revell, 1913), each chapter is an in-depth report on one of many lowly jobs. The book is illustrated with precise black-and-white photographs of lone working women; Hutchins Hapgood, *Types from City Streets* (New York: Funk & Wagnalls, 1910); Garry Gaines, *The American Girl of the Period: Her Ways and Views* (New York: J. B. Lippincott, 1878); Sue Ainslie Clark and Edith Wyatt, *Making Both Ends Meet: The Income and Outlay of New York Working Girls* (New York: MacMillan, 1911); Esther Packard, *A Study of Living Conditions of Self-Supporting Women in New York City* (New York: Metropolitan Board of the Young Women's Christian Association, 1915); Carol B. Schoen, *Anzia Yezierska* (Boston: Twayne, 1982); Louise Henrikson, *Anzia Yezierska: A Writer's Life* (Piscataway, N.J.: Rutgers University Press, 1988); Robert A. Woods and Albert J. Kennedy, *Young Working Girls: A Summary of Evidence from Two Thousand Social Workers* (Boston: Houghton Mifflin, 1913); Derek and Julia Parker, *The Natural History of the Chorus Girl* (London: David and Charles, 1975).

Store and office culture:

Susan Porter Benson, *Counter Cultures: Saleswomen, Managers and Customers in American Department Stores, 1890–1940* (Urbana: University of Illinois Press, 1986); " 'The Customers Ain't God': The World Culture of Department-Store Saleswomen," in Michael H. Frisch and Daniel J. Walkowitz, eds., *Working-Class America* (Urbana: University of Illinois Press, 1983); John William Ferry, *The History of the Department Store* (New York: Macmillan, 1960); Robert Hendrickson, *The Grand Emporiums: The Illustrated History of America's Great Department Stores* (New York: Stein and Day, 1979); Lisa M. Fine, *The Souls of the Skyscraper: Female Clerical Workers in Chicago, 1870–1930* (Philadelphia: Temple University Press, 1990); Helen Woodward, a successful advertising woman who began as a secretary, argued that stenography was "a woman's shortest cut to a big job," in *Through Many Windows* (New York: Harper Brothers, 1926); Grace Dodge, *A Bundle of Letters* (New York/London: Funk & Wagnalls, 1887); Florence Wenderoth Saunders, *Letters to a Business Girl: A Woman in the World of Business* (". . . *replete with Practical Information Regarding the Perplexing Problems of a Girl Stenographer . . .*") (Chicago: Laird & Lee, 1908); Mary S. Fergusson, *Boarding Homes and Clubs for Working Women*, *Bulletin No. 15* (The U.S. Bureau of Labor, 1898).

Working-girl novels:
Dorothy Richardson, *The Long Day: The Story of a New York Working Girl* (1905; Charlottesville: University Press of Virginia, 1990): the controversy surrounding the authenticity of the author's account was never officially resolved, although it seems she likely did as she said: had some early experiences as a working girl, then later in life went back as an undercover reporter. The sticking point was how much time she could possibly have spent as a young penniless girl in the factories. In her hometown, she worked for the *Pittsburgh Dispatch*; in New York she wrote for many publications, including Eugene Debb's *Social Democrat*, and in 1899 she began a ten-year engagement at the *New York Herald*. That's when she did her research for what's been called—and I think, accurately—an autobiographical novel. Richardson published another novel in 1924, *The Book of Blanche*, this one about a single woman, a musician, trying to establish herself in New York City. The book, less socially conscious, had more traditionally romantic and sexual concerns, but as in *The Long Day*, the heroine never marries.

Sinclair Lewis, *The Job*, 3d ed. (1917; Omaha: Bison Books/University of Nebraska Press, 1994), *Main Street* (1920; New York: Dover, 1999), and *Ann Vickers* (New York: P. F. Collier, 1933); Christopher Morley, *Human Being* (New York: Doubleday, Doran, 1932) and *Kitty Foyle* (Philadelphia: J. B. Lippincott, 1939); Theodore Dreiser, *Sister Carrie* (1900; New York: Penguin Classics, 1986) and *Jennie Gerhardt* (1910; New York: Penguin, 1994); Anzia Yezierska: *The Breadgivers* (1925; New York: Persea, 1999) and *The Open Cage: An Anzia Yezierska Collection* (New York: Persea, 1999).

Prostitution:
Ned Buntline, *G'hals of New York* (New York: Dewitt and Davenport, 1850); Ruth Rosen, *The Lost Sisterhood: Prostitution in America, 1900–1918* (Baltimore: Johns Hopkins University Press, 1982); Kathy Peiss, "Charity Girls and City Pleasures," in *Powers of Desire*, Ann Snitow, Christine Stansell, and Sharon Thompson, eds. (New York: Monthly Review Press, 1983); George Ellington, *Women of New York* (New York: New York Books, 1869).

Periodicals:
Edgar Fawcett, "Woes of the New York Working Girl," *Arena* (Dec. 1891); Lillian W. Betts, "Tenement-House Life and Recreation" (*Outlook* 61, Dec. 11, 1899); Mary Gay

Humphreys, "The New York Working Girl," (*Scribner's* 20, Oct. 1896); Barbara Schreier, "Becoming American: Jewish Women Immigrants, 1880–1920," *History Today* (Mar. 1994); Mark K. Maule, "What Is a Shop-Girl's Life?" *World's Work* (Sept. 1907); "A Salesgirl's Story," *Independent* (July 1902); "The Shopgirl," *Outlook* (Feb. 1908); "After Business Hours, What?—Pleasure!" *Ladies' Home Journal* (Feb. 1907); "What It Means to Be a Department Store Girl," *Ladies' Home Journal* (June 1913); "Glimpses at the Mind of a Waitress" (*American Journal of Sociology* 13, July, 1907); Belle Lindners Israel's "The Way of the Girl" (*Survey* 22, July 3, 1909).

The early bohemian periodicals:
Mary Gay Humphreys, "Women Bachelors in New York," *Scribner's* (Aug. 1896) and "Women Bachelors in London" (*Scribner's*, Aug. 1896) in which we learn "Women are everywhere; climbing down from omnibuses; coming up in processions from the underground stations. They are hurrying along Fleet Street . . . Chelsea and South Kensington are peopled with petticoats. . . . This new figure has no place in fiction. That is why we know so little of her. . . ."; "Feminine Bachelorism," *Scribner's* (Oct. 1896); Olga Stanley, "Some Reflections on the Life of a Bachelor Girl," *Outlook* (Nov. 1896); Winifred Sothern, "The Truth About the Bachelor Girl," *Munsey's* (May, 1901); "The Matinee Girls," *Metropolitan* (June 1900). For the origins of the Trilby character, see Lois Banner, *American Beauty* (Chicago: University of Chicago Press, 1984).

Novels:
From *The Folks* (1934; Iowa City: University of Iowa Press, 1992), the "Margaret" section: I. "The Hidden Time," II. "Basement Apartment," III. "And It Had a Green Door," IV. "After the End of the Story."

Ruth McKinney, *My Sister Eileen* (New York: Harcourt, Brace & World, 1938). Enormously popular novel turned play and musical film featuring two sisters who daringly take a basement apartment in the Village. Tragically, just after publication, the author was killed in a car accident with her husband, Nathanael West, who was, ironically, the author of *Miss Lonelyhearts* and other novels.

CHAPTER 3: THIN AND RAGING THINGS

Social crusaders:
Jane Addams, *The Spirit of Youth and City Streets* (New York: Macmillan, 1909), *Twenty Years at Hull House* (New York: Macmillan, 1910), and *The Second Twenty Years at Hull House* (New York: Macmillan, 1930). For more general information, Allen Davis, *American Heroine: The Life and Legend of Jane Addams* (London: Oxford University

Press, 1973); the section on Hull House in Roy Lubove, *The Professional Altruist: The Emergence of Social Work as a Career* (Cambridge: Harvard University Press, 1965); Karen J. Blair, *The Club Woman as Feminist: True Womanhood Redefined, 1868–1914* (New York: Holmes & Meier Publishers, 1980); William Dean Howells, *The Minister's Charge* (Boston: Ticknor, 1887).

New women:
Judith Schwarz, *The Radical Feminists of Heterodoxy* (Lebanon, N.H.: New Victoria, 1982); Elaine Showalter, *These Modern Women: Autobiographical Essays from the Twenties* (Old Westbury, N.Y.: Feminist Press, 1978); Lila Rose McCabe, *The American Girl at College* (New York: Dodd, Mead, 1893); June Sochen, *The New Woman: Feminism in Greenwich Village, 1910–1920* (New York: Quadrangle, 1972); Leslie Fishbein, *Rebels in Bohemia* (Chapel Hill: University of North Carolina Press, 1982); Ellen Trimberger, *"Feminism, Men and Modern Love: Greenwich Village, 1900–1925,"* in Ann Snitow, Christine Stansell, and Sharon Thompson, eds., *Powers of Desire* (New York: Monthly Review Press, 1983); Lewis A. Erenberg, *Steppin' Out: New York Nightlife and the Transformation of American Culture, 1890–1930* (Westport, Conn.: Greenwood Press, 1981) provides an overview of attitudes among middle-class urban kids in the teens; Terry Miller, *Greenwich Village and How It Got That Way* (New York: Crown, 1990); Lillian Federman, *Odd Girls and Twilight Ladies: A History of Lesbian Life in Twentieth-Century America* (New York: Columbia University Press, 1991); Lydia Kingsmill Commander, "An American Idea: Does the National Tendency Toward a Small Family Point to Race Suicide or Race Development?" *The American Idea* (1907; New York: Arno Press, 1972).

The tea-dancing modern girl, circa 1913:
Susanne Wilcox, "The Unrest of Modern Women," *Independent* (July 8, 1909); "Why Educated Young Women Don't Marry," *Independent* (Nov. 25, 1909); Juliet Wilbor Tompkins, "Why Women Don't Marry," *Cosmopolitan* (Feb. 1907); "The Passing of the Home Daughter," *Independent* (July 13, 1911); Margaret Deland, "The Change in the Feminine Ideal," *Atlantic Monthly* (Mar. 1914); Ethel W. Mumford, "Where Is Your Daughter This Afternoon?" *Harper's* (Jan. 17, 1914); "New Reflections on the Dancing Mania," *Current Opinion* (Oct. 13, 1915); "Turkey Trot and Tango—A Disease or a Remedy? *Current Opinion* 55 (Sept. 1913); Charlotte Perkins Gilman, "The New Generation of Women," *Current History* (Aug. 18, 1923).

White slaving:
"Five White Slave Trade Investigations, *McClure's* (May 1910); "The White Slave Films" *Outlook* (Jan. 17, 1914); "The White Slave Films: A Review," *Outlook* (Feb. 14, 1914); John Stanley, "Traffic in Souls: The Horror of White Slavery," *San Francisco Chronicle* (Oct. 21, 1990).

The Gibson girl:

Ann O'Hagen, "The Athletic Girl," *Munsey's* (Aug. 1901); Richard Harding Davis, "The Origin of a Type of the American Girl," *Quarterly Illustrator*, vol. III (winter 1895); "Charles Dana Gibson, the Man and His Art," *Collier's* (Dec. 1902); Winifred Scott Moody, "Daisy Miller and the Gibson Girl," *Ladies' Home Journal* (Sept. 1904); "Gibson Girl Would Fit in Fine in the '90s," *Roanoke Times and World News* (Apr. 9, 1995).

The flapper and 1920s youth:

Ann Douglas, *Terrible Honesty: Mongrel Manhattan in the 1920s* (Farrar, Straus & Giroux, 1995); Robert S. Lynd and Helen Merrill Lynd, *Middletown: A Study in Contemporary American Culture* (New York, Harcourt, Brace & World, 1929) was cited routinely for decades as the preeminent microcosmic view of American middle-class society; Paula Fass, *The Damned and the Beautiful: American Youth in the 1920s* (New York: Oxford University Press, 1977); Anita Loos, *A Girl Like I* (New York: Viking, 1966); John Keats, *You Might as Well Live: The Life and Times of Dorothy Parker* (New York: Simon & Schuster, 1970); Eric Partridge, *A Dictionary of Slang and Unconventional English*, 7th ed. (New York: MacMillan, 1970); *A Flapper's Dictionary, as Compiled by One of Them* (Pittsburgh: Imperial, 1922).

Periodicals:

George Ade, "Today's Amazing Crop of 18-Year-Old Roues and 19-Year-Old Vamps," *American Magazine* (March 1922); "Says Flapper Aids Church," *New York Times* (Sept. 2, 1922); "An Interview with a Young Lady," *New Republic* (Jan. 1925); "A Doctor's Warning to Flappers," *Literary Digest* (Oct. 1926); Judge William McAdoo, "Young Women and Crime," *Ladies' Home Journal* (Nov. 1927); Zelda Fitzgerald, "Eulogy on the Flapper," *Metropolitan* (1929); Ruth Hooper, "Flapping Not Repented Of," *New York Times Book Review* (July 16, 1926).

The new spinster:

We know the former flapper "new spinster"—her frustrations, joys, successes, snipey conversations with wives, and wardrobe changes—from articles published in magazines and newspapers. Primary information about her sex life—and she apparently had one—is found in *Factors in the Sex Life of Twenty-two Hundred Women* (1935, a privately funded study, Vassar College) and in Daniel Scott Smith, *The Dating of the American Sexual Revolution*, part of the collection *The American Family in Social-Historical Perspective*, Michael Gordon, ed. (New York: St. Martin's Press, 1973). Also Ellen Rothman, *Hand and Hearts: The History of Courtship in America* (New York: Basic Books, 1984); and portions of Beth L. Bailey's highly enjoyable *From Front Porch to Backseat: Courtship in Twentieth-Century America* (Baltimore: Johns Hopkins University Press,

1986); there are wonderfully frightening images of the late flapper down and out in two Jean Rhys novels: *After Leaving Mr. MacKenzie* (New York: Harper & Row, 1931) and *Quartet* (1928; New York: Vintage, 1974).

Periodicals:

Grace M. Johnson, "The New Old Maids" (*Women Beautiful*, May 1909); Elizabeth Jordan, "On Being a Spinster," *Saturday Evening Post* (Apr. 1926); Dorothy Dunbar Bromley, "Feminist—New Style," *Harper's* (Oct. 1927); Lillian Bell, "Old Maids of the Last Generation and This," *Saturday Evening Post* (Dec. 1926); "Feminism and Jane Smith," *Harper's* (June 1927); Lorine Pruette, "Should Men Be Protected?" *Nation* (Aug. 1927); Lillian Symes, "Still a Man's Game: Reflections of a Slightly Tired Feminist," *Harper's* (May 1929) and "The New Masculinism," *Harper's* (June 1930); "And Now the Siren Eclipses the Flapper" *New York Times Magazine* (July 28, 1929); Margaret Culkin Banning, "The Plight of the Spinster," *Harper's* (June 1929); Mrs. Virginia Kirk, "A Tale of Not So Flaming Youth," *Literary Digest*, no. 105 (Oct. 10, 1930).

CHAPTER 4: THE SUSPICIOUS SINGLE

Susan Ware, *Holding Their Own: American Women in the 1930s* (Boston, Twayne, 1982); Joan Hoff-Wilson and Marjorie Lightman, *Without Precedent: The Life and Career of Eleanor Roosevelt* (Bloomington: University of Indiana Press, 1984); Anne Hirst, *Get and Hold Your Man* (New York: Kinsey, 1937); Don Congdon, ed., *The Thirties: A Time to Remember* (New York: Simon & Schuster, 1962); Ben L. Reitman, *Sister of the Road: The Autobiography of Box-Car Bertha* (New York: Sheridan House, 1937); Susan M. Hartmann, *The Homefront and Beyond: American Women in the 1940s* (Boston, Twayne, 1982); Karen Anderson, *Wartime Women: Sex Roles, Family Relations and the Status of Women During World War II* (Westport, Conn.: Greenwood Press, 1981); Sherna Berger Gluck, *Rosie the Riveter Revisited: Women, the War and Social Change* (Boston: Meridien, 1987) includes oral histories of women in all areas of the war industries; Maureen Honey, *Creating Rosie the Riveter: Class, Gender, and Propaganda During World War II* (Amherst: University of Massachusetts Press, 1984); Ferdinand Lundberg and Marynia Farnham, *Modern Woman: The Lost Sex* (New York: Harper & Row, 1947); Elizabeth Hawes, *Anything but Love: A Complete Digest of the Rules for Feminine Behaviour from Birth to Death, Given Out in Print, On Film, and Over the Air, Read, Seen, Listened to Monthly by Some 340,000,000 American Women* (New York: Rinehart, 1948).

Periodicals:

Mabel Barbee Lee, "The Dilemma of the Educated Woman," *Atlantic* (Dec. 1930); Genevieve Parkhurst, "Is Feminism Dead?" *Harper's* (1935); "Anxious Ladies: To Be

(Wed) or Not to Be," *Mademoiselle* (1938); Juliet Farnham, "How to Meet Men and Marry," book excerpt, *McCall's* (1943); "Somebody's After Your Man!" *Good House-keeping* (Aug., 1945); "In Marriage, It's a Man's Market!" *New York Times Magazine* (June 17, 1945); "Your Chances of Getting Married," *Good Housekeeping* (Oct. 1946); "U.S. Marriage Rate Zooms to All-Time High," *Science Digest* (Oct. 1947); "How Feminine Are You to Men?" *Women's Home Companion* (May 1946); "No Date Is No Disgrace," *Women's Home Companion* (Nov. 1946); George Lawton, "Proof That She Is the Stronger Sex," *New York Times Magazine* (Dec. 12, 1948); "The Unwilling Virgins," *Esquire* (May 1949); "The High Cost of Dating," *Ladies' Home Journal* (Sept. 1949).

Advice/conduct guides:
Steven Hart and Lucy Brown, *How to Get Your Man and Hold Him* (New York: Dover, 1944); Cora Carle, *How to Get a Husband* (New York: Hedgehog Press, 1949); Jean and Gene Berger, *Win Your Man and Keep Him* (Chicago: Windsor Press, 1948); Judson T. and Mary G. Landis, *Building a Successful Marriage* (Englewood Cliffs, N.J.: Prentice-Hall, 1948).

On the emergence of bobby-soxers, see *This Fabulous Century: 1940–50* (New York: Time-Life, 1969).

CHAPTER 5: THE SECRET SINGLE

Alfred Kinsey, *Sexual Behavior in the Human Female* (Philadelphia: Saunders, 1953); David Reisman, *The Lonely Crowd*, 2d ed. (Cambridge: Harvard University Press, 1964); C. Wright Mills, *White Collar: The American Middle Class* (New York: Oxford University Press, 1951); Mirra Komarovsky, *Women in the Modern World: Their Education and Dilemmas* (Boston: Little, Brown, 1953); Lawrence and Mary Frank, *How to Be a Woman* (Indianapolis: Bobbs-Merrill, 1954); Norman Hamilton, *How to Woo and Keep Your Man* (New York: William Fredericks, 1955); Robert O. Blood, *Anticipating Your Marriage*, the classic marriage text (New York: Free Press, 1957); Nicholas Drake, *The Fifties in VOGUE* (New York: Henry Holt, 1987); Rona Jaffe, *The Best of Everything* (1958; New York: Avon, 1976); Joyce Johnson, *Minor Characters: A Young Woman's Coming of Age in the Beat Generation* (New York: Washington Square, 1983); Herman Wouk, *Marjorie Morningstar* (Garden City, N.Y.: Doubleday, 1955); Winnie Dienes, *Young, White and Miserable: Growing Up in the 1950s* (Boston: Beacon Press, 1992); J. D. Salinger, *Franny and Zooey* (Boston: Little, Brown, 1961).

Periodicals:
"What You Should Know About Women, Even if You're a Woman," *Collier's* (Nov. 1951); "No Right Age for a Girl to Marry," *New York Times* (Oct. 19, 1952); Patty

DeRoulf, "Must Bachelor Girls Be Immoral?" *Coronet* (Feb. 9, 1952); "Her First Date," *Look,* (Dec. 1953); Juliet Tree, "When a Girl Lives Alone," *Good Housekeeping* (Mar. 1953); *"Life* Calls on Seven Spinsters," *Life* (June 8, 1953), in which *Life* went out and found spinsters as it might earlier have found the Dionne quints (seven sisters, thirty-eight to fifty-one, all wait on Dad and dress alike—quirky Mousketeer sensibility or psychopathology?); "How to Be Marriageable," *Ladies' Home Journal* (Mar. 1954); James A. Skardon, "Room, Board and Romance," a series on new coed boardinghouses in San Francisco, *New York Herald Tribune* (Oct. 20, 1954); "Is Marriage the Trap?" *Mademoiselle* (Dec. 1955); Anita Colby, "In Defense of the Single Woman," *Look* (Nov. 29, 1955); "The Date Line," *Good Housekeeping* (Oct. 1956); "Some Persons Should Stay Single," *Science Digest* (May 1956); *Life* Magazine Special Issue on "The American Woman," *Life* (Dec. 24, 1956); Polly Weaver, "What's Wrong with Ambition?" *Mademoiselle* (Sept. 1956); "Will Success Spoil American Women?" *New York Times Magazine* (Nov. 10, 1957); Gael Greene, "Lone Women," series, *New York Post* (Nov. 18–Dec. 1, 1957); Earl Ubell, "Pressure and Tension Beset the Lone Woman," *New York Herald Tribune* (Dec. 6, 1957); James H. S. Brossard, "The Engagement Ring: A Changing Symbol" *New York Times Magazine* (July 14, 1958); Gloria Emerson, "The Lives of a New York Career Girl" *Holiday* (May 1958); "If You Don't Go Steady, You're Different," *Ladies' Home Journal* (Dec. 1959); "Bachelor Girls—They Play by Their Own Rules," five-part series, *New York Daily News* (Apr. 1959).

Novels:

Gail Parent, *Sheila Levine Is Dead and Living in New York;* (New York: Putnam, 1972) Judith Rossner, *Looking for Mr. Goodbar* (New York: Simon & Schuster, 1975); Erica Jong, *Fear of Flying* (1973; New York: NAL, 1995); Mary Gordon, *Final Payments* (New York: Ballantine, 1978).

CHAPTER 6: THE SWINGING SINGLE

Books:

Helen Gurley Brown, *Sex and the Single Girl* (New York: Bernard Geiss/Random House, 1962); Betty Friedan, *The Feminine Mystique* (1963; New York: Dell, 1973); Charles Abrams, *The City Is the Frontier* (New York: Columbia University Press, 1965); Joan Didion, *Something Toward Bethlehem* (New York: Farrar, Straus & Giroux, 1968); Howard Bahr and Gerald Garrett, *Women Alone: The Disaffiliation of Urban Females* (Lexington, Mass.: Lexington Books, 1976); Suzanne Gordon, *Lonely in America* (New York: Simon & Schuster, 1976); Jean Baker Miller, *Toward A New Psychology of Women* (Boston: Beacon Books, 1979).

Periodicals:

Joan Didion, "The Great Reprieve," *Mademoiselle* (June 1960); "Do Women Provoke Sex Attack?" *Cosmopolitan* (Mar. 1960); "The Non-Woman, A Manhattan Enigma, *Cosmopolitan* (Mar. 1960); Sylvia Porter, "Women Alone," *New York Post* (Sept. 13, 1960); Carol Taylor, "East Side, West Side, They Flock to New York for Job, Dream, Dream Man," *New York World-Telegram* (Jan. 3, 1960); "Go West Young Woman if You Wish to Wed," *New York Herald Tribune* (May 10, 1961); Phyllis Rosenteur, "Unwed Woman a Likely Cynic," (*Newsweek*, book excerpt, May 1962); Gloria Steinem, "The Moral Disarmament of Betty Co-ed," *Esquire* (Sept. 1962); "How Nice to Be a Pretty Girl in Washington, D.C.," *Life* (Mar. 23, 1962); Marion K. Sanders, "The Case of the Vanishing Spinster," *New York Times Magazine* (Sept. 22, 1963); "Two Girls Murdered in E. 88th St. Flat," *New York Times*, (Aug. 29, 1963); Nan Robertson, "Where the Boys Are Not: At the Barbizon," *New York Times* (Oct. 19, 1963); on Kitty Genovese, Loudon Wainwright, "The Dying Girl That Nobody Helped," *Life* (Apr. 10, 1964); Sylvia Porter, "Girls Without Jobs," *New York Post* (Mar. 25, 1965); Nina McCain, "New York and the Single Girl!" *New York World-Telegram* (Dec. 14, 1965); "Cities and the Single Girl," *Newsweek* (Nov. 15, 1965); "Students in the Free Sex Movement," *Time* (Mar. 11, 1966); Judith Viorst and Dorothy Gilliam, "Washington and the Single Girl," *Washington Post* (June 22, 1966); "Where the Singles Are!" *Newsweek* (Sept. 26, 1966); Douglas Sefton, "The Girl Ghetto: East Side, West Side, Gals Buoying It Up on Broads-way," *New York Daily News* (May 10, 1967); "New Rules for the Singles Game," *Life* (Aug. 18, 1967); "The Pleasures and Pain of the Single Life," *Time* (Sept. 15, 1967); Jean Baer, "The Single Girl in the City," *New York Post* (Sept. 21, 1968); Shelby Coffey III, "Single Style Yesterday and Today,'" *Washington Post* (Jan. 14, 1968); Christina Mirk, "Mingle but Stay Single!" Sunday *Daily News* (Mar. 23, 1969); "The Politics of Sex: Who's Come a Long Way, Baby?" *Time*. (Aug. 31, 1970); Jon Nordheimer, "Vacation and the Single Girl: Tireless Pursuit of a Dream," *New York Times* (July 29, 1970); "A Very Nice Kind of Ski Bum," *Life* pictorial on single girls, living together in Aspen (Mar. 8, 1971); "Gloria Steinem: A Liberated Woman Despite Beauty, Chic and Success" *Newsweek* (Aug. 16, 1971); see also "The Thinking Man's Jean Shrimpton," *Time* (Jan. 3, 1969); Judy Klemesrud, "Single Women Against a Dangerous City," *New York Times* (Jan. 12, 1973); Grace Lichtenstein, "Slain Woman's Neighbors Express Both Horror and Detachment," *New York Times* (Oct. 25, 1973); Leslie Maitland, "The Singles Scene Has Sordid Side," *New York Times* (Nov. 1, 1974); Susan Jacoby, "Forty-nine Million Singles Can't All Be Right," *New York Times Magazine* (Feb. 17, 1974); Gloria Emerson, "In a City of Crowds, So Many Lonely Women," *New York Times* (Jan. 28, 1974); Wendy Shulman, "Singles Becoming More Stable Tenants," *New York Times* (July 1974); Judy Klemesrud, "Bachelor's Life: Things Aren't Always Hunky-Dory in Paradise," *New York Times* (May 3, 1974), "Margaret Mead Puts Single Life in Perspective," *New York Times* (Jan. 25, 1974), and

"They Tell How They Feel About Being Single Women," *New York Times* (Dec. 1974); Robert J. Levin and Amy Levin, "Sexual Pleasure: The Surprising Preferences of 100,000 Women," *Redbook* (Sept. 1975); "Men Bite Back," *New York Times* (Aug. 1978), a response to Nan Robertson's controversial essay "Single Women Over 30: Where Are the Men Worthy of Us?" (to quote from one typical male subject: "I am bored with women who claim all that liberation, self-realization, self-fulfillment pap and blame all the woes of women since Eve on me."); John Kifner, "Hospital at Last Identifies Its Shopping Bag Lady," *New York Times* (Jan. 10, 1979).

CHAPTER 7: TODAY'S MODERNE UNMARRIED—HER TIMES AND TRIALS

Nancy L. Peterson, *Our Lives for Ourselves: Women Who Have Never Married* (New York: G. P. Putnam's Sons, 1981); Dr. Connell Cowan and Dr. Melvyn Kinder, *Smart Women, Foolish Choices: Finding the Right Men, Avoiding the Wrong Ones* (New York: Signet, 1986); Molly McKaughan, *The Biological Clock* (New York: Doubleday, 1987); Sylvia Ann Hewlett, *A Lesser Life: The Myth of Women's Liberation in America* (New York: Warner Books, 1987); Peter J. Stein, *Single Life: Unmarried Adults in Social Context* (New York: St. Martin's Press, 1981); Barbara Levy Simon, *Never Married Women* (Philadelphia: Temple University Press, 1987); Cynthia Heimel, *Sex Tips for Girls* (New York: Simon & Schuster, 1993).

The terrorizing Yale/Harvard study that so inaccurately predicted my life's outcome is best dissected in Susan Faludi's still-brilliant *Backlash* (New York: Crown, 1991). Two of the hundreds of paralyzing "You lose!" documents: Eloise Salholz et al., "Too Late for Prince Charming," from the cover story "The Marriage Crunch," *Newsweek*, June 2, 1986; Barbara Lovenheim, *Beating the Marriage Odds: When You Are Smart, Single and Over 35* (New York: William Morrow, 1989).

Marcelle Clements, *The Improvised Woman: Reinventing Single Life* (New York: W. W. Norton, 1998); Louise J. Kaplan, *Female Perversions* (New York: Doubleday/Nan A. Talese, 1991); Lee Reilly, *Women Living Singly* (Boston: Faber and Faber, 1996); on hypochondria, the only documented disease of the unwed, Susan Baur, *Hypochondria: Woeful Imaginings* (Berkeley: University of California Press, 1988).

Modern conduct guides in all earnestness:
Ellen Fein and Sherrie Schneider, *The Rules: Time Tested Secrets for Capturing the Heart of Mr. Right* (New York: Warner, 1995).

Modern conduct guides with attitude and irony:
Cynthia Rowley and Ilene Rosenzweig, *Swell: A Girl's Guide to the Good Life* (New York: Warner, 1999).

Periodicals—1980s/1990s–present:
Christine Doudna with Fern McBride, "Where Are the Men for the Women at the Top?" *Savvy* (Feb. 1980); Peter Davis, "The $100,000 a Year Woman," *Esquire* special issue on women (June 1984). The author, in correspondence with editor, searches for a New Type who earns more than the average man—what is that like? What is she like? He finds her. Somehow convinces her to let him follow her through life for several months, and to interview her bosses, colleagues, ex-husband. She takes him on a driving trip with her parents, and gives him access to her diary; she comes off after all this exhaustive day-in-the-life attempt at finding "new pathos" as a demanding, difficult but truly remarkable, memorable person; Janice Harayda "Unwed Women Needn't—and Don't—Despair," *Wall Street Journal* (June 27, 1986); Claudia Wallis, "Women Face the '90s" *Time* (cover, Dec. 4, 1989); Richard Cohen, "What About Alice?" *Washington Post*, (July 28, 1991); David R. Williams, David T. Takeuchi, Russell K. Adair, "Marital Status and Psychiatric Disorders Among Blacks and Whites," *Journal of Health and Social Behaviour*, vol. 33 (June 1992); "Advance Report of Final Divorce Statistics, 1989 and 1990" (The U.S. Department of Health and Human Services, 1995); Torri Minton, "Road to Modern Romance Is Paved with Potholes," *San Francisco Chronicle* (Feb. 12, 1993); Florence King, "Spinsterhood Is Powerful," *National Review* (July 19, 1993); John Tierney, "Picky, Picky, Picky," *New York Times Magazine* (Feb. 1995); Cynthia Heimel, "Solo Contendre," *Playboy* (Feb. 1995); Judy Abel, "Sisters: The New Generation Gap: Twentysomethings Are Choosing Mom's Family Values and Not Their Siblings' Career Paths," *New York Post* (Aug. 6, 1996); Katie Roiphe, "The Independent Woman (and Other Lies)" *Esquire* (Feb. 1997); "Why Marriage Is Hot Again," special section, *Redbook* (Sept. 24, 1997); "American Marriage Today," special supplement, *Brides Magazine: The Heart of the Bridal Market* (Sept. 26, 1997); Lois Smith Brady, "Ready to Propose? Make it Short, Sweet and Real," *New York Times* (Oct. 1997); Elizabeth Cohen, "They Don't Want Kids: Why Women Are Opting out of Motherhood" (with a quiz: "Should You Become a Mom?") (May 14, 1998); Sarah Bernard, "Early to Wed," *New York* magazine (June 16, 1997); Jim Yardley "Going on Full Alert for a Dream Dress," *New York Times* (Feb. 1, 1998), on the frenzy at Kleinfeld's, the famed Brooklyn wedding gown emporium.

Novels
Gail Parent, *A Sign of the Eighties* (New York: G. P. Putnam's Sons, 1987); Margaret Diehl, *Men* (New York: Simon & Schuster, 1988); Alice Hoffman, *Seventh Heaven* (New York: Ballantine, 1990); Lorrie Moore, *Like Life* (New York: Knopf, 1990) and *Birds of America* (New York: Knopf, 1998); Susannah Moore, *In the Cut* (New York: Knopf, 1995); Candace Bushnell, *Sex and the City*, collected essays (New York: Atlantic Monthly Press, 1996); Helen Fielding, *Bridget Jones's Diary* (New York, MacMillan, 1998).

INDEX